Praise for *The Art of Effortless Living*

"Here is a Book of Changes—a profound and potent guide to making transformative shifts in body, mind and spirit. At once wise and passionate, *The Art of Effortless Living* offers state-of-the-art knowledge and practice in the development of the inner life. The author's journey from mainstream to deepstream presents a model for our own self-discovery. The result can only be new ways of being for self and society."

> —**Jean Houston, Ph.D., bestselling author of fifteen books,**
> **including *The Possible Human* and *The Search for the Beloved***

"This book contains a piece of essential wisdom—that by letting go we gain more, not less. Because most of us are obsessed with the idea of making things happen, we seriously need the lessons of *The Art of Effortless Living*."

> —**Larry Dossey, M.D., author of *Reinventing Medicine* and**
> ***Healing Words***

"Dr. Ingrid Bacci's marvelously readable and immensely practical book shares decades of her own experience exploring and developing a wide range of ways of healing and enhancing health—physical, emotional and spiritual. I loved reading it, and continue to draw upon its resources of wisdom."

> —**Elaine Pagels, Ph.D., author of *The Gnostic Gospels*,**
> ***The Origin of Satan*, and *Adam, Eve and the Serpent***

"Bacci deftly describes addictions to fear and anxiety . . . She offers many suggestions for developing an alternative, 'effortless' lifestyle . . . She skillfully presents the bodywork she's been performing with clients since the early 1980s and explains the philosophy behind it in calm, accessible prose."

> —*Publishers Weekly*

"Along with profound as well as practical suggestions for healing, *The Art of Effortless Living* cultivates a confidence in the path of knowing, feeling, sensing and releasing all that is in the way of our own healthy self-empowerment."

> —*Spirit of Change*

THE ART OF

Effortless
LIVING

Do Less, Let Go, and Discover Health,
Emotional Well-Being, and Happiness

INGRID BACCI, Ph.D.

A Perigee Book

Dedicated to you,
because you wish to treasure life.

◆

A Perigee Book
Published by The Berkley Publishing Group
A division of Penguin Putnam Inc.
375 Hudson Street
New York, New York 10014

Vision Works hardcover edition: September 2000
Perigee trade paperback edition: June 2002

Perigee trade paperback edition ISBN: 0-399-52793-1

Visit our website at www.penguinputnam.com

The Library of Congress has catalogued the Vision Works hardcover edition as follows:

Library of Congress Card Number: 00-190156.

ISBN 0-9678507-1-1

First edition

Printed in the United States of America

10   9   8   7   6

Contents

It's time to replace stress, struggle and effort with effortless, creative living. Let go of the tension you bring into living and find the road to health, emotional fulfillment, productivity and creativity.

Part I
The Way of the Effortful Warrior: A Cultural Addiction

We each face a fundamental choice: to live according to other people's rules or to own ourselves. While the first choice often leads to effort, frustration and failure, the second brings peace, happiness and personal success.

We can find radiant health and deep fulfillment instead of illness and life without passion. To do so, we have to let go of

an unconscious cultural addiction that encourages us to focus
too much on how others see us, to fill our lives with endless
tasks, and to accept anxiety and fear as normal.

Part II
The Way of the Effortless Warrior: Transcending Cultural Addiction

**Part III
The Power of a Higher Life: From Effortlessness
to Self-Creation**

Acknowledgments

At the core of my life are the friends without whose support this book would never have seen the light of day. My deepest love, gratitude, and thanks go to Susan Lanzano. As both my dear friend and the editor of this book, she has been steadfast in her enthusiasm and delightfully insightful in refining and improving upon my sometimes amorphous creations. In more ways than can be enumerated, this book is truly our joint venture.

The support and endorsement of colleagues Dr. John Upledger, Dr. Larry Dossey, Dr. Jean Houston, Professor Elaine Pagels, and Dr. Peter D'Adamo—individuals whose professional writings and work I deeply admire—have been a special gift for me.

I offer my heartfelt thanks to Keith McGinnis, for his ongoing technical assistance and for his friendship. I am also indebted to my colleague Joel Fishman who, in the early stages of the writing of this book, both suggested its title and offered suggestions for its improvement.

Often we learn most from those we teach, and I am no exception to this rule. My students have contributed profoundly to my work. Most especially, I would like to thank the small band of women who met with me for a number of years in a weekly meditation group, and who supported me in developing the ideas and techniques presented here: Joan Alfano, Betty Ebzery, Elaine Gandal, Peggy Greenawalt, Helene Imber, Alice Lengers,

Henrietta Poehlmann, and Maura Walsh. Our meetings, filled as they were with peace, joy and humor, provided an opportunity to create the sacred space that is the essence of community.

I am fortunate to have a number of good friends, each of whom has contributed to my work in a unique way: Stephanie Von Hirschberg, Ron Bacci, John Kennedy, Bill and Marta Greenleaf, Jan Johnsen, Jane Marks Hart, Michael Lanzano, Robert Curry, and Nellie Sabin. Thank you for sharing yourselves with me.

Finally, the members of my family—my father, Edgar Raymond (now deceased), my mother Else, my step-mother Maristella, my sisters, Madeleine, Lavinia, Donatella and Claudia, and my brother Duncan—form part of my own foundation. Thank you for your love.

Foreword

Healing is a term that may be applied to many aspects of our lives. We may heal a physical illness or an emotional pain. We may heal enough so that we approach our creative potential much more closely. In any case, *healing* describes an internal process of transformation that releases us from binding energies, removes obstacles and enhances those processes that help us further evolve.

The Art of Effortless Living is a book about healing. The author's fundamental premise states that a perceived need for healing indicates that we must cleanse ourselves of fear. Fear fosters disease. It may also complicate intimacy, inhibit achievement, destroy integrity and limit creativity. The idea that fear is our primary enemy is not itself new. The uniqueness of author Dr. Bacci's approach is a method of developing an awareness of the manner in which fear infiltrates and takes up residence in our cultural unconscious. Once established within us, this fear creates a psychological commitment to effort and stress that may then pattern the way we think and live physiologically, psycho-emotionally and spiritually. Dr. Bacci believes that because the commitment to fear is not conscious, we cannot release this commitment without embarking on a journey into self-awareness. That journey is a journey into our bodies. When we go deeply into our bodies we discover that the body, the mind and the spirit are all one. The divisions are man-made and artificial.

The ability to live effortlessly unfolds as you learn to be present to your body. That happens when you make your internal experiences primary and external factors secondary. Dr. Bacci describes a step-by-step process for achieving "flow," a process that teaches you continually to deepen bodily relaxation, release somatic tensions, and engage and express unrecognized emotions that are stored in your tissues. This process of release sets the foundation for the development of authenticity, which is the ability to create your life individually and communally according to your own inner preferences rather than reacting to life as you think you are supposed to according to external judgments and priorities.

You will probably recognize yourself in some of the descriptions the author offers of the effortful lifestyle that is the cultural norm. More important, you have every opportunity to benefit from reading about and following the practices she suggests as tools for transforming effortful into effortless living, and generalized malaise into pleasure. Some of these tools, such as the use of meditation or of visualization, may already be familiar to many of you. What may be unfamiliar, however, is the level of practical detail that Dr. Bacci provides on how to utilize those techniques effectively and for the most powerful results. All the techniques described she has used herself in the process of meeting major personal challenges, as well as in coaching clients in her private practice. The results are evident in both the sensitivity and the concreteness of her suggestions. This book can be a very useful manual for personal self-transformation.

Ingrid Bacci is a pattern maker. She identifies a single, deep-seated and self-destructive pattern and traces its holographic impact on all aspects of our lives, ranging from physical, mental, emotional and spiritual health to relationships and professional performance. She locates the key for transforming this pattern into bodily responses. After demonstrating how we alienate our bodies, she then guides us through the processes that help us to shift the relationship to our bodies in a way that once again spreads the body's empowering influence holographically through all the other dimensions of our lives. The focus is on achieving personal empowerment and interpersonal community. The rewards of listening to and utilizing the language of the body are well worth the effort.

John E. Upledger, D.O., O.M.M.
Palm Beach Gardens, Florida

Introduction:
The Life We Are Meant to Live

Why is it that life often seems to be more like a treadmill than like a pathway to life, liberty and the pursuit of happiness? As we go about our daily lives, many of us are dogged by feelings of emotional and personal dissatisfaction. We have a nagging sense that there must be more to life than what we are getting. We apply ourselves to reaching our goals, only to find that even the best achievements sometimes seem thin relative to the price we pay in the form of tension and stress. And as if that weren't enough, the tension endangers our health and our bodies suffer. Is it any wonder that sometimes we ask ourselves whether, in keeping up with the pace of life, we have missed something less tangible but more important? What keeps us traveling down a road whose rewards carry such a cost?

It is time to ask ourselves whether we need to live this way, or whether there may not be some other more fulfilling way, a way that is rich in personal and professional achievement, yet comes without such a loss of energy, creativity, and health. We all have a dream of the good life that includes visions of fulfillment, personal intimacy, and commitment to a meaningful profession of our own choosing. But as a society we'll never get to where we want to go if we keep on going the way we've been going. Deep in our cultural unconscious there are embedded assumptions about life that

are destructive to our health, our personal and professional fulfillment, and the satisfaction of our innate creative drives. These
assumptions sabotage our attempts to explore our potential. They
deny us our capacity for commitment. They limit us. They make us
small rather than big inside.

How do we uproot these self-destructive assumptions and
replace them with more life-enhancing ideas? The answer comes
from taking a closer look at ourselves. A culture is made up of the
people who live in it. Most of us unconsciously accept and live by
principles that limit our possibilities, foster less than optimum
health or even disease, lead to emotional dissatisfaction and sometimes even engender despair. We don't fully realize what we are
doing. And that's not new. Centuries ago, in writing about the
quest for the good life, the philosopher Plato described the problem this way: imagine a society of people in a cave who are seeking to understand how to live well. They have their backs to the
sun, which shines through the cave opening and projects shadows
onto the wall. The people in the cave see the shadows and take
them for reality, for the good life. But reality and goodness lie in
the sun, not in the shadows. Those cave dwellers who are capti-
vated by the dance of shadows on the wall will never see the sun
unless they turn around and look at their life source.

Like the cave dwellers, we will never find another way unless
we let go of the way we are used to living, make a hundred and
eighty-degree turn, and start from a healthier foundation. In the
meantime, we are stuck. We may want to achieve at our peak, but
we approach day-to-day living in a manner that underutilizes the
vast potential of our minds. We long for emotional depth, but we
avoid it and find ourselves mired in anxiety, frustration, and
anger. We are increasingly concerned for our health, yet we live a
lifestyle that is killing us. It's time to uncover our self-limiting
assumptions. It's time to embrace our extraordinary potential. It's
time to replace stress, struggle, and effort, with effortless, creative
living. This book is the story of how to make effortless living a
reality in our lives. And it is accompanied by step-by-step proce-
dures for finding that ease and achieving our potential.

First, I want to show you how we actually create for ourselves
the life we don't want: a life of too much strain with too little satisfaction. We do this to ourselves unconsciously, but once we

become conscious, we can set about changing this pattern. Second, I want to show you step-by-step how we can create the life we do want, how we can move beyond effort and into the art of effortlessness. The effortless life is the life that brings light into our eyes, an expanding warmth into our hearts, a sense of pride into our bellies, and an assurance that we can manifest something truly meaningful through what we do. It's the life we are meant to live.

My Personal Breakdown: A First Step toward Living Well

But why should you take it from me? Why should you believe what I have to say? The only answer I can give you is my personal journey. That's what the rest of this introduction is about. It's the story that launched me into learning about and teaching the art of effortless living. It's also the story of a person whose life seemed to be totally on track until something happened that ground her beliefs into dust. Like so many of us, she had to take a long look at what she was doing and construct her life in another way.

I was born in New York City, the daughter of a mathematics professor and a literary editor. Both of my parents had immigrated to the United States from Europe, and since my father was both multi-lingual and well established in the intellectual community, he was frequently invited to teach abroad. By the time my twin sister and I were ten, we had spent several years in Europe and spoke both French and Italian fluently. Then the family moved back to New York City. My parents divorced, and my sister and I lived with my mother, while visiting my father on weekends.

I was accepted on scholarship to a prestigious private girls' school called Brearley, located on Manhattan's affluent Upper East Side. Classes were small and intensive. I especially loved science, ancient Greek, and the excellent choral and instrumental instruction offered by the school. When I completed high school, I attended Radcliffe College, the sister to Harvard University that merged with Harvard in 1977. I graduated first in my class and with highest honors in 1967, and went to England to study for two years on a fellowship at Cambridge University. My father had strongly encouraged my academic aspirations. When I returned to the United States I enrolled at Columbia University, and within four years I had earned a doctorate in philosophy.

By all standards, I had had a privileged life and had done well. By the age of twenty-seven I was an assistant professor of philosophy at the State University of New York. I had been a serious student and was rewarded for that. I published well-reviewed articles and taught popular, well-attended classes. I received several post-graduate fellowships. While I was teaching, I married an old college flame from a wealthy family. I had absolutely no financial worries. Everything seemed to be on course. I was looking at early success both in my career and in my personal life, and felt I was on my way to achieving those things that I had grown up thinking were important to achieve.

And then, over a few short months, my world collapsed. The early signs were bothersome but not enough to engender panic. I began to notice that when I came back from bicycling, running or shopping, my legs felt unusually tired. Then, one overcast October day I woke up feeling strange. When I swung my legs around to the edge of the bed, they wouldn't support my weight. I stumbled when I tried to stand. I have a vivid memory of feeling ridiculous as I got down onto my hands and knees to crawl to the bathroom. I didn't realize that I would be spending a lot of time with my nose close to the floor in the months to come.

I recovered some of my strength as the day wore on but I was shaken. Over the next few weeks my symptoms multiplied and visits to my regular doctor brought no relief. I struggled to regain my stamina but my body rebelled. I had never been out of control in this way. I was used to calling the shots with my body but now it was having its own way. Day by day I felt weaker. Soon, every inch—from my neck, shoulders, and chest down to my fingertips and toes—felt like it was burning. Sitting in my office, when I would reach for a ballpoint pen or a cup of coffee, sudden jabbing pains would shoot from my shoulder to my wrist and fingers. When I stood up, I had to strategize how I was going to get across the room without my back collapsing.

I wasn't concerned anymore. I was panicked. Even so, I didn't think that whatever was wrong with me would be long lasting. Someone could fix it. After all, I lived in New York City, home to some of the best medical experts in the country. I made appointments with highly recommended neurologists, orthopedists, rheumatologists, and internists at the best hospitals in the city. But each visit was inconclusive. No one seemed to know quite what was going on. I was hospitalized for extensive tests, bed rest, and pharmacological treatment. Then I went back home for several more months of bed rest. Since my health didn't improve, I returned again to the hospital. Once more, nothing changed. The doctors agreed that I was suffering from some kind of collagen disorder but the diagnosis was unclear. Anti-inflammatories didn't help. Anesthetics dulled the pain but knocked my mind out of commission, leaving me unable to work. Mood elevators lessened my growing depression but left me with the same physical problem. If there was a drug that could have helped me, none of the doctors came up with it. I returned home with neither a diagnosis nor a cure.

All my rescue lines had failed me. And for a long time, no avenues for healing opened up. For three years, I remained trapped in a nightmare from which I could not wake. Seriously incapacitated, I spent most of my time in bed. Three years—that's over a thousand days. It's difficult even for me to imagine now that I have left that agonizing time behind. As I look back, however, those thousand days of unending misery were part of the universe's plan to put me on a road of learning. Those hard times forced me to solve some big puzzles about living and to apply what I learned to helping others solve their own puzzles.

The old saying that we get what we ask for has a lot of truth to it. It's just that we often don't understand what it is we are asking for. My own interest in the larger questions about life had led me to a career in philosophy. I had spent a lot of time reading and thinking about questions like what is the purpose of living, what is consciousness, what does it mean to be free? Now it was as if a higher intelligence were saying, "You're going to have to do your learning from a lot more than scholarly texts. And it's not enough for you to sit back and think about these things with your high-powered analytic mind. That's cheating. It's superficial. But since you're interested, we're going to take you through some major twists and turns, and see what you learn about life, consciousness and freedom from all of that!"

Just like thousands and thousands of people over the centuries, pain, frustration, and despair were going to force me to grapple with some pressing issues on a real level. Eventually they were going to lead me to explore and develop techniques for leaving behind that pain, frustration, and despair. Looking back today, I wouldn't have had it any other way.

But back in 1978, nobody was available to tell me about the universe's plan. Nobody was there to paint a picture either of the labyrinth I was in or of the way out of that labyrinth. Nobody was there to help me reflect on the relationship between my illness and my life, and to show me that all my apparent successes had come at the price of an inner failure to own a richer, more authentic part of myself. No one was there to tell me that my job now was not to be academically brilliant but to learn about the inner arts, the arts of self-awareness, arts that can be used to change our lives from the inside out. And nobody could predict that I would later help other people, whether they were suffering from physical disease or just from a sense of unease about their life. I had no inkling that I was going through something that I would one day bless as one of the most useful experiences of my life. As far as I knew, I was just wretchedly sick.

My husband would leave for work early in the morning, depositing fruit and other snacks by the bed, along with a jug of water and a carafe of tea. I would sleep until sleep evaded me. Then I'd read, draw, talk to my therapist or to family members on the phone, smoke compulsively, play solitaire, watch soap operas on television and feel miserable. Friends visited, but they soon discovered that it's boring to keep company with someone who is sick and depressed. On my worst days, the pain and weakness were so intense that we had to invest in a bedpan for home use. During good streaks, I could build up my strength enough to take short walks in our New York City midtown apartment. At my best, I could even go out accompanied by a friend or family member for a long walk of a block or two. At thirty years of age, I was living the life of an inmate in a nursing home.

During this dark and seemingly unending corridor of time, I continued to seek out medical assistance. If some doctor came recommended, I visited him. I also devoured all the literature on health and nutrition that I could find. I eventually gave up smoking and coffee, both after a struggle. Then I found a naturopath, a rare species on the East Coast of the United States in those days. Dr. Cursio was in his eighties, had close to fifty years of practice under his belt, and was a mine of knowledge. I met with him on a monthly basis. He would prescribe in the minutest detail what I was to eat for each meal of the month ahead. I embarked on a strict vegetarian diet, complete with juiced raw fruits and vegetables, steamed vegetables, raw nuts, and legumes. My diet was one hundred percent free of salt, sugar, caffeine, and any other stimulants. Those steps were essential to my healing, and I believe the diet created a background against which the healing could take place. But I discovered over time that it was not enough. It did not provide the critical ingredient for change. Purely physical treatment wasn't returning me to physical health. I had to embark on a journey into my own consciousness. It was deep in my consciousness, and in my assumptions about life, that the real problem lay.

Early Explorations of Consciousness

It was when I opened the door to working with my consciousness that I began to find untapped inner resources. The story of those inner resources, what they are and how to develop them, is the subject of this book. Over time, I learned that the development of those inner capacities is profoundly neglected by our culture. I also found that exploring and cultivating them and strengthening the power of the mind provided the key not only to health but also to emotional well being, happiness in relationships, peak performance, and creativity. I discovered that if we paid attention to learning about and developing our inner power we would find our way to adopting an enriching lifestyle that grew from our deepest potential.

My physical problems put me on a journey of self-discovery that led me far from the conventional values and aspirations that I had cherished up to that point. They took me into studies in religion, bodywork, and the alchemy of self-transformation that to most of my acquaintances seemed weirdly esoteric if not downright ridiculous. I didn't choose to be offbeat. The simple truth was that the mainstream wasn't healing me. I had a choice between staying where I was and being sick or looking to unknown waters and seeing where that would take me.

The initial three years in bed were years that I was living in the mainstream. Even my turn to naturopathy was still mainstream in the sense that it didn't require me to take control of or to change my situation or my consciousness. I was still fully embedded in the cultural tradition that views disease as something that happens to you. That tradition says that if you get well, it's because a doctor does something to fix you. I had to get to the place of owning my own power in dealing with my illness, and that took time and personal change. Yet one thing became clear to me. Only when I began to experiment with my lifestyle and with my consciousness did my body choose to live again and my life begin to change.

Space for healing started to open up when I left both academia and my husband. I had already been on sick leave from my job for several years, so walking away from the academic life wasn't that hard on a practical level. On a psychological level it was more difficult, because it meant abandoning my professional identity and letting go of being the person my parents wanted me to be. But all of this paled in comparison to the difficulty of leaving my husband. I had become totally dependent on him financially, and he tended to most of my physical needs as well.

Nonetheless, some voice within me was whispering that so long as I relied on the security of life with him, I would not heal. Without either of us recognizing it consciously, our marriage contract held a hidden, subversive clause: we could stay together only as long as I stayed dependent. It wasn't any malicious scheme on my husband's part that made this so. Our relationship just happened to be part of a sociological archetype that valued feminine dependency, and we were both unconsciously committed to that archetype.

Ironically, my husband was his most caring with me when I was at my physical worst. And since I was completely dependent, I missed him a great deal when he was away. I was also deeply indebted to him. My dependency and my sense of indebtedness made it difficult for me to face the underlying truth: When I would start getting better, instead of rejoicing together over the change, we would start having trouble. We would quarrel and fight. I had to clear away a lot of guilt and fear before I got to the place where I could see that I could only keep my husband in my life if I kept myself out of life. Eventually I had to make a choice.

I left the midtown apartment that had been my home and the marriage that seemed to fulfill every childhood romantic dream on one of those days when crawling was easier than walking. I moved into a small studio apartment. My husband couldn't understand,

and who could blame him? He was very angry and not inclined to
be generous, and I was not in a mood to fight for myself. Within a
year, we were legally separated and I was close to penniless. Yet it
was under those unlikely circumstances that I began to get better.
I hadn't planned things that way. I hadn't known that leaving my
husband would begin the process of healing. I had just known that
I couldn't continue with him, and out of despair I had taken a leap
and had changed my circumstances. My body had responded,
telling me I had done the right thing.

Leaving the security of my marriage was my first real step in
owning my own healing. I had let go of a piece of what I had
thought I wanted—marriage to someone who offered me financial
security and who unconsciously required emotional dependency as
well. But after changing my outer circumstances I had to do something more difficult: I had to deal with my consciousness, the part
of me that stayed with me no matter where I went. I had to come
to grips with what it was in the way I approached my life that was
contributing to my trouble. What was I doing physically, emotionally, mentally, and spiritually? How was I harming myself against
my conscious intention? I had to walk that fine line that so many
of us have to walk. Like other people on a healing path, I had to
learn how to take responsibility for my life, including my illness,
without plunging into guilt, self-blame, or self-criticism.

I also had to own my illness by seeing it as a taskmaster and a
teacher. Instead of staying in depression, every day I had to
approach my predicament as a challenge to develop insight, personal power, and perhaps certain unique skills. I had to learn how
not to go into collapse.

I began working on myself by joining a meditation group. I did
not have a clear map of where I was going. But I did know that I
was a bundle of anxiety and fear. Getting quiet and developing a
little more inner calm seemed to be a good place to start.
Meditation helped with that and it gradually became an everyday
staple of my life. It wasn't a panacea and it didn't change my life
overnight. But day by day, incrementally, the changes that meditation brought into my life completely transformed who I was. It
was meditation that over time taught me how to relieve and eventually release anxiety, depression, anger, tension, and pain.

The more I meditated, the more aware I became of deep levels
of tension that I had been holding in my body without even

knowing it. To a certain extent, I had been unaware of that tension because it was culturally normal—accepted and unquestioned—taken as a necessary, and sometimes even a positive, fact of life. Now I could see similar tension reflected everywhere around me: in colleagues, friends, family, and the stranger on the street. The lack of softness in people's faces; the frequently intense, worried, aggressive or fearful look in the eyes; the bunched-up muscles and raised shoulders; the non-stop talking. All of that was about tension. I could see that if our culture had a hallmark, this was it: unnecessary and chronic tension and stress. Everywhere I turned, people were holding on to stress like children clutching their precious lollipops.

Rejecting the Cultural Addiction

Over the years that followed, the thought pressed itself more and more insistently into my mind that our culture actually fostered an addiction to stress. The medical community was offering us techniques to relieve stress, but the culture itself was geared to rewarding stress. The more you pushed yourself at work, the more you got rewarded. The more competitive you were, the more you got rewarded. The more you did for your spouse or children, the more kudos you got in their eyes. The more you accumulated, the more recognition you got.

Television, movies, and the print media addicted people to stress by over-stimulating them with scenes of sex, violence, and fear. People learned to associate happiness with being hyped up, even though that didn't feel particularly comfortable. The food industry added to over-stimulation by addicting people to foods saturated with sugar or salt and to stimulants like caffeine, all of which contributed to stress.

Most of the people I saw around me weren't especially happy. A lot of them were successful and fortunate enough to be financially stable. Most were married and some of them lived on tree-lined suburban streets with tennis courts and health clubs down the road. They were living the American dream. But they lacked contentment. And it seemed that they couldn't get enough of what was making them less than happy: the bad food, the negative images in the media, the competition, and more than anything else the drive to prove themselves in other people's eyes. They had the same stuff inside them that I had been discovering in myself.

I had the weird impression that their lives were stuck in a record groove, just as mine had been. They kept on playing the same tune endlessly, until you'd think that they would go mad. And in their own way many of them were going mad, but they couldn't help it. They didn't know anything else. They couldn't see how much they were hurting themselves because they didn't have a point of comparison, and they lacked adequate tools for changing. I began dreaming of what society would look like if we all decided to jump out of that maddening, repetitive groove that we were in and tried a fundamentally new melody.

In the meantime, I was trying to find that new melody for myself. My health still wasn't good, and after working for a while with meditation, Yoga also became a staple of my life. There were long periods of time when Yoga was too challenging for me, but I kept on coming back to it and gradually, in that cyclical up and down way that is part of getting over chronic illness, I got better.

By now it was becoming very clear to me that my healing lay in becoming more conscious of how I was living in my body. I had to learn how to be at ease in my own skin—a skill that on the surface might seem simple, yet clearly involved the highest of arts. I decided to explore more forms of bodywork that could teach me how to live in my body with less tension and more pleasure. I had already tried the types of bodywork that didn't involve working directly with my consciousness: acupuncture, massage, chiropractic, and so on. Now I was looking for approaches that would engage my spirit.

When people think of working with the body, they often think of developing greater body strength. I had always loved sports, and I longed to be strong again, to run and swim and bicycle whenever I was inclined, but I wasn't interested in the exercise mania that is part of a Western cultural obsession with beating the physical body into shape. I knew by now that a manipulative relationship to my body was part of what had made me sick in the first place. I was looking for something deeper. I wanted to change the way I experienced my body. I wanted to explore the mind-body connection.

Exploring the Mind-Body Connection

The superficial understanding of the mind-body connection suggests that mind-body work is about thinking nice thoughts in order to boost your immune system. But that's not really it. More than anything, mind-body work involves tuning in to your body and using your awareness to directly influence the way your body feels and through that, the way you feel as a whole person. Mind-body work is about getting really comfortable, feeling alive, expansive, and free. I had been dead all my life, even when I thought I was well. I wanted to break that pattern and become fully alive. I knew I would be healthy when I was alive.

A friend suggested that I explore the Alexander Technique. Like other forms of mind-body work, in the Alexander Technique someone else does not do something to make you feel better. Instead, you learn how to make a shift within yourself so as to release effort and access inner calm combined with power. A form of movement therapy, the Alexander Technique teaches students how to let go of unconscious physical tension and to increase vital energy.

An Alexander Technique teacher utilizes both her voice and her hands as teaching tools, and guides a client into changing the way he performs basic, everyday movements. These movements—sitting, standing and walking—are part of our unconscious repertoire. We execute them, but we don't really notice how. Most of the time, we execute them less efficiently and fluidly than we might. Not surprisingly, the way we move from day to day is intimately connected to our own hopes, fears and self-perceptions. The more fluidly we move, the more likely we are to be free of self-destructive tendencies that express themselves unconsciously through body tensions. By teaching a person how to change basic movement patterns, an Alexander Technique teacher can trigger profound personal changes. The Technique is also well known for working miracles with relieving back pain. In addition, actors, dancers, and professional musicians take Alexander Technique lessons to improve their poise and expressiveness, and convey a fluid sense of power.

When I went for my first lesson, my teacher welcomed me into a spacious room. Mirrors covered one entire wall, and a bodywork table occupied the center of the floor. She showed me in the mirror where my body was out of alignment. One hip was higher than the other, my shoulders were pulled forward, and I had a swayback. Although I had occupied my body day in and day out for my entire life, I had never really noticed these things before. The teacher told me we would be working to change my inefficient alignment patterns, but we would not be doing that through exercises, pushing or pulling. I was going to change my body, she informed me, through "letting go."

My Alexander Technique teacher put me on a bodywork table and gently moved my limbs around. She took my right leg in her hands and as she placed one hand under my thigh and the other under my heel, she asked me to imagine my leg getting longer. Amazingly, it felt like that was exactly what was happening! She continued moving my legs around in this way for a while, and then had me get up. She worked with me on sitting down and standing up, and to my surprise I discovered that there are many different ways to perform and experience this basic movement pattern. As she guided me in and out of a chair, the teacher asked me to imagine my neck lengthening or my knees releasing. Simultaneously, she touched me lightly in different places. My whole body began to feel like a finely oiled machine, graceful and fluid. Since I was new to the work, I couldn't really understand what was going on, but I certainly absorbed the fact that it felt terrific. I felt so comfortable, light and free! Needless to say, my pain also diminished. After just one lesson, I was hooked.

A Passion for Letting Go

I knew I needed this work—lots of it—to improve physically. But I also knew, with my very first lesson, that I had found a doorway into a new kind of life. Here was something I could study that would stimulate infinite interest and passion on my part. There was nothing as intoxicating as learning about, practicing, and possibly even teaching "letting go." It was so practical in its effects, and at the same time so viscerally satisfying and liberating. I recognized immediately that the study of letting go held far more attraction for me than the academic studies that had absorbed my professional life up to that point. And although I was making a living at that time consulting for academic institutions, an academic career no longer drew my interest. I had become a professor because I was being my father's daughter instead of being true to myself.

I committed myself to the three-year training program for certification as a teacher of the Alexander Technique. I was both healing myself and making the first steps into a new profession. This was a period full of realizations. For example, the more I used the Alexander Technique to release my own physical tension, the more I relaxed emotionally. I was amazed to see that if I could consciously let go of physical tension, that would automatically relieve emotional distress.

As I explored myself more deeply, I realized that for me, fear was identical with a contraction in the back of the neck and the gut, and anger was a tension in the chest and jaw. If I started getting angry with someone, I would tune in to my chest and jaw, and use the Technique to release some of that tension. That not only helped me feel better, it also enabled me to communicate more effectively, since I could express myself without that edge of tension and anger that makes it difficult for someone else to accept what you are saying. And I began to feel that instead of my emotions always having the upper hand, I could gain some control over them: I could decide to stay with emotions that served me and to let go of the ones that were toxic. The bodywork training gave me a powerful tool for letting go of negative emotions.

I was also fascinated by the fact that there seemed to be a direct connection between releasing tension from my body and improving my focus and concentration. I could actually utilize my expanding control over my physical state to improve my concentration by leaps and bounds. The more physically calm I was, the more powerful my concentration was. This discovery had a profound impact on me. I had attended one of the best private schools in the country. Then I had gone to some of the world's premier universities: Harvard, Cambridge University in England, and Columbia. Yet nowhere had anyone told me about this connection between concentration and physical relaxation. No one had trained me or my classmates to improve focus and performance through disciplined physical relaxation. On the contrary, in the high-pressured academic environment of my childhood and young adulthood, I had learned to associate concentration and performance with stress. Now I was finding out that concentration and tension were not good bedfellows, and that if I was genuinely committed to becoming all that I could be mentally, I would have to learn how to leave tension behind.

It began to dawn on me that learning how to navigate the connection between our physical bodies, our emotional states and our mental focus is what gives us power and makes us free. I kept a journal that mapped this connection. By the time I was certified as a teacher of the Alexander Technique, I had left behind the darkest period of my illness and pain. I opened my own private practice in a suburb of New York City.

A New Life and Career

I began teaching the Alexander Technique and meditation, while continually looking for and incorporating new tools into my work. I wanted to understand every dimension of letting go, and to help clients navigate the mind-body connection in a way that would maximize their well being. I explored and trained in many forms of bodywork, including Craniosacral Therapy, a powerful form of healing through subtle touch that can help a person release emotional traumas held in the body's tissues. I read every book and listened to every experiential tape I could find on the mind-body connection. I attended motivational seminars, studied Neuro-Linguistic Programming, and delved deep into the study of Buddhism, Theosophy, and contemplative Christianity.

In addition to my private practice, I began to consult for schools, churches, corporations and country clubs. My prior experience as a professor and my strong left-brain education served me well. I was teaching people about right-brain learning, showing them how learning to take charge of our sensations, our inner vision and our imaginative faculties can generate dramatic changes in our health and productivity. Because of my background, I was blessed with the ability to translate right-brain truths for left-brain minds. My audience grew. Often, people were drawn into working with me because what I said sounded intellectually plausible. Then the work itself moved them from intellectual to experiential consent.

Even so, I remember feeling like an outlaw for a while after I opened my private practice and consulting business. I had left behind everything that I had originally trained for, and everything I thought I valued. My family didn't understand what I was doing, and they were disappointed that I had abandoned what seemed to be a brilliant career. What was all this meditation and bodywork stuff about? Why not just go back to being an intellectual?

I wasn't getting much respect. And even with my intellectual training, it was not always easy to explain to people what I did. After all, mind-body work was not recognized by the mainstream at that time. How could I tell someone that if he changed the way he held his body he would solve his problems with anger, sadness or fear? He would think I was crazy. How could I tell someone that meditation, or tuning in to the rhythm of his breathing, would provide a quick ticket to improving his mental concentration? He would label me as unbalanced and "New Age." But I had to keep going in the direction I was headed. The more time I spent exploring mind-body disciplines, the more my health, emotional state, concentration and creativity improved. The more I taught other people the disciplines I was learning, the better their lives became. That had to be motivation enough.

I saw that understanding the mind-body connection completely could provide all the answers we need for developing physical vitality, emotional balance, productivity and happiness. Today, I continue to work with people who have physical problems that range from back pain to heart disease to cancer, identifying the physical, emotional and cognitive sources of these illnesses in my clients, and teaching them how to transcend their illnesses through developing their own powers of awareness. I also work with people who aren't sick, teaching meditation, intuitive self-development, and creative self-transformation to professional business people, artists and athletes seeking to maximize their productivity, and to many men and women interested in bringing greater quality and satisfaction into their lives and relationships.

The people who seek me out all want to enhance their ability to take charge of their lives. They are also all unconsciously committed to mental, emotional, physical, and behavioral patterns that sabotage their efforts at growth. My job is to show them experientially how they are limiting themselves, and how they can shift their consciousness in order to empower themselves. I use dialogue, bodywork, breath work, emotional repatterning and visualization training to help them find more freedom.

Consciousness: The Road to Self-Transformation

The same mind-body methods that help heal the body of chronic illness also heal emotional trauma, provide spiritual insight and direction, open the doors of self-expression, motivate performance and optimum concentration, and help people develop stronger relationships. These methods are profoundly different from the ways that we in our society have been taught to approach our lives. The tools we have been given for living, and the techniques we have been trained in for achieving personal and professional success, are sometimes inefficient and at other times downright counterproductive to life enhancement.

My own physical crisis forced me to learn how to tap into the deeper powers of my mind. It also showed me that nothing in my upbringing, which was among the best that my society could offer, taught me how to enhance self-awareness or to reach into that deeper potential that is our human inheritance. My upbringing emphasized getting a lot done, often at the expense of exploring the landscape of my mind, or seeing how my consciousness affected my life. And I am a product of my culture, just like all the people who come to me. Just as I did, they lack self-awareness and have no idea how to access their internal resources beyond the most superficial level. They know something is wrong and are looking for techniques to heal and enrich their lives. And they, like every one of us, deserve to find those techniques.

Our culture actually discourages inner growth and self-awareness, stifling the ultimate source of our sense of fulfillment. I myself earned success at the cost of deadening my sensitivities, my consciousness, and my body. My illness was an inevitable and natural product of the cultural values I grew up with. I followed the rules to the letter and they made me sick. All around me I see other people who, like me, are seriously sick as a result of living lives enslaved to the cultural norms. Others who are not sick are nonetheless suffering. They are saddled with dissatisfying relationships, or with demanding but unrewarding professions, or with a loss of creativity. The same dynamic works its way through many people's lives. What happened to me through those long years of my disability was just a very dramatic result of living by unconscious social rules and patterns that others also live by.

Making those unconscious rules conscious stimulates the process of healing, and opens the door to more expansive living. If you have read this far, then you are already committed to finding a richer and more authentic life. To help you in that process, I invite you to join with me in asking and answering some fundamental questions. What is it about our culture that simultaneously cultivates stress-based disease, emotional dysfunction, impoverished relationships, limited creativity and spiritual malaise? How are the physical, emotional, interpersonal and spiritual costs of everyday living related to each other and to our cultural attitudes? How can we adopt a new set of skills that simultaneously promotes radiant health, emotional authenticity, and enriching relationships, and that also allows us to reach our maximum potential? And where can we find a map for the journey into healing?

The answers to those questions are the subject of this book. The next section, Part I, paints a more complete picture of the problem we all face. Parts II and III then explore the dynamics of self-transformation and personal fulfillment. The goal: to offer you a comprehensive, practical and also pleasurable map of the journey into becoming more fully yourself.

The Way of the Effortful Warrior: A Cultural Addiction

chapter 1

To Do or To Be

Every culture seeks to provide answers to some of the fundamental questions we face in the course of a lifetime. How can we become everything that we need to be? How do we tap into our potential and go in a direction that matches our deepest needs? These questions reflect another even more fundamental question: How do we master the art of living? There are only two basic answers to this question. Each culture pledges primary allegiance to one of these answers. That answer then becomes the driving force behind individuals' choices and accomplishments. It defines their value systems. It creates criteria for success and failure that determine how society's members perceive and value themselves. It enters deep into the core of each person's being.

The first answer to the question is that living well is a function of what you *do*. It embodies a philosophy of *doing*. It says success at living is measured by what you *accomplish externally*. The second answer is that living well is a function of who you *are*. It embodies a philosophy of *being*. It says success at living reflects your *internal state*, or how you experience yourself inside.

When we define ourselves by what we do, our focus is on achieving concrete external goals. We also assume that by achieving those goals we will find internal contentment. We think that the external activities that absorb our attention will create a desirable internal result. We become professionally successful, or gain the recognition of colleagues so that we can feel internal states called happiness, confidence or self-esteem. We search for a mate and create a family for the same reason: to feel internal satisfaction. We always assume that external accomplishment, or *doing*, comes first. Our internal state, or how we feel, comes second, presumably as a consequence of what we do.

The second answer to the question of right living is exactly the opposite. According to this philosophy of *being*, achieving a desirable internal state comes first. When we define ourselves by *who we are* instead of by *what we do*, our focus is on achieving inner qualities like serenity, strength, balance, passion or insight. The inner reality is the most important thing. External success, which is the primary focus of a philosophy of *doing*, comes second, presumably as a result of achieving a desirable internal state.

The Cultural Commitment to Doing

Our culture overwhelmingly embraces the first approach to right living and life mastery. We live in a culture based on doing. We have very few reference points for achieving internal fulfillment or success at being. We are all willing to sing the praises of poise, passion or courage, but most of us spend relatively little time thinking about what these terms mean, or about what we would have to do to develop these qualities. Naturally, we hope to attain noble character traits as a result of our activities. But that is not quite the same thing as devoting ourselves each day to using the events of the day to pursue inner growth. Instead, even while we are interested in inner growth, most of us still define our day in terms of a "to do" list: getting the next deal closed, the obligatory phone calls completed, the children fed and shipped off to school, or the next meal arranged.

Society also doesn't offer us many institutionalized opportunities for pursuing inner goals. We have to look to our extracurricular volunteer activities, recreation or religious life if we want to devote time to character cultivation. It's in our time off that we try to find the inner qualities we long for. But the rest of the time, all the time that is not leisure, gets focused mostly on achieving. And so we have lots of criteria for making it in the arena of doing. Financial stability, recognition in the professional field of our choice, marriage, children, service to the community, social status, are all signposts for external success. We spend a great deal of time working to meet these criteria, and to a large extent we measure our success as individuals by how effectively we have done this.

No one would deny that external goals can be extremely important. There is nothing wrong with doing things. After all, we do live in a physical world and things do have to get done. And the Western industrialized focus on external accomplishment has until recently fostered unparalleled levels of abundance for at least certain portions of the planet. But there is a problem. It is not at all true that achieving external goals will guarantee internal satisfaction. This may be what the philosophy of doing claims, but things don't work out that way. There is no guarantee that by accomplishing the external goals we set for ourselves we will achieve internal fulfillment. In fact, nothing could be further from the truth. Over-focusing on external achievements can cause us to ignore the deep personal changes and challenges we must confront in order to feel we have lived life well.

How many people do you know who are successful yet are gnawed by feelings of insecurity and failure? The road to external success is not necessarily the road to depth of character and self-realization. You can amass millions to assuage feelings of insecurity yet never resolve that inner sense of worthlessness. You can become an entertainment celebrity and the envy of all around you, a Marilyn Monroe or a John Belushi, and be so ridden by feelings of despair that you take your own life. Storing up the external symbols of success just isn't the whole answer.

Our culture is in crisis, and the crisis we are in is due in part to this terrible gap between external success and internal satisfaction. Carried to an extreme, the focus on external accomplishments and achievements produces the opposite of a satisfying life. We accumulate external proofs of our value at the cost of a deep inner sense of emptiness and what often amounts to despair over the meaning of life. If we try to quench our inner emptiness by accomplishing more, that inner emptiness only grows. As a guiding principle, the philosophy of doing is at best limited and at worst bankrupt. And there is something about our focus on achieving that is distorted, that expresses a sickness of the soul. Why do we think that we have to pile up achievements in order to be okay?

The truth is that we would not feel that we had to prove ourselves by what we did unless we already believed that we were unworthy. Yet if we are unworthy at our core, no amount of achievement will solve our problem.

The Alternative of Being

The only way we can find the pathway to satisfaction is by lessening our obsessive grip on doing and focusing more on being. But what does being involve? What would individuals who practice being be like? These people are all too rare, but I have met a few. They are balanced and at peace, yet also courageous, strong and not afraid of taking risks. They blend authority with gentleness, patience with dynamism, the capacity for joy and laughter with an ability to experience deep recesses of personal pain. They integrate a passion for self-expression with the ability to listen intently, and are leaders who can also follow. They are their own person, uninfluenced by public opinion, yet also capable of deep partnership and companionship. They are profoundly committed to inspiring causes, and able to evoke that sense of commitment in others. They are mentally sharp, emotionally vibrant and vitally alive. They make every moment of life count and contribute in a big way, not because they need to pile up accomplishments but because they care deeply. They can give and receive love abundantly, and be of genuine service from a spirit of self-giving rather than of obligation. Their many strengths combine *yin* and *yang*, softness and strength, independence and the capacity for loving interdependence. They are totally comfortable in their own skins.

Spiritual writings extol the virtues of being. In the *Old Testament*, Job was great not for what he possessed but for his ability to endure with strength through all he lost. It was his struggle to achieve internal freedom and faith that gained him God's grace and that eventually returned him to material prosperity. Job represents the spiritual principle that internal achievement, or focus on being, brings about external achievement and success. The *New Testament* is also a teaching of being. It guides us toward purifying ourselves of inner weaknesses like envy, greed and fear, and replacing them with the light of love. In a different tradition, Buddhism teaches us not about achieving externally but rather about developing detachment in the face of life's restless striving, and committing ourselves to the inner quest for peace. The ancient masterpiece of China, the *I Ching* or *Book of Changes*, which became a source for the teachings of both Confucius and Lao-Tse, teaches the way of inner balance in the midst of constant external change. Its oracles guide the sincere seeker into right living through learning the personal security, tranquillity and power that come from aligning oneself with the forces of life and the reality of the *Tao*.

The philosophy of being is about self-transformation. The consequences of our culture's total failure to value self-transformation are deadly. A pessimism about human potential pervades Western society. This pessimism tells us that we cannot amount to much, that we must lower our sights, and that great feats are not for the common man or woman.

A lack of faith in the human spirit underlies our obsession with keeping busy. We learn to over-focus on details and avoid responsibility for the big picture. We learn how to do more but we don't necessarily learn how to become bigger and better people, to conquer the anxieties that drive us, or to set our sights on high ideals. Our lack of faith in ourselves limits our ability to challenge ourselves. We admire greatness of character in others, yet often assume that we cannot develop this greatness within ourselves. Almost nothing around us tells us what the pathwork of self-transformation and empowerment looks like or how we can embrace it.

Cultural voices counsel defeat rather than challenge us to grow. These crippling voices even masquerade as scientific fact. Here's a typical so-called objective scientific argument: We are born with unalterable genetic traits. Therefore, our personalities are largely under the control of our biochemistry. And if biochemistry rules us, how can we change ourselves for the better? How can we change our internal states? How can we conquer anxiety, depression or fear if these are biologically determined? In fact, since biochemistry is our master, then when anxiety or depression hails our way, shouldn't we take a drug to control it rather than find out how to transform it from within? According to this view, we are victims of our biochemistry, and the best we can do is to manage our states with the use of external agents.

Our nation is not only the biggest consumer of illicit drugs in the world, it is also the biggest consumer of prescription drugs. We rationalize this fact by saying that our brain synapses rule our lives, and so all we can do is biochemically influence those synapses. The problem with arguments like these is that they use so-called science to limit us instead of helping us to grow. They are also misleading. It is a fact that biochemistry affects our mental and emotional states. But it is just as much a fact that our mental, emotional and spiritual states influence our biochemistry. Our beliefs can create health or disease, self-doubt or self-confidence. There's no doubt that our beliefs have power. When we embrace self-limiting, fearful beliefs and ground them in cultural superstitions that we call science, we use our mental capacities for outright self-destruction.

Each of us has the power to use our own mind to transform our internal states and create a life that is physically healthy as well as emotionally and mentally rewarding. But we can't create this life for ourselves unless we place our priorities where they belong: with being rather than with doing. That's the responsibility we face. And it's not a question of sacrificing one thing for another. Focusing on being will take us where we actually want to go when we focus on doing, because both the philosophy of doing and the philosophy of being are aiming at the same goal: inner satisfaction. But people who focus on becoming happy by achieving external goals are going about their lives in a confused way. They're putting the cart before the horse. They think that they can get away with focusing on their achievements first and deal with themselves afterwards, when what they really should do is the opposite. This confusion over what comes first is the problem. It makes for a lot of poor choices in life.

The Key to Happiness

Long ago, the Buddha recognized the confusion in the way human beings pursue happiness. He observed that a restless striving after goals is part of human nature. People are constantly seeking to get something or to do something, operating with the notion that what they get or what they do will give them satisfaction. At the same time, what they are really looking for is something they can achieve only by ceasing their striving, by ceasing to think in terms of what they can get and do.

The Buddha identified a paradox. In all the frenzy of our activity, no matter what we are trying to do or where we are trying to go, what we are actually seeking is not an external achievement but an *internal feeling*. It is our internal state that we are trying to manage, and not something else. We believe that by achieving something—finding the right mate, getting the perfect job, etc.— we will attain the internal state of satisfaction that gives us a feeling of meaningfulness. We look to the outside, but we are looking there to heal the inside. External goals simply become a means for producing internal results. After all, it is our *internal state* that we live with moment by moment and day after day. It is the only thing that never leaves us. It *is* us.

In the end, everything we do is motivated by the desire to achieve an internal state that makes us feel better. What differentiates us one from the other is not whether or not we are seeking internal fulfillment, because all of us are doing that. What makes us different from each other is how we go about seeking to create that inner well-being, what kind of results we actually achieve, and whether we learn from the results.

The drug addict takes drugs to change his internal state, to get rid of pain, anger or anxiety and feel more pleasure, more freedom, more joy. Like everyone else, he wants to find happiness and release from pain. But he has a fairly low criterion of success and is prevented from learning and growing. The addict is also dependent on something external for changing his internal state. The external thing that changes his state—the drug—produces short-term satisfaction and leads to long-term disaster. The more he relies on the drug for feeling good, the more the rest of his life falls apart. He gets symptomatic relief from a cancerous problem he's feeding. His approach to managing how he feels is short-sighted, creates a more and more unmanageable life, and doesn't meet his real needs—needs that have more to do with feeling safe in the universe than with feeling high.

Imagine the opposite extreme from the drug addict: the Tibetan yogi who wraps his naked body in a dripping wet sheet and sits in sub-zero temperatures on a Himalayan mountain top throughout the night. He practices a fairly intense inner discipline by training himself to heat his body with his mind, drying the wet sheet that envelops him. He's remarkably adept at maintaining a comfortable body temperature in an uncomfortable world. There's a similarity between the Tibetan yogi and the drug addict. Both of them are working on getting control of how they feel on the inside. But the yogi is doing it in a way that's very different from the drug addict. Instead of looking for something outside him to warm him up on the inside, the yogi trains his mind to raise his body temperature so that the outside world doesn't bother him. He is using an adverse external circumstance as a tool for developing an internal skill. Instead of changing from the outside, he changes from the inside. Instead of trying to get something outside himself to satisfy him, he satisfies himself by changing his normal response pattern to the outside. And if he keeps it up, he'll even influence his environment by melting the snow he's sitting on.

We may not all want to develop the ability to dry wet sheets in Arctic conditions. But there is a lesson in the yogi's approach. The ability to maintain control of our internal states in the face of difficult circumstances, instead of being tossed to and fro by the winds of the moment, is basic to leading a fulfilling life. And there's more. Inner balance is a key ingredient for meaningful external achievement. People with inner balance train their minds to be powerful allies in the pursuit of their goals, instead of weak companions or even foes.

When we focus on being instead of doing, we explore and strengthen the power of our minds. The mind is the greatest resource we have. Because our culture asks us to focus excessively on doing, it neglects the cultivation of our greatest resource, the internal faculties of our minds. What's more, when we over-focus on doing, we actually end up achieving far less in the outside world than if we focused on being. That's the real rub: if you go with doing you lose on all fronts. You're less happy and you achieve less. But if you go with being, you find that by working on your internal state you're not only happier, you also achieve far more than you would have imagined possible. Focusing on doing is self-destructive and inefficient. It undermines our peace and makes our life stressful. It encourages self-hatred, fear and shame. It is totally ineffective, crippling and painful. We are suffering from a cultural disease that is making us sicker than we know.

It's impossible to live in today's world and not be affected by this disease. We need to understand the enemy we live with fully before we can free ourselves. The next three chapters explore how living a life that overfocuses on doing and on external success weakens every aspect of our lives, from our health to our emotional life, our relationships and our creative potential. I call the life path of doing *the way of the effortful warrior*, because over-focusing on doing eats up our lives. Let's look at how we commit ourselves to an effortful lifestyle that then destroys us.

chapter 2

Doing: An Addiction to Effortful Living

Linda over-focuses on *doing*. When she heads for the early morning train into the city, getting to the station on time becomes more important than whether she goes into a state of anxiety on the way. By the time she reaches the station her shoulders are up around her ears and her mind is full of worries. At the office, her main focus is on getting all those memos or deals out of the way. If that comes at the cost of tension, anxiety or indigestion, she assumes it's the price she has to pay. And there's no time on the job for real contact with other people, especially since chatting with colleagues doesn't have a payoff in getting things done.

With Linda's children too, doing takes top priority. Linda loves her children and wants the best for them, so she unwittingly passes along to them her commitment to doing. Exhibiting the virtues of parenthood by marshalling them through soccer games, music lessons, competitive schooling and timely nutrition takes precedence over finding goofy moments together or relaxing in an open-ended, unplanned way. Getting the kids to do a lot, and coping with doing a lot for them, is more important than something less concrete but very real: sharing time and space in a way that deepens communication and brings joy.

On a psychological and spiritual level, when we define ourselves by what we do rather than by who we are, we confess to feeling powerless. If this sense of powerlessness is not always conscious, that is only because it forms the framework of our perception, the lens through which we see the world. Our identity becomes tied to accomplishing what is expected of us by a pervasive yet vague "somebody else." We put our attention on gaining recognition and approval and measure ourselves by how we stand relative to others.

The growth of technology compounds this alienation from ourselves by increasing the pace of life. Technology can be liberating, but so far it has favored the life of external achievement far more than the life of internal growth. It encourages us to emphasize speed and quantity over quality. And our economic employment structure worsens the problem by making it difficult for people to live creative lives. It is easier to find employment as a data processor than as a dancer, even though being a dancer offers more venues for self-awareness and self-expression.

When employment possibilities don't seem to feed the human spirit, people give up on dreams of turning their avocation into their vocation and of finding themselves through their work. But since our jobs take up a big part of our lives, we have to validate ourselves somehow through them. If we can't work at what we love, we find validation in another way. We replace loving what we do with a second best: accomplishing a lot of whatever it is that we are stuck doing. If the work isn't intrinsically rewarding, then let's at least feel good about ourselves by getting a lot done! So we close a lot of deals, package a lot of foods, sell a lot of real estate, or perform a lot of surgeries. We look back at the end of a long day, pat ourselves on the back and say, "Well, you sure did accomplish a whole bunch!" We feel a glimmer of satisfaction, even as we realize that feeling okay about ourselves tomorrow will require the same piling up of unending and sometimes questionable results.

In day-to-day life, we succumb to a relentless feeling of pressure. We wake up in the morning asking ourselves what we are supposed to do that day. We spend most of our day doing one thing and simultaneously thinking about what we are supposed to do next. We come to the end of our lives, still thinking about what it is that we have to do next. We are in a constant battle with time.

The Battle with Time and Its Cost in Disease

Our battle with time has a heavy cost. In the 1950's, two doctors named Meyer Friedman and Ray Rosenman became interested in how different personality types relate to time, and how that affects health. It was Friedman and Rosenman who identified and named the Type A personality, and launched the first extensive investigation into the relationship between personality and heart disease. In 1974, they published *Type A Behavior and Your Heart*, in which they claimed that emotional factors play a prominent role in cardiovascular disorders. Their discovery is now part of cultural lore. And their research underscored two basic truths about compulsive performing. First, over-focusing on external achievement is physically and emotionally destructive. Second, the obsessive doer's need constantly to move on to the next goal does not make him more successful, even though he may think it does.

A couple of clues led Rosenman and Friedman to investigate the role of personality in heart disease. One odd clue came from a woman who was upholstering the chairs in the doctors' waiting room. She was curious about the fact that all the chairs seemed to be worn in the front but not in the back. Apparently, patients sat on the front of their chairs as they waited for their appointments. Why? Because they were always in a hurry! They couldn't sit back, be patient and take a break.

Another clue emerged when the doctors investigated the eating habits of men with heart disease and of their wives. Husbands and wives had identical diets, but the women tended not to have coronary problems. The doctors were puzzled. They had assumed that the eating habits of the men were an important factor in their disease, and finding out that the wives had similar diets seemed to contradict that hypothesis.

Friedman and Rosenman wondered if there was anything else that might account for the fact that the men developed heart trouble while their wives did not. As it turned out, the lives of husbands and wives were significantly different in one respect: the men worked in highly competitive environments. Their wives' lives were certainly not free from stress, since raising children carries its own challenges. But because most of the women did not carry full-time jobs, it was the competitiveness of the men's lives that distinguished them. This fact loomed even more important when the doctors sent out a questionnaire that asked the patients themselves to identify what they felt were important factors behind their illness. Seventy percent of the respondents claimed excessive competitiveness and deadline pressure as a contributing cause. This was extraordinary because prevailing medical paradigms did not recognize job stress as a source of heart disease.

The doctors eventually concluded that the most significant personality factors contributing to heart disease were a chronic sense of time urgency and excessive competitiveness, along with the hostility that this competitiveness breeds. "Type A Behavior Pattern is an action-emotion complex that can be observed in any person who is *aggressively* involved in a *chronic, incessant* struggle to achieve more and more in less and less time, and if required to do so against the opposing efforts of other things or other persons. It is not psychosis or a complex of worries or fears or phobias or obsessions, but a socially acceptable—indeed often praised—form of conflict."[*] Type A suffers from what the doctors called "hurry sickness."[**] He's always in future time, sacrificing now for where he is going. Today, he—or she—is the average person in society.

If we measure who we are by what we do, we end up sacrificing creativity and the pleasure of doing things well for the sake of doing them faster. We put aside higher values that make life meaningful for the sake of getting the job done. And since we're in a hurry, we don't get to experience true involvement and concentration. But these are what make work pleasurable!

It's the subjective feeling of pleasure that helps us make right choices for ourselves. When we're healthy, we commit ourselves to activities, friendships, and professional work that give us joy. Yet to a remarkable extent, many of us have learned to eliminate enjoyment as a critical guide in our life choices.

Instead of measuring our worth by the organic feeling of satisfaction that comes from engaging in something meaningful, we look at how much money we're making or at whether we're receiving social recognition. We get pleasure not from what we do but from the tangential results of what we do. If the result is money,

---

[*] Meyer Friedman, M.D. and Ray Rosenman, M.D., *Type A Behavior and Your Heart* (New York: Fawcett Columbine, 1974), p. 68.

[**] Ibid., p. 70.

then we find our pleasure through what money can buy us: elegant clothes, fancy houses with swimming pools, or vacations on Caribbean islands. If the result is social recognition, which is usually tied to money, then we also get to feel important in other people's eyes. In either case, the reward of work lies not in the work but in what we can lay claim to as a result of the work. The consequences are insidious. We enter into a bottomless pit of effort. We start having to measure ourselves not only by how many goals we achieve but also by how many of those goals we achieve compared to others. We become competitive because we have abandoned any internal standard of our own worth.

The compulsive doer inside us needs to be in control. We need to control ourselves so that we can meet other people's demands, including that vague other called "society," or "convention," or "the next door neighbor." And we need to control others, and get them to do what we think they must do, so that they don't create problems for us and so that we can accomplish what we think we need to accomplish. The possibility that nobody might be in control, and that this could be just fine, doesn't occur to us! We think that either we have the power or someone else does, and so we're afraid of losing power. The Type A personality is run by fear, even though he or she may not realize this consciously.

Rosenman and Friedman estimated that approximately 60 percent of the population was Type A. Heart disease has become more prevalent since they wrote their book, and so has the incidence of Type A personality. With women more active in the workforce today than in the 1970s, for both women and men cardiovascular illness is the top killer in the United States. Yet our society does not address the truth underlying that fact. Diseases of the heart reflect the dis-ease, or lack of comfort, of *living without heart*—of living a lifestyle that is inwardly self-destructive and of struggling to achieve in terms that amount to spiritual and psychological malnutrition.

Type A personality doesn't show itself only in cardiovascular problems. Those of us who have a compulsive performer inside may develop any one of a number of chronic stress-related diseases that are endemic in a society committed to hurry sickness. A full 70 percent of doctors' visits today are stress-based. This means that patients' complaints result from their mental and emotional responses to the demands of everyday living. The mental framework through which most people approach their lives is downright harmful to their physical well-being.

Treadmills, Emotional Stress and Illness

Stress-based illness is the result of life lived on a treadmill. We get on that treadmill because we think we have no choice; we think we're being forced to effort our way through our lives. We become *reactive* instead of *proactive*. When we are proactive, we determine our direction and shape our environment. We assume that our own decisions and values can have a strong influence on the world around us. When we are reactive, we think events around us have the dominant influence, and we confine ourselves to coping with and defending against those events. We don't see that we are constantly influencing the world as well as being influenced by it. We assume that our best stance is a defensive one and we adopt a fight or flight response to daily life.

Biologically, the human animal isn't well adapted to continual fight or flight responses. If we're going to be healthy, the stress response has to be the exception and equilibrium must be the norm. If we lived in a way that matched our biological inheritance, then most of the time we would be in balance or at rest. Occasionally, a difficult situation would put us into fight or flight. But today, the fight or flight response is the statistical norm rather than the exception. It's the norm for people to live with anger or fear close to the surface. It's the norm for them to approach their daily lives with the feeling that at any moment they might need to defend themselves or attack someone else. It's the norm for our bodies to remain in the biochemically aroused and muscularly contracted state of a creature in danger. Is it any wonder that a constant fight or flight response to life compresses the body, depresses the immune system and eventually leads to long-term disease?

It's easy to trace the dynamics of the connection between emotions and physical illness. In the case of heart disease, the biochemical consequences of stress lead directly to the symptoms of the illness. Heart disease is associated with high blood pressure. So is the fight or flight response. A healthy person, who can balance his emotions and move from action to rest and from rest back into action, will react to a stressful situation with a momentary rise in blood pressure. Then that blood pressure will return to normal. The endangering situation is dealt with and left behind. But what happens to a person who experiences life itself as endangering? For this person, there is no point of equilibrium. There is no point at which anxiety and tension are put to rest and body and mind return to a tranquil state. Instead, the blood pressure rises and it stays elevated. Then high blood pressure becomes the norm instead of the exception, and the person eventually develops cardiovascular disease.

Many of the chronic diseases of our culture are a direct result of physiological imbalances created by emotional stress. Back problems and arthritis, one or both of which eventually afflict up to three quarters of the population, are often long-term manifestations of stress. When we are under stress the muscles in our body contract in an attempt at self-defense. We get tight, literally as well as figuratively. We pull all our energy inward, shut down, and put a barrier between ourselves and the world. If we get tight often enough and for long enough, our muscles stay tight. We experience this as pain, rounded shoulders, herniated disks, and hip, knee and foot problems. Our tight muscles also create friction around the joints, and that friction encourages the calcification that leads to osteoarthritis. We often attribute our physical discomfort to aging but it has nothing to do with aging itself. It has to do with how we respond to our experiences day after day. If we develop a habit of tightness and defense, after a while we no longer can find our way back to the sense of release and ease that are our birthright.

Our society is witnessing an epidemic of breathing disorders. Atmospheric oxygen depletion and pollution play a role in the rise of asthmatic and other bronchial conditions, but stress is also a major contributor. When we are frightened or angry, we breathe shallowly and rapidly, cutting off the supply of oxygen to our tissues. If we do this often enough and long enough, we forget how to breathe normally. Most people in our society exhibit the shallow, thoracic breathing of a frightened animal.

The normal rate of breathing for a fully relaxed person is *between four and six breaths a minute*. Yet very few people breathe at this relaxed, optimal level. It is not unusual for people to breathe between twelve and thirty breaths a minute. They may experience this as normal because it is their habit. But it is a sign of a body in distress, and if it is not corrected, then after years of shallow and rapid breathing a person will end up in the doctor's office with either heart disease or a chronic respiratory ailment.

Another increasingly pervasive chronic lifestyle disease that may be tied in part to poor breathing habits is cancer. Loss of oxygen to the cells is an important factor in the growth of carcinogenic tissue, and that loss of oxygen can be a direct result of restricted breathing.

Type A's Effort: A Study in Counter-Productivity

The prevalence of serious stress-based illnesses in our society is glaring evidence of the astronomical physical price that the Type A personality pays for over-focusing on doing. The problem is that most of us accept struggling our way through life as if it were inevitable. We feel we have to strive ceaselessly. We feel we have no choice. We think that the demands of life force us to be in a rush and to produce. We ignore the fact that if we want to improve our lives, we must each choose individually to get off the treadmill of effort.

There might be at least a modicum of sense in our attitude if rushing got us anywhere. But it doesn't! It may sound logical to the person in the existential pressure cooker to say that he has to keep hurrying. But being in a rush has no relationship to getting things done, even though the person who is in a rush may think so. There is no proven relationship between being in a rush and being vocationally successful. When Friedman and Rosenman researched the relationship between Type A personality and professional accomplishment, they found no significant correlation. Someone who was not Type A was just as likely, if not more likely, to succeed materially as the Type A person. In fact, hurry sickness can be a liability if you are interested in maximizing your abilities. We may not be aware of it, but when we tell ourselves we have to rush in order to succeed, we lie.

In his *New York Times* bestseller, *The Seven Habits of Highly Effective People,* Steven Covey points out that the behavior pattern of hurry sickness is antithetical to success. According to Covey, highly effective people master the illusion of being chased by time. They may have to respond to the normal pressures of everyday living, but they are not overwhelmed by them. Instead of seeing life as a constant effort to deal with demands made upon them, they direct their energies creatively toward building what they think is important. They spend a good portion of each day shaping their life rather than reacting to it.

Effective people are creative, and creative people make time their ally. When any of us have individual moments of creativity, we taste the truth of this description. We experience ourselves in the flow, we tame the perpetual wave of external events and ride it from a place of inner balance. But when we get into compulsive doing, time becomes a turbulent force pushing us one way or another. We find ourselves reacting to a series of external constraints and demands instead of acting to implement ideas and values that we believe are important. Every wave becomes a tidal wave that threatens to knock us down. So we thrash around, making much ado about those waves and feeling generally urgent.

The more we feel pressured by time, the more we get irritated and upset by the smallest event, and the more trouble we give ourselves in accomplishing whatever we are doing. I am reminded of a flight attendant I met once when I was flying on business from New York to Salt Lake City. As she approached down the aisle with her beverage cart, I noticed that her voice was loud, urgent and grating. She asked me what I wanted to drink, and I told her, "Orange juice, no ice please." She reached for the orange juice carton, saw it was almost empty, and turned down the aisle to get some more cartons. When she came back, she hurriedly pulled open a drawer, stuffed the extra juice cartons inside, and then plunged a plastic glass into the ice bucket, filling it full of ice. I reminded her, "No ice please." She dumped the ice, filled the glass, and promptly spilled one third of its contents onto my tray, my book, and my lap. Without apologizing (I guess she didn't have time for that!) she hurriedly wiped up the spilled juice and refilled my glass. As she rushed to pull the juice cart down the aisle, she bumped it solidly against the base of my chair and had to retreat to free it.

Some time later, she came by again, serving drinks with dinner. She stopped at the seats in front of mine, went to open a drawer in her cart to reach in for some canned beverages, and pulled the drawer so hard that she dumped the entire contents right in the aisle. That irritated her plenty, and she picked the cans up, dropped them in the drawer, and shoved it brusquely back in place. Then she yanked the cart forward, jamming it a second time into the base of my seat.

Perhaps the flight attendant was thinking about how many people she had to serve. Perhaps she was feeling her job was endless. Whatever was going on inside her, she was definitely giving herself a hard time. She was the one who was dropping juice on my lap, bumping carts against seats, banging drawers or pulling them so hard that she dropped their contents on the floor. She was the one who had to clean up after herself. She was the one who was doubling her work, all because she was so focused on getting through with one customer and moving on to the next. You would think that she would realize she was creating problems for herself and would slow down. You would think that she would learn from the other flight attendant, who was calmly and efficiently accomplishing a great deal, or that she would step back and laugh at the whole situation. But she didn't seem to be learning from her failed efforts. Instead, she pushed harder. And that made her mad.

The next time I saw this flight attendant she was marching down the aisle serving after-dinner beverages. She would rap out, "Coffee? Tea? Milk?" in an insistent voice, demanding the attention of the passengers, most of whom didn't care too much one way or the other or who were fast asleep. Instead of remembering that she was there to offer a service if they wanted it, she seemed to be irritated that the passengers weren't wide awake and on their toes, ready to help her do her job! A group of Russian tourists who spoke no English occupied the seats ahead of me. Her method of communicating with them was to repeat her questions at an increasingly rapid staccato pace. "Coffee? Tea? Milk? Coffee? Tea? Milk? Coffee? Tea? Milk?" Each time she repeated the question she became more irritated at the fact that the Russians didn't understand. After all, how many times was she going to have to give out the same information? By the time she had moved down to my end of the plane, her scowl was so intense and her voice so brusque that I wanted to shrink away.

This flight attendant spent the trip becoming increasingly tense and angry. It was remarkable to see how she persevered in making her situation worse. The more haste she was in, the more mistakes she made. The more mistakes she made, the angrier she got. The angrier she got, the more she seemed to blame the passengers for her state of mind. The more she blamed the passengers, the less she acted in a way that would invite cooperation. She was completely oblivious of the cycle she was in, and of how she was creating it. She also had no perception of the amount of frustration she was putting into accomplishing something that was not very demanding. Hers was a classical example of the type of urgency and crisis orientation we can bring into our lives when we are consumed by small tasks, all of which we experience as being imposed on us by somebody else!

The Internal Dynamics of Endless Effort

It is easy to laugh at compulsive effortful behavior and striving when we see them in someone else. Yet aren't we laughing at something that we can also recognize in ourselves? Our own compulsive doing comes in a million guises. Perhaps it takes the form of getting home from a long day's work and being unable to stop moving. Instead of relaxing and enjoying ourselves, we fuss, fret and fix things around the house, moving kinetically from one task to the next. Perhaps our over-focus on doing shows its face when we feel like exploding at someone who keeps us waiting on the phone. After all, we have so much to do! And of course, it is true that most of us carry a lot of responsibility. But the level of anger we feel is often not justified by the situation. There's something else going on when having to wait at the end of a telephone line makes us want to explode. And that something else is internal pressure.

Perhaps this pressure builds with each request from a spouse or child. It's because we're programmed to see life's events as imposing pressure on us that we so readily experience other people's needs as demands on us. Otherwise, couldn't we calmly and firmly say no? Perhaps we experience our compulsive doing when we go to bed, and instead of being able to sleep—even if we're sleep deprived—we spend much of the night thinking about what we have to do next, or about how someone is reacting to us. Finally, we may act out our own compulsive performing by becoming workaholics, even at the cost of our health.

I remember counseling a woman who had quite a successful career in the media business. Since childhood, she had suffered from chronic illness, and maintaining her health required watching her diet and getting a decent night's sleep. But giving herself permission to truly take care of herself (and who else is going to do that, if we don't?) was extraordinarily difficult for this woman. She felt called upon to perform socially as part of her job. She thought that she had to appear at events, to drink with the higher-ups, to go to late night parties. Even while she dreaded doing these things because of the toll they imposed, she had a hard time politely drawing a boundary and saying no. She felt that if she didn't sacrifice her own needs—including the needs of her fragile health—to the demands of the job, she would fail to make the grade. And while the costs of poor personal health management in her case were immediate, the statistics on stress show that it is the norm to sacrifice our health to what we experience as the pressures of our lives. Compulsive performing is everywhere, and is extremely difficult to give up. Deep down we equate doing and more doing with success. Whatever is deep down is hard to eradicate.

We all share four characteristics when we put too much value on doing and too little on being. First, we overfocus on results and neglect to pay attention to mastering how we feel inside. Second, we act from a place of anxiety and tension; our actions become a knee-jerk response to tension. Third, we project our tension outside ourselves, objectifying it in the form of demands that we think the situation is making on us. Fourth, we assume that getting the job done is inevitably linked with tension, and so we accept the tension as normal. The flight attendant who was so anxious and angry on my flight out West displayed all these characteristics.

In contrast, American tennis champion Pete Sampras provides an excellent example of a non-compulsive approach that yields genuine peak performance. Here is someone who is committed to a high level of accomplishment but without the strife that accompanies most of our efforts at achieving external success. As he serves and volleys, or drives a backhand down the line, his body is a picture of effortless ease. He looks as if he is really enjoying what he is doing, and even at the height of competition, he rarely seems to lose his composure.

An observer would be able to tell how well Sampras would do on the next point by noting how relaxed his body and face were. Sampras seems to monitor his mental and physical state and to work to achieve a quiet mind and an alertly relaxed body. He seems to know these are synonymous with concentration and confidence. He also seems to know that moment-by-moment poise creates the proper conditions for achieving a maximum result with minimum effort. He doesn't give his desire for the goal greater importance than the process he uses to achieve the goal. He knows that if we keep on thinking about where we want to get to, we lose our ability to be one hundred percent involved with what is happening.

The famous golfer Arnold Palmer lost the 1961 Masters golf tournament on the last hole by one shot. When he was interviewed after the tournament, he told the newsmen that in the last crucial moment before making his shot he started to think about the score he needed to make instead of focusing on hitting the ball. His energies were taken away from where they needed to be, and by focusing on the end result he wanted to achieve, he worsened his game. When peak performers are at their best, they refuse to allow the seductions of the goal to disturb the balance they need to reach it.

The four characteristics of endless effort that I mentioned earlier have a flip side: the four characteristics of effortless performance. First, when we are effortless, we focus more on how we feel inside than on the results we want to achieve. Second, we keep our attention on maintaining inner calm, and not giving way to anxiety. Third, we refuse to lose our composure in the face of external pressures. Instead, we use those external pressures to strengthen our inner balance. Fourth, we assume that performance is intimately connected to pleasure, and keep our attention on finding enjoyment in our activities.

These four characteristics distinguish Pete Sampras' performance, just as they are likely to characterize our own performance when we abandon doing and open the door to performing at our best. Instead of focusing purely on his goals, Sampras is process-oriented. He's interested in taking a look at and taking charge of how he feels on the inside. He also works from an internal state of calm, because he knows that being in this state contributes to reaching his goals. He associates achievement with relaxation rather than tension, and has learned to train himself to use relaxation in order to achieve. In addition, instead of projecting internal anxiety outward into perceived demands, Sampras uses the pressures of the situation to strengthen his ability to maintain internal balance. His primary focus is on keeping an optimum internal state, and every external situation is a challenge to improve his internal abilities. He doesn't make his situation responsible for how he feels. Finally, he follows the rule that success is intimately linked with enjoyment, and associates what he is doing with pleasure rather than anxiety. He has trained himself to identify not just the result of performing but the performing itself with satisfaction.

The Addiction That Underlies Needless Effort

Why do we put so much effort into living in a way that makes us less productive than we might be? At bottom we are addicts. Hurry sickness and compulsive performing are addictive behavior patterns. Addictive behavior is behavior that we persist in with the hope it will get us what we need, *despite evidence to the contrary*. Hurry sickness doesn't work as a technique for becoming successful, and it's also unpleasant. But we still hurry, convinced that piling up our plates, managing ourselves and others, will get us the success, the love, and eventually the internal satisfaction we want. We are looking for something we really need, but looking for it in a way that creates failure.

Addictions are behavior patterns that perpetuate underlying problems while providing symptomatic relief. They are ways of avoiding and bandaging over instead of resolving underlying feelings. The compulsive eater gets away from his inner feelings of pain and anxiety by eating. But while his uncomfortable feelings may be temporarily blocked and pacified by the food, they are not resolved. They're just stuffed under. And so they build up inside, creating a greater need for suppression through further compulsive eating. The life of the compulsive eater becomes absorbed in trying to flee from feelings instead of dealing with them.

Like compulsive eating, hurry sickness and compulsive effort don't resolve the underlying feelings that motivate them either. We keep on hurrying or doing because of inner anxiety, but our activity only dissipates the anxiety temporarily. And over the long run it actually aggravates that anxiety. Like other addicts, we need to acknowledge the reality of our pain and fear and allow ourselves to feel them. We also need to own our responsibility for our fear and pain, and instead of reacting to them, learn how to transform them.

Is it really true that we are addicted to effort if we are just trying to handle all the things on our plate: the needs of our spouse and children, work pressures, aging parents, vacation plans? Are we addicts when we find ourselves home in the evening after a stressful day of work, unable to sit down and relax despite our best intentions, unless we put on a television program that hypnotizes us? Are we addicts when we can't sleep at night, and our mind goes around and around the things we have to do or our concerns about the future?

The answer is both yes and no. It is a question of degree. It is normal for things to get pressured now and then. But if pressure becomes a lifestyle, if every day is full of demands that you feel you must meet, and if your mind races on a regular basis, then you are engaging in addictive behavior. You are doing something to yourself, though you may think it is being done to you. And what you are doing to yourself is not fun. You may not think of yourself as an addict, but remember that addictive behavior perpetuates itself through denial. We deny that our behavior makes us strangers to ourselves and breeds anxiety and fear. We refuse to see that it is impossible to find inner worth by meeting external standards.

In *When Society Becomes An Addict*, Anne Wilson Schaef points out that the primary addiction underlying other addictions is the addiction to non-living and powerlessness. Addictive effort hides another, deeper addiction: an addiction to fear. *We are attached to fear and we are afraid to take the steps that will take us out of fear.*

We are afraid to take responsibility for ourselves, to fully define ourselves in our own terms. So we give responsibility for defining who we are to someone else, and then we struggle to live up to those standards. We avoid our fear of being ourselves by identifying ourselves in terms of achievements that give temporary relief and leave the primary problem unsolved.

Most of all, we are afraid of feeling our feelings, because if we were to acknowledge and take responsibility for our feelings, we would also have to leave the treadmill of our lives behind and take responsibility for creating something more meaningful. Our list of things to do is never ending, and so is our avoidance of ourselves. We become hyperactive in order not to come in contact with our deeper needs. That hyperactivity helps us pretend that something meaningful is happening when it really isn't. Instead, we're living with a semblance of what we really want in order to avoid taking responsibility for creating it.

I once shared a room with a hyperactive woman I'll call Amanda who was attending the same conference as I was. This was a person who was quite committed to seeing herself as spiritually developed, and since we spent a week in the same room, we got to know a fair amount about each other. The conference we were attending also included group discussions on personal growth issues, and we all had opportunities to express ourselves. Amanda approached everything with boundless enthusiasm. She would sing songs to me in the morning to accompany my rolling out of bed. In our group sessions, she had one realization after another, all of which were important to share. She repeatedly wanted to "process" whatever she was going through. After a while, I was quite exhausted from the display. Amanda meant well. She was a good-hearted person. But her moods all came in the same key: the key of excitement. To her, everything was significant, everything was insightful, everything was profound. That's why she was fundamentally false.

Amanda was unable to find her inner variety, to move through the endless modulation of tone that gives our experiences a quality of truth and makes us interesting to others. Instead, she splattered herself all over the situations she entered. Despite her exclamations about how meaningful everything was, she had difficulty feeling things profoundly. You can't feel anything deeply unless you can give yourself the time to digest it. And that means down time. Time where you're not having yet another experience.

Amanda couldn't face down time, the time when we really learn from experience. She had to keep on the move. She couldn't move through a range of moods: from peace to excitement, to playfulness, to seriousness, to grief, to contemplativeness, to tenderness. She didn't understand that the more fully we live, the more instruments we have in our personal orchestra of expression. Amanda was an addict, and like other addicts, she avoided her feelings. She was afraid of her feelings, especially her feelings of fear. Unfortunately, it's when we avoid feelings that they stay with us.

The main way we avoid our feelings is by projecting *outside* ourselves what we feel *inside*. Then instead of taking responsibility for how we feel, we make the world responsible for what's happening to us. I remember counseling a woman I'll call Mary who had created painful difficulties for herself at work through her projections. She was unable to see how her mental framework generated the troubles she experienced. Mary had been fired for getting too wound up and angry while on the job. The root of her dysfunctional behavior stretched back into childhood. Mary's parents had regularly told her two things when she was performing tasks: On one hand, they constantly told her, "It's important that you get this right!" But on the other hand, they belittled her, saying, "You're not good enough to do that!" They put her in a double bind over and over. They told her that whatever she did, there was a right way to do it, and it was her job to discover that. They also implied, however, that she was inept.

As an adult, Mary unconsciously held on to the framework she had learned as a child. Whenever she had a task, she assumed that it was overwhelmingly important to do it well. She also assumed that she would fail. With that kind of framework, her only option was panic. Even routine tasks raised feelings of anxiety about her ability to perform and feelings of rage about being asked to do the impossible.

Mary was not aware that her problem lay in her mental framework instead of in the situation. She could not take responsibility for her panic because she always thought something outside herself was causing it. She perceived her employer as difficult, demanding and frightening. When she was fired, she couldn't understand what had happened. She thought she had been trying terribly hard and then the sky had fallen, justifying her worst fears. Mary kept on assuming that there was an objective reason for her fear, and that this was her boss' demanding nature and abruptness. But Mary would have found anyone abrupt and demanding, because her unconscious commitment to fear paralyzed her, guaranteeing her boss' frustration and creating the failure she feared.

The Shadow of Fear

Owning and transforming our fear is the most important step we can take in developing independence and strength. When we do that, we stop seeing the cause of our fear as outside of ourselves. We see our fear as coming from within, and we begin the alchemical process of transforming it. That's when we begin to move from a lifestyle of doing to a lifestyle of being.

In her wonderful novel *The Wizard of Earth Sea*, Ursula LeGuinn weaves a fantasy tale on the transformational impact of owning our inner states. The story is set in the mythical isles of Earthsea. When a young boy named Ged, born in a lonely village on the island of Gont, displays an early talent for sorcery, he is sent off to a School for Wizards to undergo training in the inner arts. Gifted as he is, however, Ged also suffers from excessive pride. He needs to prove himself to others, and to do that by showing them that he is superior. Taunted by an older classmate, Ged challenges the youth to a demonstration of prowess. As he throws himself into a battle of egos, Ged unwittingly invokes into being his own demon or shadow. The shadow side of Ged, the part of him that needs reclaiming and transformation, takes on a life outside of him, becoming a terrifying external force that over the next few years chases and torments Ged. His life becomes consumed with escaping from the demon. It is not until Ged turns to face his demon in a frightening battle on the open seas that he finds victory and peace. He reclaims and masters the negativity he had projected into the outside world. This opens the door to his becoming a great wizard and healer. When he conquers his own fear, nothing outside him seems terrifying anymore, and he is free to develop his power of inner vision.

Transforming fear-based patterns is the road to freedom, but recognizing those patterns in ourselves is not easy. It's human nature to assume that our fears are rational, and to take the products of our fears as objective facts. I once spent an evening with a very successful tort lawyer whose fear-based behavior completely escaped his awareness. We met at a dinner party. He was an interesting man, and at a point in our conversation he began telling me how worried he was for his son. He thought his son, who was quite gifted, also wasn't realistic and wasn't prepared for dealing with the real world. The son didn't want to go to the college his father recommended because he found the competitive environment too cutthroat. Instead, he had chosen for himself an institution that focused on a more collaborative approach to learning but that the father felt was less prestigious. This son was also an exceptional sportsman and team player. After games, he took pleasure in speaking with members of the opposing team, treating them as people with a common interest stemming from their love of sports. He was critical of the hostile approach that often pitted opposing team members against one another and that sometimes led to fights. The father admired his son's attitude, but also said, "My son is going to get hurt because he thinks too highly of people." Instead of encouraging his son's behavior as setting an ideal, he both admired it and fretted about the consequences for his son in a dog-eat-dog world. He actively discouraged his son from becoming a model for others because he found his son's behavior naïve and unrealistic.

Our conversation turned to the father's professional work. He said that he didn't in principle approve of the hostile, competitive approach but had no problem with this at work because as a lawyer, if he didn't thrash his opponent, his opponent would thrash him. He also told a story about some investment bankers who had come to him for advice on whether or not to invest millions of dollars in the tobacco industry. The investors were concerned that the legal action taken by a number of the U.S. states against tobacco companies in 1997—action that cost the tobacco industry close to four hundred billion dollars—would hurt the profitability of their investments. While the lawyer I was speaking with was not himself a smoker, and personally felt smoking was bad for one's health, he found it perfectly acceptable to deal with this situation from a purely financial perspective. Upon investigating the financial situation of the tobacco companies, he came to the conclusion that the tobacco companies would not be substantially damaged by the actions against them. He strongly recommended to the wealthy investors that they continue to put their money into the tobacco industry.

In the small decisions of his life, this man was well-intentioned. He loved his children and wife and worked hard. But he was deeply enmeshed in an approach that justified doing things that another part of him felt were not acceptable. He loved his son's courage and idealism but sought to discourage them as unrealistic. He felt aggression and hostility were bad, but rationalized his own competitive ethic as a lawyer by saying the profession made him act that way. He knew smoking was destructive for health, including the health of his own children and future generations, but recommended investing in the tobacco industry. Like so many people, he had built a financially and professionally successful life by looking the other way, sacrificing inner integrity and consistency on the grounds that he couldn't survive if he lived according to his ideals.

The story is painful because it is so common. This man was subtly addicted to his fear. He rationalized his life decisions on the grounds that he could not do otherwise. And why could he not do otherwise? Because of what "other people" did, or because of the "demands of his profession," or because that was just "the way life is." He excused his own inability to stand for what inwardly he felt was a higher ideal by saying that something else—in particular other people, society, or human nature—was forcing him to behave the way he behaved. I was not surprised to find, toward the end of the evening, that he had developed serious joint pain. After a while the spirit rebels, and if the heart does not listen, the body bears the cost.

chapter 3

The Addiction to Effortful Relationships

The tension most people accept as normal and the incessant drive to achieve in ways that may not match their deeper needs are both rooted in fear. They are both expressions of fear and Band-Aids for that fear. We keep on moving and driving ourselves so as not to feel our fear. We also operate under the illusion that if we push hard enough, do enough, or achieve enough, we will be able to escape from our fear. And like the lawyer who violated his own personal ethics when he recommended that his clients invest in the tobacco industry, we rationalize our fear-based behavior on the grounds that we have to compromise our values because otherwise, we could not survive and thrive in the world. Fear becomes an addiction—a pattern that we reinforce at the same time that we seek to escape it—when we blame the outside world for what really originates inside ourselves.

When we project our fear onto the outside world, it inevitably infects every part of our lives. In our significant relationships, our fear fosters co-dependency and wound-based behavior. It is in our intimate relationships that we look for healing from our inner pain and loneliness, but it is also in those relationships that we act out our pain, validating our feelings of loneliness or accepting makeshift love in place of the real thing.

Ideally, relationships are about learning and practicing transparency. They involve becoming authentic in the presence of another person and inviting that person also to be authentic. This is the high road of relationships. But so long as the motivating force behind our relationships is fear, we will cling to masks even in our closest relationships and then wonder why our experience of intimacy is so empty.

How We Embrace Our Masks

Fear-based relationships require masks. It is in our very earliest relationships that we learn to fear and to develop masks. When we are born, there is no separation between who we are for ourselves and who we are in front of others. Our sense of ourselves is as close as our own skin. It's natural for us to act spontaneously, to chortle, cry, suckle, eat, sleep and play according to an internal, unobstructed rhythm. We don't hold anything back and we don't judge, evaluate or monitor ourselves. We're transparent. We also approach life with wide-eyed fascination. We absorb and explore. Just as we are open to the experiences that rise up inside us, we are also open to the experiences that come from contact with the external world. But as we grow up, we close down. We begin to live in the brittle shell that separates us from ourselves and from one another.

It all starts when as children we begin to distrust our natural impulses and our environment. We become frightened of being ourselves and begin to experience the world around us as dangerous. The cause can be as simple as Daddy scolding us one too many times for wiggling around when we sit on his lap. It can be as traumatic as experiencing abuse, illness or abandonment. We then begin to inhibit our self-expression and curiosity, and we focus on figuring out what we need to do to get love, approval or security from the people we depend on. We become as afraid of ourselves as of anything outside us that might cause us fear. We repress the feelings that we think our parents will disapprove of and try to become the people we are supposed to be. We stop being and start calculating and doing. We lose our innocence. Now we start to identify who we are with the masks of how we appear to other people. We split ourselves in two: our deeper selves and the selves we develop in order to survive.

Once we go to school the problem gets worse, because our educational system is predicated on the assumption that learning requires accepting and digesting somebody else's version of the truth. This false assumption is so deeply entrenched that we hardly ever question it. Yet real learning has always been about something far more profound: assimilating, growing and changing through our own experience. It entails a lot more than absorbing information; it involves going through something that changes our framework of perception.

Learning is about experiencing metamorphosis. Neurobiology confirms this view of learning. The brain continually evolves, responding moment by moment to stimuli by revising the neural maps that encode its perception of the world, then using those revised maps to influence the environment, and again taking in new stimuli and reformatting itself. This is a very experiential and change-oriented view of learning. But traditional schooling tells us learning is non-experiential, and that it involves accepting somebody else's information, somebody else's rules of the game.

Too much of school learning is about forgetting how we see things and seeing them as someone else sees them. By the time most of us finish school, the combined experience of infantile dependency and traditional education have pretty much convinced us that doing well in our lives is tied to meeting someone else's standards. Instead of being ourselves, we assume we have to be someone else's version of a person. Achievement of any kind becomes associated with *performing*, and since someone else decides how well we perform, performing becomes associated with *anxiety*. Now we are hooked on anxiety, and since that anxiety is linked to success in any endeavor, it drives not only our professional lives but also our intimate relationships with other people.

Performing: A Deadly Recipe for Intimacy

Performance anxiety pushes us down the road of meeting other people's needs, and being focused on meeting other people's needs can create a lot of problems for intimacy. Janice and Bob, a married couple in their fifties, are struggling with letting go of the performance anxiety that has turned two people who really want to love each other into housemates besieged by conflict. Janice grew up in an affluent country club environment, in a world where appearances counted for a great deal. Her mother associated her own standing and success in the community with how well her daughter stood in comparison with the other daughters in the sub-urban community. When Janice shone, her mother felt vindicated and when she didn't, her mother felt insecure. A sensitive child, Janice recognized that she would be rewarded if she could take care of her mother's needs. When she sang, danced, acted, and studied, all of which she did well, she did these things for Mom.

The conscious ethic of Janice's family was an ethic of helping others, and in addition to being a great achiever, Janice became an adviser and cheerleader to siblings and friends. Along with doing for her mother by performing, Janice did for others by helping them. Being helpful toward others is a wonderful quality, but it can be destructive if the real reason we help others is because we *have* to, and not because we *want* to. Advising, helping and sup-porting were part of the role that Janice adopted to receive the approval a little child desperately needs. Unfortunately, the two roles of helper and successful mother's daughter put her in con-flict, and no matter what she did, she couldn't win. She learned to perform to meet her mother's needs, but this encouraged her to be competitive with others instead of supportive. She learned to sup-port other people, but this required her to take herself out of the limelight, which was where her mother wanted her.

When Janice did well, she felt guilty about whom she might be hurting. When she supported and helped others, she felt secretly judgmental and critical because of her competitiveness. Then she criticized herself for her own judgmentalism. It was hard for Janice to allow herself to feel her feelings at all, because they were always in conflict with what she thought she was supposed to do.

As an adult, Janice developed a business as a consultant, meet-ing clients' often close to impossible demands. She continued to respond exceptionally well to what other people needed. She mar-ried Bob, who also had grown up the star of his family. Bob had been taught it was important to shine. An emphasis on accom-plishment can motivate us to explore inner talents, but it can also make us excessively dependent on the public eye. For Bob, his fam-ily's interest was less in his real talents and potential and more in how others perceived him. So he grew up looking to others for his sense of importance. In addition to building a booming business,

Bob searched for the public recognition he craved by involving himself in local politics.

Janice worked hard to meet what she perceived to be Bob's needs. Along with running her own full-time consultancy, she organized dinners for political guests, attended long-winded meetings on Bob's behalf, and accompanied him to his golf tournaments. She wanted to do these things for Bob as an expression of love, but she couldn't help feeling overburdened, drained, frustrated, and angry. And she had difficulty getting him to return the favor and help her. He would often get angry if she asked him to wash the dishes, or yell at her if he had to wait for her when they were going out together.

Janice skirted a lot of issues to avoid possible confrontation. She let Bob keep control of the remote when they watched television, so he wouldn't get unhappy if she chose a channel he didn't like. She made a point of not taking a shower when he might want to do that. And even in making love, she avoided telling him what would please her because she was afraid he would see this as criticism and take it badly. She accommodated Bob because that was what she thought love was about, but then she felt frustrated, rejected and angry. When the feelings built up, instead of backing away from the overload that she had brought on herself, she blamed Bob for how angry she felt when she did so much for him.

If Bob was touchy and ungenerous to Janice, he didn't see it that way. He worked long hours at the office, and by the time he got home, he was exhausted and irritable from the effort of fighting his own anxiety and presenting the appearance of brilliance to colleagues and clients. When his wife asked him for something or said anything that sounded critical, he saw it as one pressure too many. If she asked him to clear his papers off the living room table, he heard anger and rejection in her voice and took the opportunity to storm out of the house.

Bob was acting out instead of confronting his own anxiety. He alternated between feeling excessively responsible and blaming the people around him, especially the person he loved most. He was self-centered because his own concern about how other people saw him created too much internal pressure to be able to respond to anyone else's real needs. Because both Janice and Bob were too focused on deriving their own sense of self-worth from meeting other people's expectations, they actually gave less and less real affection to each other, squeezing an occasional drop of kindness from a sponge full of tension and anger.

Instead of *caring about* Bob, Janice was *taking care of* Bob. She was so involved in what she had to *do* for Bob to show her love that there wasn't too much room to get in touch with *feeling* for him. It was the same for Bob with Janice. When we take care of people rather than care about them, we caretake. When we caretake, we drain ourselves. We don't grant ourselves basic respect because we feel we have to prove our worth by ministering to the other person's needs. At the same time we don't grant basic respect to the person we take care of because we assume that that person can't take care of himself. Janice and Bob improved their marriage when they stopped taking care of each other so much and also stopped making each other responsible for their anger and resentment. They began to care about each other far more when they became responsible for taking care of themselves.

What kept Janice and Bob in their unrewarding pattern of behavior was *guilt*. As soon as Janice took on so much that she felt angry at Bob, she would also feel guilty about her own anger. She would compensate by stuffing her feelings and making up for being a bad girl by working even harder. Instead of letting go of some of the obligations she had piled on herself, she would criticize herself for being ungenerous and try to prove that she was a lovable person by doing more. And this only worsened the problem for her.

Bob's explosions were also caused by guilt. When he heard Janice's requests for assistance, instead of just hearing them as simple requests, he would react by feeling totally inadequate and guilty. But this was intolerable to him, and so he would explode.

How Guilt Perpetuates Victim Consciousness

Guilt is the psychological mechanism that keeps victim consciousness in play. When we feel guilty, we criticize our own feelings and behavior, calling them wrong. We attack ourselves for our own feelings without resolving them. Instead of figuring out what we really want and need to do, what would be appropriate for us, we keep on guiding ourselves by what we *should* do. Listening to the voice of guilt guarantees that we will repress our feelings. *But repression always backfires because it encourages negative, reactive feelings.* When we fail to be honest and our actions fail to come from our heart, we become a breeding ground for anger, resentment, self-pity, and fear. We hold on to our negative feelings because we tell ourselves that it's the other person's fault that we feel this way. Then we hate ourselves for our negative feelings and tell ourselves we're bad. All of this makes us not very good at relationships.

It's ironic that the more we define ourselves in terms of what other people think of us, the less we feel our deeper impulses and the more self-involved we become. Janice became self-involved when she blamed Bob for her anger instead of changing her own behavior so that she wouldn't do things that made her angry. Bob became self-involved because his need for approval turned him into an emotional volcano who couldn't pay attention to what was happening with his wife. Since he was insecure, he also demanded that his wife prove her affection by doing all sorts of things for him. He didn't see that this imposed a strain on their relationship. When we are overly dependent on other people's perceptions of us, we often become overly demanding. We expect proofs of love.

One of my clients told me a very funny story about her ex-husband, a man who exhibited an extreme version of self-involvement. The two of them were sitting in the kitchen, and he happened to notice a potato chip on the kitchen floor. He said, "There's a potato chip on the kitchen floor." In the earlier days of her marriage, she would have felt guilty and reacted by going to pick up the offending object, but this time she decided to take another tack. In a neutral voice, she queried "So?" He replied, "Someone has to pick it up," apparently meaning her, but she parried this thrust by saying, "Go ahead." "Oh, I can't do that," he said. When she asked why, he said, "There are ants on the potato chip," something which apparently was too offensive for him to deal with. She described to him how he might go about getting the potato chip off the floor without getting ants on himself, and then quietly left the room. Her husband never did go after that potato chip. A friend who was visiting completed the onerous task. Instead of seeing what needed to be done, and then just doing it, my client's husband felt that for him to do it would be demeaning. He therefore expected whoever loved him to do it for him.

Self-Involvement, Fear and Neediness

Excessive self-involvement is always an expression of fear. It's also generally unconscious. One of my clients who had grown up with manipulative and ungenerous parents suffered from a lot of fear in her interactions with people. By nature, she was imaginative and humorous. But her exaggerated concerns about how other people saw her hid these wonderful qualities from view. When she went out shopping or stopped at a gas station or restaurant, she felt people were looking at her disparagingly or commenting on her peculiarities. She had difficulties at work because she thought people were talking about her behind her back, and this made her fearful and sometimes explosive. In her eyes, everyone around her was unkind and demeaning.

In our sessions, this woman worked on letting go of the illusion that she was the center of everyone else's negative interest. She became aware that people around her had their own concerns that had nothing to do with her. She began to see that it was burdensome for them if she made their behavior responsible for how she felt every time she ran into them. Perhaps they weren't thinking about her at all! Perhaps they had problems of their own that they were dealing with. Over time, my client became less fearful and more outgoing. Her colleagues began to like the interesting, funny person she was at heart.

While doing some consulting work for a male colleague, one of my woman friends was very drawn to him. Although he was married, the attraction was mutual and they ended up having a passionate affair. In an ideal world, perhaps such things shouldn't happen, for they are recipes for pain. Yet if they do happen, the most important thing is that the people involved deal with one another with integrity. While the feeling between this man and woman was intense, the man, who was not only married but also had two young children, was understandably conflicted. To make matters more complex, he was of Catholic background and was a financially successful member of a very conservative social group. Doing things in proper form was very important to him. He no doubt found himself in a situation that he had never imagined would be his lot. Yet this gentleman's most fundamental problem was that he had so thoroughly internalized feelings of guilt and of socially proper behavior for years that he had learned to reject his own feelings long before he ever met his lover. That was why the love affair became inevitable. It was also why he dealt with it, once it happened, in a manner that lacked integrity and good will.

As the man's feelings of guilt began to bother him more and more, he expressed his ambivalence by relying on his lover to call him to make dates. That way, he could pretend that he wasn't as involved as he was, and this eased his guilt. But she stopped calling and taking the initiative because she felt the asymmetry was inappropriate. She wanted him to deal with his feelings instead of masking his conflict. Then, because he didn't want to lose her, he would call and ask to see her. She would agree to a date because she still loved him. After they had set a time, more often than not he would get cold feet and leave a message for her saying a business problem was causing him to cancel and that he would call the next day. Then he wouldn't call. A week or so later, he would call again, tell her he was dying to see her, and make an appointment.

This man was unable to make the simple, obvious and decent gesture: be straightforward about his conflicts and treat a woman he loved as an equal who both deserved respectful treatment and who would be able to understand. He couldn't even call to say, "I'm having a lot of trouble with this relationship," and add, "I'm sorry." Instead, he acted afraid of his lover, as though it were her fault that he was in this predicament.

This man's professional conduct was ethically irreproachable, and in business he was respected for his standards. His personal conduct, however, lacked self-respect and honesty. His need to keep up appearances made him oblivious both to my friend's feelings and to her capacity as a mature woman to handle frank discussion. Needless to say, if he could not handle open discussion with his lover, he no doubt could not do this with his wife either. After a while, my friend let go of the relationship, not so much because of hurt feelings as because of the fact that the man's lack of honesty undermined her affection for him. Another woman would have felt abandoned and unworthy, but my acquaintance saw her lover's behavior for what it was: an expression of his weakness and victim-consciousness and not a problem of hers. In his own way, the man was needy. He needed his lover to hold up more than her share of the relationship, and to excuse him from his own responsibility toward her and toward himself.

Being needy keeps us on the merry-go-round of unfulfilling,

self-destructive patterns of intimacy. As long as we're on that merry-go-round, we act from the wounded place in ourselves and encourage the people we are with to act from their own wounded place. However, people can transcend this neediness and create healthier relationships. A friend of mine once described to me a relationship with a man in which both of them learned to confront the addictive neediness that was making their relationship painful.

Peggy and John had been seeing each other for six months, spending weekends and sometimes weekday evenings together. John was having a hard time with some professional changes he was going through, and he began to express his own tension by taking it out on Peggy and by being generally irritable with her. One evening she said that this was no longer acceptable to her and revealed that she was very close to ending the relationship. After first getting defensive, John apologized profusely and they spent that night together.

The next morning, John begged Peggy to stay longer than usual so that they could hold each other. He told her he was afraid of her leaving him. She was going to be away on professional business for the rest of the week, but promised to call when she got back in town. On her return, she did call him, and left a message on his answering machine. After two days, he had not called back, and she called again, once more leaving a message. Despite the fact that the two of them had been in the habit of calling each other every day to touch base, she didn't hear from him for two weeks. Since her phone services included Caller ID, she knew that he had not been in an accident or in some other kind of trouble because he telephoned twice without leaving a message.

Peggy's reaction was to go into deep pain, like an infant deprived of its milk. She craved to hear from John. She was close to desperate. She cried into her pillow at night. It was difficult for her to resist calling him repeatedly or rushing over to his apartment. Yet as she became conscious of her craving, instead of just reacting to it she began to see that she had spent a lifetime associating love with this internal craving, reducing herself to begging for the crumbs of love. Just because John was being withholding, she felt pummeled into dependent submission.

One of the things that helped Peggy release herself from the addictive need to beg for love was a discussion we had on what had to be going on inside John. Clearly, his own behavior was need-based and full of fear. The last time they had spoken, he had asked her to call and told her he needed to see her. But since this happened after an argument in which she asked him not to take out his own frustrations on her, he was afraid of being abandoned. Instead of coping with his own fears or sharing them, he withdrew into a shell and basically said, "Prove you love me!" Proof for him meant that she had to bend over backward to reach him, overcoming his resistance. If Peggy had responded as her addictive need made her want to do, she would have supported his needy behavior instead of compelling him to look at it and grow up. She would have begged to see him until he felt she had paid for his suffering. Then she would have gone back into a stifling relationship, holding onto smoldering resentment herself.

Once Peggy understood that John was withholding his affection because of his own fear and not because of something in herself, she could more easily let go of her neediness and of the feeling that there was something wrong with her. Though it was painful for her, she took responsibility for conquering her own anxiety and refrained from calling John after she had made the two phone calls that weren't returned. After two weeks of withdrawing into his own rebellious shell, John, too, came to see that his behavior was fearful rather than loving, and that fear-based behavior was no way to build intimacy. The two of them eventually came to a richer and more productive understanding of their relationship.

In their own ways, Peggy and John both discovered that our society places far too much emphasis on achieving happiness through another person. We are brought up on myths of romance, finding our soul mate, or some other fantasy that has us wait to find fulfillment until the right person comes along. However, *others do not create our happiness. They cannot fill the hole in our lives*. If we ask others to fill that hole, our own need too easily turns to resentment, anger and even hatred. When love is an addiction, its other face is hate.

chapter 4

The Effortful Lifestyle: A Holographic Pattern

The addiction to effort rests on a deeper addiction to fear. We feel afraid because we make others the arbiters of our lives. We accept an external standard for our internal self worth. As long as an external source holds this power, we are trapped in fear and resentment. This expresses itself in an effortful lifestyle that affects every aspect of our being, from our biochemistry through our emotional, mental and spiritual lives.

The preceding pages have traced the effects of our effortful lifestyles on our health, emotional attitudes, relationships and performance. These aspects of our lives are not separate. In fact, the commitment to doing creates a *holographic pattern* that radiates through our entire lives. In a hologram, parts of an object that seem to be independent of one another are really not. The entire hologram can be reconstructed from the smallest of its parts. The holographic nature of our lives is evident in the way that our physical health reflects itself in our emotional lives, and vice versa. Similarly, our cognitive potential, interpersonal relationships and spiritual ideals all influence each other. And they all manifest the fundamental addiction to fear and to struggle that expresses itself through them. That is why, if we let go of doing and move toward being, every part of our lives will change for the better.

Let us look back and review the network of interacting influences fostered by an overemphasis on doing. The first and most obvious place where we see the holographic influence of the focus on doing is in our relationship to time. If we identify *who we are* with *what we do*, we end up in a battle with time, pushing ourselves to get things done. On a physical level, this translates into all the biochemical and physiological components of the stress response. The result is a tendency toward chronic illness, including heart disease, back trouble, breathing disorders and cancer, along with a loss of vitality. Our addiction to effort is literally killing us. We rationalize killing ourselves by saying we can't do anything else, that someone or something is making us be this way. We feel we have to struggle, push and drive.

The holographic pattern of self-destructive doing keeps its grip on our lives through an addiction to fear that underlies the addiction to effort. So long as we are tense and tight, we will be afraid. And as long as we are afraid, we will be tense and tight.

When we are addicted to fear, we repeat and repeat behavior patterns that keep us in fear, and avoid dealing with resolving our feelings. We project our negativity outside ourselves and blame the world. This pattern of fear projection also affects our relationships. Because we give other people power over who we are and how we see ourselves, instead of using relationships as opportunities for mutual growth, we become needy, blaming, and co-dependent in our interactions with others. Instead of building ourselves into beautiful people and then sharing our beauty with other beautiful people, we ask other people to patch up our lives and tell us we're okay. Others' attitudes become way too important for our sense of self-esteem. And just as we ask others to patch up the hole inside ourselves, we also assume that our job with other people is to patch up their lives.

When we give our power over to other people by giving them too prominent a role in our sense of self, we can't help destroying our own relationship to ourselves. Living with fear means we hide our own deeper feelings and needs from ourselves. We're so involved in defending ourselves from how we feel on the inside that we end up not feeling much at all. As a result, we accept superficial excitement in place of depth. We talk a lot, but we don't really say much. We'd rather have the pretense of meaning than the real thing, even though it is unsatisfying. We witness this truth every day when we turn on the television and watch one program after another filled with characters whose apparent intensity substitutes for their lack of depth. When we turn off the television we rarely feel educated or enlarged, and we often feel drained. Witnessing shallow feelings exhausts us. Witnessing deep feelings opens us up. But unless we are willing to face the deep feelings inside ourselves, including feelings of grief, fear and rage, we can't accept deep feelings at all. We can't live from a place of depth and personal power.

Our mental life is not immune to the radiating influence of the holographic pattern of doing. Focusing on doing limits our mental capacity and takes us far away from exploring our peak potential. We lose the concentration, sense of center and power of presence that contribute to great achievements. We also lose the love of life that fosters mental focus and that underlies satisfying accomplishment. We may push our way through life in the name of achieving success, but we destroy our minds in the process. Tension is antithetical to mental focus.

The most intense period of learning in a person's life occurs between birth and the age of eight. That is the time when alpha waves predominate in the brain of the child. Alpha waves are the brain wave pattern corresponding to deep meditation or inner quietness. It's in that quietness that we can be fully aware and present. Inner quietness is synonymous with the mind functioning at a higher level. Yet as adults we sacrifice awareness and presence in the name of performance, and then we fail to perform at our best because we lack focus. It is time to recognize that our effortful, anxious, performance-based approach to life systematically undermines our potential.

On the spiritual level, the influence of the holographic pattern of doing shows itself through absence. We fail to ask ourselves the most basic questions, such as: "What are my ideals?" "What am I willing to stand by?" "What do I want to create in the world, regardless of public opinion?" "How can I genuinely make myself and the world a better place?" These are the types of questions that help us make our own lives worth living and that generate an abundance of challenge and joy. When we focus on doing, instead of asking what we think is worthwhile, we ask what others think is worthwhile. Or we tell ourselves we can't go for what we value, because others won't value it as well. Yet if we dare to ask basic spiritual questions, we will join together to create a world we want to live in rather than a world that makes us sick at heart.

How can we create that world? How can we rediscover health, emotional authenticity, rewarding relationships, and realistically grounded spiritual idealism? How can we ground ourselves in a lifestyle of being and holographically express that being in all the dimensions of our lives? The answer to those questions fills the rest of the book.

Since focusing on doing commits us to tension and effort, and since tension and effort are nourished by fear, then undoing addictive effort has to constitute a first and major step toward letting go of fear and finding an authentic approach to living. What would it be like to be effortless rather than effortful? What would it be like to explore how to live free of tension? What would it be like to move through our lives from a deep place of physical ease and inner strength? What would this mean for the emotional tenor of life, for the way we approach learning and emotions, and for how we live in relationships? What would it be like to abandon the way of the effortful warrior and replace it with the way of the effortless warrior? How to commit to the way of the effortless warrior, and what happens when we do that, are the subject of Part II.

The Way of the Effortless Warrior: Transcending Cultural Addiction

chapter 5

The Effortless Way

What is it like to let go of effort and become effortless? Are there people who actually know how to do this? Can we recognize them when we see them? The quality of effortlessness is instinctively and profoundly appealing. For example, it's what makes for the magnetic attractiveness of great performers. When world-famous musicians like Itzhak Perlman or Isaac Stern play the violin, they seem totally relaxed even though playing classical music on a stringed instrument is physically demanding. These gifted artists' faces reflect an abandonment to some higher power, not the difficulty of an arduous job. Great athletes also often look effortless. During the 1984 and 1988 Olympics, Greg Louganis seemed to flow into his dives, giving the lie to the extraordinary strength, power and control that he needed to execute his moves. I also remember once watching a video of the golf champion Freddie Couples. One of his long drives seemed so easy, that for a moment I was convinced the camera had recorded it in slow motion.

For the person watching, effortless action looks fluid, graceful and easy. For the person performing, that appearance corresponds to a quality of deep and total absorption. The person who is effortless isn't thinking about other people and how they see him. And he isn't in a race against time or in a struggle to achieve. He's just one hundred percent involved. He may also feel as though what he is doing is happening without his having to make it happen. That's why he feels effortless.

Effortlessness is intensely attractive. People who master difficult disciplines and execute them with high levels of poise are often driven by a passion for the effortless experience of surrender. They want to experience life as though a force is manifesting itself through them and they're just the channels for that force.

The experience of effortlessness is sometimes called being "in the zone." Everyone experiences this sense of effortlessness at times, when they trust enough to let go. For one person, this may be when he is presenting a speech to an audience. He becomes effortless when he enters a space where he is no longer delivering prepared content and the words simply move through him. He's not thinking and then speaking. His speaking is his thinking. For another person, running or dancing becomes effortless when the body gets into its own rhythm and just takes over. Making love becomes effortless when two people forget about pleasing each other and enter into the current of the rising energy. Self-consciousness and ambivalence disappear. Something is happening, but we are so relaxed that it feels like we aren't making it happen. We are accomplishing more but trying less.

Effortlessness and Concentration

The profound sense of relaxation that accompanies effortlessness is a mark of true concentration. Concentration involves absorbing ourselves so completely in something that our mind becomes empty and we become channels. This is exactly the opposite of how our linear culture approaches concentration. We're taught to bring our thinking mind into everything we do, to plan, prepare and analyze. Analysis and planning have their place, but we tend to think obsessively. For example, we start talking with someone, and before we know it we're not even listening to that person because we're thinking about what we're going to say next. Or we're playing golf or tennis, and we ruin our shots because we analyze them to death and only get uptight.

It's a scientific fact that the more we think, and the more verbal chatter is going on in our minds, the more physical tension we have in our bodies. Physical tension makes both for poor performance and for poor concentration. True concentration happens when we stop thinking. We relax and become present. Performing at our peak is about letting go of trying.

Researchers who study human potential know that concentration, effortlessness and deep relaxation go together. They recognize that mental focus depends on physical relaxation, and they teach people how to improve concentration and performance by practicing physical relaxation.

In the 1960s, a Bulgarian doctor named Georgi Lozanov became internationally recognized for developing an approach to accelerated learning whose foundation was the use of breathing techniques, rhythmic music and gentle Yoga exercises, all of which put the body into the relaxed state that's necessary for rapid learning. The Silva Mind Control method, founded by Jose Silva and most widely used for corporate training in the 1970's, uses hypnotic relaxation techniques as the first step in developing extraordinary powers of focus. Peak performance training for athletes frequently includes intensive programs in deep relaxation in order to help athletes align themselves consciously with the goals they want to achieve.

In this country, interest in the use of mind-body training for sports competition was spurred by the events of the 1976 Olympics, when the Soviet Union won more gold medals than any other country. The United States had placed third, and while the Soviets were suspected of using steroids, this turned out not to be the case. Instead, the key to the Soviets' success was their use of mind-body techniques, including deep relaxation. The Soviets had discovered that athletes who spent as little as twenty-five percent of their time in actual physical training and devoted the other seventy-five percent of their time to mind-body training out-performed athletes who spent most of their time in physical training. All the mind-body training techniques began with deep physical relaxation.

What is relaxation? Our culture associates it with leisure activities—for example watching television or having a drink—that often are closer to spacing out than they are to true relaxation. These activities are passive, and true relaxation is not. It is a discipline of the body and mind in which extraneous tensions and thoughts are eliminated, creating a profound calm in which one is also totally alert.

Relaxation involves the ability to live fully but without struggle. It is a central goal of numerous spiritual disciplines. Buddhism, Taoism and Zen are all devoted to helping create a sense of deep inner peace, or calm aliveness. The Western Christian tradition of contemplative prayer is also aligned with this type of relaxation. Contemporary spiritual work invokes the same theme. For example, in her lectures based on *A Course in Miracles*, author and public speaker Marianne Williamson says that the message of this dense book of Christian spiritual and psychological teachings could be boiled down to one word: *relax*!

The true meaning of relaxation is a combination of peace and power, inner calmness and complete self-expression and focus. How ironic that we need to learn how to relax, how to stop trying so hard. We can't just do it because we are addicted to our struggle and to the concern about how we appear to others that underlies that struggle. We have to learn to let go and become ourselves, become effortless.

Most people admire the quality of effortlessness, of total ease or being "in the zone," when they see it in others. Yet they assume they can't cultivate this quality in themselves. Spiritual traditions, however, have amassed entire disciplines focused around training followers to develop effortlessness. In all of those traditions, this training is *a very visceral and physical experience*. It involves changing the way we live in our bodies, letting go of the push and pull that creates everything from low quality performance to chronic disease.

Effortlessness and Non-Doing

Effortlessness is about what Zen traditions call "non-doing." Non-doing is not a concept. It is an experience that happens in our bodies. Non-doing involves moving deeper and deeper into a gut feeling of physical ease. That sense of physical ease then gets reflected in mental clarity and emotional detachment.

In order to discover non-doing, to get into the effortless zone, we have to make being at ease in our bodies more important than getting something done. We have to let go of the addiction to pushing and pulling. That is the bottom line, and it can be a difficult line to toe. After all, aren't we always rationalizing our tension? We get tense *because* we have a lot to do, or *because* we're caught in traffic and are late for an appointment, or *because* someone isn't treating us the way we want to be treated. We have a million reasons for tension. Most of them boil down to saying it's more important to get a certain result than to feel balanced inside ourselves. When we commit to effortlessness, we decide we are going to learn how *not* to let our interest in getting something done trigger us into tension. We're going to learn how *not* to let our needs in relation to other people trigger us into anxiety. We're going to learn how *not* to let other people's needs trigger us into tension.

The martial arts offer the clearest examples of disciplines that are single-mindedly devoted to training their practitioners in effortlessness. They can teach us how important it is to let go of all the things that we use to rationalize our tense and effortful responses to life.

Eugen Herrigel's *Zen in the Art of Archery,* published in 1953, offers a close-up view of this training. An American professor of philosophy, Herrigel lived in Japan and studied archery with a Zen master long before interest in Zen was common in the West. In his first lesson with his Master, he watched as his teacher gracefully and fluidly demonstrated drawing the bow. When Herrigel was invited to follow his teacher's example, he found to his dismay that despite his strength he could not draw the bow without straining and pulling, even though he was much bigger than his teacher. The Master observed and said nothing.

For months, Herrigel struggled unsuccessfully to draw that bow. When he was about to quit in despair, his teacher demonstrated some breathing techniques that opened up and relaxed his body, with the result that he drew the bow easily. The Master showed Herrigel how to change himself physically on the inside to get an external result. All of a sudden, with some simple internal shifts that brought more flow and energy into his body, Herrigel could do what he had been unable to do for months.

Herrigel learned two important lessons from this experience. First, he learned that he could improve his external performance by altering his internal state in a way that induced greater relaxation. By changing the way he breathed so that it felt deeper, more open and less labored, he increased his strength, energy and power. When the Master helped him change his automatic way of doing things, he realized that he actually had unconsciously been applying more effort and tension than was necessary. It was the excess tension that caused his failure. When Herrigel worked less, he achieved more. Second, Herrigel learned that he was able to work less and achieve more when he withdrew his attention from what he wanted to accomplish externally and made how he was feeling internally the main focus of his interest. When he focused on effortlessness—on developing greater relaxation—and let go of focusing on the result he wanted to achieve, he achieved external results more easily.

Herrigel was learning about the Zen of archery. He was learning that one's internal state is everything, and that the external focus is at best a distraction from the real goal. This is an enormous lesson, and like any life-changing lesson it has to be learned again and again to be absorbed.

Three years into his training program—a program which lasted through six years of daily practice—Herrigel had another series of difficult experiences. The Master had been demonstrating loosing the shot from the bow. His body stayed completely quiet even though the force of discharge when the arrow released jerked his right arm back at a tremendous speed. Try as he might, Herrigel was unable to imitate his Master's achievement. He became obsessed with figuring out a technique to loose the shot without his body jerking. The more he did this, the less he paid attention to his inner state. He stopped being and started trying. He made the cardinal but all too tempting error: he focused on the result he wanted to achieve instead of on his process.

One day, Herrigel developed a special technique to make loosing the shot look effortless. In order to do this, he had to take his attention off how he felt inside and focus instead on doing a manipulation with his right hand. The result looked effortless to the untutored eye, but the Master exploded and threatened to expel Herrigel from the school. Instead of remaining true to the intention of the martial art, Herrigel had fallen prey to the desire for the goal. The temptation to abandon an internal state for external results is constant. Herrigel learned that his best chance of achieving an external goal lay in letting go of it. He also learned that the only thing that ultimately mattered was commitment to the internal experience of release.

Making Letting Go the Most Important Thing

In order to let go of the addictive effort or commitment to stress that characterizes our culture, we have to focus on one thing only: how we feel inside, the quality of our internal state. We have to focus on letting go of the tension response. We have to stop thinking so much about where we want to go and what we're going to accomplish. We also have to stop thinking about how other people see us and react to us, or about how we want to affect other people. We have to make our internal experience of ease and peace all-important.

We have to learn to make internal tranquillity and relaxation the backdrop for anything we do in life. We have to cherish inner relaxation more highly than we cherish achieving a result. That doesn't mean that we become couch potatoes. It means that as we go about doing the things we do, we pay attention to how we are doing them. We pay attention to whether we are going into tension, and we learn how to inhibit that tendency. Herrigel's experience demonstrates that instead of decreasing our achievement level, this practice actually improves our ability to achieve. We get further if we stop thinking so much about where we want to go and focus instead on releasing the addiction to effort.

The commitment to letting go of effort is the cornerstone of undoing the addiction to fear. It's a fun and pleasurable commitment. It is also fascinating because in the process of learning to let go of effort we learn many interesting lessons about ourselves and find surprisingly simple ways to release negative patterns. The next two chapters explore techniques for pursuing effortlessness, show how these techniques have changed other people's lives, and suggest how you can use them for yourself.

chapter 6

Effortlessness: Discovering Our Breath

Herrigel studied the Zen of archery, became a master archer, and discovered effortlessness by combining his training sessions with deep, open breathing. Esoteric traditions throughout the ages have focused on breathing techniques as an avenue to self-transformation, and for good reason. They work because they teach you how to let go.

To get a sense of what truly relaxed breathing is like, take a moment and imagine seeing a lazy cat stretched out on the floor, basking in the rays of the sun. Watch the way the cat's belly rises and falls, rises and falls, rises and falls. Notice how soft it is and how the cat's breathing fills its entire body. Imagine now that you are that cat, feeling the pleasant heat on your body and luxuriating in letting your breath fill your entire body. If you can, lie down on the floor or stretch out on a sofa and feel what it is like to be that cat. Abandon yourself to the sensation. Do you feel a shift inside yourself? You are letting go of some of the unconscious holding and resistance to living that characterize a society addicted to stress. You are using your imagination to open up the breath and go into a deeper, more relaxed state. Your ultimate goal is to develop the ability to let that relaxed, cat-like belly breathing express the way you live from moment to moment during your day, no matter what transpires.

Meditation and Deep Relaxation

The most efficient way to develop the ability to relax at will is to practice meditation. Meditation has the opposite effect on the body of the stress response. In the late nineteen-sixties, meditation rode into the United States on a wave of interest in transcendental experience, and for a long time it was viewed as a New Age practice restricted to alternative cultures. But good things have a way of spreading. Today, meditation is taught in health clinics around the country, from ghettoes to wealthy suburbs. Thousands of articles have been written on its medical, psychological and cognitive benefits. It has found its way into corporations, churches, and learning centers and has become a staple practice of many people's lives, a way of rebalancing and staying on keel in the face of ongoing pressure.

The most useful type of meditative practice to study for learning how to let go of stress comes from the Theravada Buddhist tradition and is called *Vipassana*. Vipassana meditation is the practice of simply tuning in our awareness to following the sensation of our breath. When we do this, we don't try to influence or change how we are breathing. That's a type of control, and control always creates tension. Instead, the breath deepens, and we relax as a natural byproduct of anchoring our attention in a curious, nonjudgmental way on the feeling of our breath. Whatever the breath feels like is fine. As we practice feeling our breath, thoughts float through our mind, and we don't try to push them away. We just let them be there on the periphery of our awareness and keep our focus on experiencing the sensation of the breath.

If we set aside some time every day to be by ourselves without distractions and do a simple Vipassana meditation practice (See Suggestions for Practice at the end of this chapter for detailed instructions.) for five to twenty minutes, we find ourselves becoming a lot calmer. After a little practice, following the breath reverses the stress response to which we are all addicted. The impact of this self-quieting practice then extends into our day.

These are enormous benefits, but the biggest benefit is yet to come. Once we learn how to relax and get rid of some of our habitual mental and physical tension by sitting quietly by ourselves in this focused way every day, we are ready to expand our self-mastery. We can begin to use our ability to tune in to our breathing to help ourselves while we're in the midst of going about our day's activities. This is where we truly begin to change our lives. Whereas initially we were just getting quiet by sitting alone and following our breathing, now we are centering and calming ourselves during the daily battle of life. We are consciously breathing in a relaxed way in our daily activities. And that changes the way we deal with everything. We learn to deal with unavoidable stresses from a strong, peaceful center.

Breathing in Daily Activities

The first time I used awareness of my breathing to influence events in my life was in the early stages of my transition from being an academic to developing a practice as a healer. I was doing some public relations consulting for the president of a college in New York City, and this president had a habit of asking for the impossible. She would give me a goal to accomplish but then wouldn't give me access to resources that would help me do what she needed to have done. The more unrealistic her expectations were, the more demanding she would get. My finances weren't in the best shape, and I needed the work, so I wasn't free to walk. But this president was making me nervous, and I had to do something. I noticed that I felt knotted up inside whenever I met with her. I decided to work on relaxing my body through practicing breath awareness when I was in her company.

Every time I sat down with this college president, I would focus my attention on training my body into a relaxation response. When the conversation got difficult, I would notice the tension building up inside me and would work on bringing my body back into deeper levels of relaxation even while we were talking. I did not have any ambitions. I just wanted to get more comfortable in my own skin. But this experiment had unexpected results. Within a month, the communication difficulties I had with this woman were resolved. By using a technique that made me more physically at ease in the president's presence, my bearing and tone of voice had changed. I was speaking more powerfully. And by focusing on relaxing, I communicated subliminally to the president that I was more confident, and less likely to respond to her attacks by feeling cowed. She stopped attacking and started respecting my opinions.

While for most people the idea of meditation evokes images of sitting alone in a quiet spot and focusing on feeling their breath, it really is a preparation for learning how to center ourselves through breathing in everything we do. This gives us power over our lives because it's impossible to breathe in a relaxed way while being reactive. When we work with our breath we spontaneously learn to let go of our own negative, disempowering behavior patterns and thoughts. Reactive patterns make us physically tight and fill us with turbulent emotions. Why not say good-bye to all that? Why not embrace effortlessness?

I start teaching clients effortlessness by giving them a basic meditative exercise to work with on their own in a quiet place every day. Once they can do this, I show them how to begin integrating what they learn about relaxation through following their breath in simple activities. I might ask them to practice relaxing into the breath while they're driving, straightening the office, cleaning the kitchen or folding laundry. They're invariably surprised to find out how much tension they had been bringing into these daily activities. They usually also discover to their surprise that by following their breathing they can relax into what they're doing and make it easier and more pleasurable.

The trick is to *commit ourselves to being with the breath and to finding a way gradually to let that breath become easier and deeper, no matter what.* That means making the feeling of inner ease more important than what we are achieving, where we are going, or whether people are listening to us.

Rachel came to me for mind-body work because of her anxiety over the pressures of life, pressures that included a successful career and three children. In our first session, practicing meditation helped her calm down. She liked feeling her breath. It felt soothing, and she noticed that as she followed her breathing it deepened. We were chatting after the meditation exercise, and I asked her to see if she could let herself feel that same, soothing sensation of the breath as she listened to me talking. At first this was hard for her to do, like rubbing her tummy and patting her head at the same time. But after a while she got the hang of it and felt more relaxed than usual. I suggested that she spend the week until our next session exploring what happened if she just tuned into her breathing and allowed it to relax during her daily routines.

Rachel was one of those people for whom things just clicked. By the next time I saw her, she had had a string of realizations. She had started by following her breathing during the morning breakfast preparations for the kids. This was usually a frenzied time, yet she found that if she paid attention to her breathing she felt much calmer. She was also surprised to find that her kids calmed down as well. Rachel had unconsciously been fueling the tension of breakfast preparations with her own tension. Once she changed her pattern, everyone else changed. Rachel learned a valuable lesson: changing the way she felt inside not only helped her feel better, it also influenced people around her.

Rachel worked with focusing on relaxing into her breathing in conversations at work. She became aware that she often tightened up or even held her breath when she was talking with someone. Sometimes this was because she was picking up the tension in the other person. We all sometimes experience this when a nervous person walks into our presence. In no time flat we're nervous too. Rachel needed to learn how to dissipate this reaction of hers so that she wouldn't keel over with every wind that blew her way. She did this by working on relaxing into her breathing.

Rachel also sometimes felt internal tension in conversations because she was making demands on herself: trying to be an interesting conversationalist, thinking of what she was supposed to say next, or trying to make a point. When we live in a culture that associates communication with performance, and performance with anxiety, it's hard not to tighten up in talking. As soon as Rachel made relaxing into her breathing more important than being an interesting conversationalist or meeting someone else's needs, both she and the person she was talking to calmed down. Her focus also improved. She could take in what the other person was saying more readily and she communicated more easily. Just by letting breath awareness be the most important thing, Rachel became quieter, more focused, more expressive and more spontaneous.

Rachel consistently found that breath awareness improved her concentration. She drove better if she focused on feeling her breathing; she played tennis and golf better; her mind wandered less when she read; and she handled professional negotiations with greater poise. The reasons are not esoteric. We function better when our central nervous system functions well. Our central nervous system functions well when our breathing is relaxed. Rachel was lessening the bodily stress of everyday performance. But she was also achieving more as she became more balanced. She was becoming effortless.

Rachel changed the way she dealt with relationships. She was very intelligent and had a habit of getting into arguments, especially when she felt she was in the right. But she noticed that when she insisted on her own point of view, her breathing got shallow. When she needed to be right, she got tight. Her desire to be right was a way of being pushy and needy.

Rachel was not a loud or aggressive person, and no one had ever told her she was pushy. But now she noticed how in a subtle way she sacrificed her inner balance for the sake of winning an argument. She had to choose. She could maintain her equilibrium by not getting into playing the "I win you lose" game. Or she could get all contracted and tight by wanting to be right. She decided that having to be right couldn't be a healthy way to operate. It was better to have her vitality and ease than to be the person to win an argument. Of course, as soon as Rachel let go of having to be right, her relationships with other people improved. They were more interested in listening to her.

Not only do we tighten up when we need to be right, we also tighten up when we need to fix things by caretaking for people around us. Rachel told me a story about one of her sons. He had come to her for advice about difficulties he was having with his studies. Her usual pattern was to rush in and engineer solutions for him, to give him lots of words of wisdom and tell him how to handle things. Rachel observed how she felt inside when she went into this pattern. She found an anxious core of tension in her belly. She might have thought she was trying to be wise, but she was really just being a nervous, overly solicitous mom. Rachel decided to focus on letting go of the tension instead of fixing her son's problems. As they talked, his problems were solved in a new way. She listened more. She was more detached. She acted as a sympathetic witness. By the end of the conversation, her son had solved his own problems and felt better about himself than if she had dashed into the trenches for him. At the same time, he felt grateful to her for helping him. Her quiet, attentive presence had helped him help himself. By focusing on her own equanimity, Rachel avoided fixing her son's life and empowered him to fix it himself.

Focusing on equanimity leads to success more quickly than focusing on the result we want to achieve at the cost of equanimity. Rachel's work with her breathing led her to one more discovery: she became aware that she suffered from *pleasure anxiety*, and that her fear of pleasure made it hard for her to relax.

It all began when I was helping Rachel with her golf swing. I asked her to forget about her targets, the golf ball and the hole for a few minutes. I instructed her just to swing the club while tuning into her breathing, letting it find its way to being more and more easy. Instead of paying attention to her swing, she was focusing on her breath. The more she did this, the more fluid her golf swing became, because she was no longer trying to control. I had Rachel continue focusing on her breathing while she hit the ball in the same fluid style. Her strokes began to improve. But she had an interesting reaction to the exercise. She said she felt so great playing in this relaxed, easy and effortlessly successful way that it made her uncomfortably guilty. She felt self-indulgent. On a common-sense level this was absurd. After all, she was already playing, so why not have it be fun instead of difficult!

Things became even more interesting at our next session in my office. I decided to help Rachel reach a deeper level of relaxation by using some imagery. I suggested that she think of the breath as a gentle caress that was entering her body and touching her deeply and tenderly inside. I was hoping that this image would help her access and release levels of tension that she had not yet become aware of. That is exactly what happened.

Rachel started crying. She told me that as she began to feel softer and softer inside, she felt more and more pleasure. For the very first time in her life she knew what it was to give herself love. Rachel saw herself as a nurturing person in her relations with other people. But she had never tried to nurture herself. The exercise taught her how to be tender toward herself, and that made her feel vulnerable. We are soft and shy in our center and as Rachel put it, "It's scary to love yourself."

Exploring softness and tenderness toward herself was new territory for Rachel because she had learned from her father to associate living with hard work. Her father had never been able to express softness, either with himself or with his family. It had been taboo, even though feeling softness is incredibly pleasurable. As Rachel said, "I'm afraid of feeling joy!" The joyfulness that is a natural part of self-love and that comes from learning to soften into ourselves was foreign to her. Rachel had learned to act appropriately or responsibly instead of joyfully. She had learned to feel shame around the joy that was a natural expression of her being. I think one reason people have resistance to relaxing into themselves is that they are afraid of feeling joy. It's such a powerful sensation, and it requires you to give up control.

When I teach classes in meditation and self-transformation, and when I work with people who have health problems, I frequently use the suggestion I gave to Rachel. I ask them to imagine their breath as a tender caress. The power this image has in releasing unconscious depths of self-denial is extraordinary.

A seventy-year-old woman named Maria once attended one of my workshops. When her time came for sharing her interests and concerns with the group, Maria spoke of how she had been through a number of crises in her life, including having to live with a back brace, arm casts and a neck brace a few years before. The pain from which she suffered had eventually dissipated, and her concern now was with how to manage living compassionately with her husband, who was suffering from chronic depression.

When the group explored breath awareness, Maria was shocked to find out that she frequently held her breath. She had never been conscious of this. Then, as I worked with her, directing her to imagine the breath as a soft and tender caress washing through her body, her entire face started quivering violently as though it were convulsed in spasms. Tears came into her eyes. She was struggling to keep all this from happening, struggling not to feel her sadness, struggling not to feel herself. When she recovered from the experience, Maria told the group that she had always been a good caretaker, but she had no sense of tenderness toward herself. When she tapped into this tenderness it opened up a well of grief. We did not speak about the fact that Maria had also unwittingly revealed the dynamics that had put her in a series of braces from the neck right down to the base of her torso a few years before. Whatever was going on in her life at that time, she had been unable to accept her feelings, and the effort of holding them back had put her in a straitjacket. Illness often reflects a refusal to love ourselves.

Summary

The most fundamental thing we learn from working with our breathing is how to live in our bodies in a more relaxed, effortless and pleasurable manner. We owe it to ourselves to learn how to live effortlessly, for developing that skill enhances both our inner and our outer lives. In this chapter, we have looked at two approaches to finding effortlessness through breathing: meditation and being present to breathing in a relaxed way while going about our daily lives. The Suggestions for Practice that follow include techniques that will help you successfully implement effortlessness in your life through breath awareness.

The techniques are simple, and have been tested by other people and other cultures for centuries. They build your ability to relax at deeper and deeper levels. All they involve is learning to pay attention to and to flow with your breathing. If you find it difficult to do this at first, remember that you are not alone. We are all addicted to anxiety. That's why it's hard to let go. But if we want to let go, we can. We simply have to practice a few new skills. As we gradually and regularly make the commitment to relaxed breathing a fundamental part of our lives, our lives begin to flower in unexpected ways.

Nothing good is won overnight. The simple techniques presented here work miracles for us when they become an everyday part of our lives. Today it may be hard to relax into our breathing. Tomorrow, it is a little easier. Three months from now, we discover that we are different people, and that without even noticing it, the weight has lifted off our shoulders.

Over the years, many of my clients have asked me to make cassette tapes for them, to assist them in integrating into their lives the simple practices that introduce them to effortless living. They find it easier to listen to a tape than to read and follow written instructions. I have therefore created an audiocassette series entitled *Effortless Practice* that you may choose to use as a companion to this book.

While it is not essential to use the audiocassettes, they can be very helpful in providing the consistent practice most people need to develop meditative and deep relaxation skills, as well as other abilities that are integral to effortless living. You may find that audiotapes provide a simpler, more complete and more readily portable tool for learning than working with the written page.

Each cassette offers exercises aimed at enabling you to learn in depth, and as easily as possible, the skills of effortless living. These exercises are modeled along the lines of the Suggestions for Practice provided at the end of each chapter, but they are more comprehensive. Wherever the Suggestions for Practice involve exercises that can be demonstrated and elaborated upon through the medium of the spoken word, you will find accompanying exercises in *Effortless Practice*, indicated by the symbol 🔲 . (For information on ordering *Effortless Practice*, see p. 240.)

*Suggestions for Practice*_____

1. Meditate. 🔲

Meditating helps you develop the ability to relax deeply by following your breathing. To learn how to meditate, follow the practice suggested below. Alternatively, use the exercise (20 minutes) on Cassette 1 of Effortless Practice, *which provides a guided meditation on the breath. (For ordering information, see p. 240.)*

- **Practice meditative breathing.**

You may wish to have someone read this exercise to you, or to record it for yourself, giving yourself plenty of time to accomplish each segment.

1. **Find a quiet place.** Begin by finding a quiet place where you can sit or lie down, without interruptions, for at least five and up to fifteen or twenty minutes. Focus on letting go of the pressures of the day. Think of your intention: to support yourself in finding greater peace. Take your time so that you can sink into the process of quieting down.

2. **Imagine stillness.** Now imagine something that gives you a profound sense of *stillness*. This may involve a scene from nature, such as looking out at a midnight sky, a wide mountain vista, the ocean or a countryside covered with snow. It may also involve a memory from your past in which you felt profoundly at peace. Whatever the image, absorb yourself in the experience of stillness. As you imagine the scene of your choice, see it vividly, feel what it feels like. Immerse yourself in the scene, until you can recall exactly what it felt like, right down into your bones. Let yourself be there. This association with an image or memory of peace moves you into a deeper state.

3. **Scan your body.** Now let go of the image and begin gently scanning your body with your attention. Start with your feet. Notice the way your toes, heels, and the balls of your feet

feel. Appreciate the sensation. There is no right or wrong here, there's just feeling. Take in the feeling of your ankles, calves and thighs. Don't try to change anything. Absorb the feeling. Be interested in the sensations, staying with them long enough to register them fully.

Continue like this up into your pelvis, abdomen, rib cage, shoulders and neck. Take all the time you need to become fully present to the sensations of the different parts of your body. Continue by scanning down your upper arms to your elbows, your lower arms, and then to your hands. Spend some time enjoying the feeling of the palms of your hands. They are full of nerve endings, and you may feel a tingling or warmth. Then come back to your face, and let yourself absorb the softness of your lips. Once you have done this, move on to the area under your eyes, then to your cheeks, and then to your whole face. If you like, imagine that your face is like the face of a baby who is fast asleep: softer than the softest. Once you have finished scanning the sensation of your limbs, torso and head, let your awareness spread to include the feeling of your entire body.

Notice how the feeling of your body has changed. Do you feel your body more clearly than when you started? Do you feel tingling or warmth? Do you feel heavy? Or perhaps light and floaty? Do you feel bigger than before? Or boundaryless? These are all typical relaxation responses.

4. **Feel the wave of your breath.** Now let your attention shift to the sensation of your breath as it moves in and out of your body. You might want to focus your attention on a particular spot, for example the feeling of the breath as it comes in and out of your nose, or the feeling of your belly rising and falling with the breath. As you focus on your breathing, you will notice thoughts going through your mind. Do not struggle with them or try to eliminate them. Let them be there, but just come back to the breath.

You will gradually become aware that the breath is a wave flowing in and out of you, and it behaves in many ways like waves in the ocean. Let yourself become absorbed in the feeling of the wave of the breath. If you were to get absorbed in watching waves hitting an ocean beach, you would become aware that each wave is unique. One wave is powerful and strong, comes crashing down on the beach, and pulls out rapidly. The next wave is gentle and soft, and lingers before withdrawing from the sand. Sitting there on the beach, you could drop into a fascinated trance absorbing how unique each wave is. Watch the breath in the same way. Appreciate how completely unique each breath is. Don't try to change it.

When you find yourself distracted by thoughts or feelings, gently bring your attention back to being anchored in the feeling of the breath. As you do this, you will gradually feel your entire body and mind becoming quieter, your breath becoming softer, slower and deeper.

5. **Imagine the breath is a caress.** Once you have truly entered into experiencing the individual waves of the breath, invite your imagination into play. Imagine that the wave of the breath is like a caress coming into your body. Each wave reaches into you and caresses you on the inside. Because it is very soft, it invites you to open up and soften inside, to feel yourself more deeply. Feel how the caress of the breath touches you on the inside, inviting you to let down into feeling yourself.

6. **Imagine the breath caressing you more deeply.** As you feel the caress of the wave of the breath, put your hands over the part of your body where you feel the breath most clearly. It may be your chest, abdomen or belly. Absorb the feeling of the wave caressing you on the inside, and you will find yourself gradually feeling yourself more and more deeply. The process of becoming more aware of internal sensation is part of letting go.

Once you have absorbed the sensation of your breath in your body under your hands, then move your hands lower on your torso. If your hands were on your chest, they will now move toward your belly. If they were on your belly, they will move toward your pelvis. Again, *imagine* that the caress of the breath is now moving deeper into your body, into the area underneath your hands. Do not try to *make* your breath deeper. This will involve you in effort and control, which is counterproductive. Allow the imagination to do the work for you. The breath will gradually move deeper, helping you rediscover a state of ease that is less contracted and closer to your natural birthright.

7. **Feel the breath filling your torso.** Continue moving your hands down your body until you feel your breath easily and quietly filling your entire torso. You can also imagine it flowing down through your legs and into your toes, down your arms and into your neck and head. Now just enjoy absorbing the feeling of open, deep breathing for as long as you like. Feel the internal pleasure this gives you.

8. **Open your eyes.** When you are ready to come to the close of your meditation, open your eyes. See if you can maintain some awareness of the breath as you look around the room. When you get up again, notice how present you can be to your breathing. This will help you carry some of the deep quietness you felt in meditation into your day's activities.

2. Practice Conscious Breathing in Your Daily Life. 🔲

Once you can follow your breathing in meditation, you can begin to incorporate relaxed breathing into daily activities. This will give you a calmer, more focused and more peaceful lifestyle. In addition to following the suggestions below, you may wish to use the exercise (15 minutes) on Cassette 1 of Effortless Practice, *which supports these suggestions by teaching you how to relax while you are at the office, doing chores, working out at the gym, or engaged in any routine activity.*

• Observe your breathing in simple activities.

Become aware of your breathing while engaging in low-stress activities: showering, taking a walk, preparing breakfast, reading a book, watching television, or driving down the highway. Observe your breathing for several minutes at a time. Be curious about how things change as you tune in to your breathing. See if you can continue to be with your breathing while you walk, read, prepare your meal, etc.

Notice whether your breathing is relaxed, or whether it sometimes feels tight. Many of us tighten up even in the simplest of activities, because we are used to bringing stress into everything we do. If your breathing is tight, don't try to change it. Just get in touch with it. You will notice if that you do not try to force yourself to relax, your breathing will begin to soften and deepen on its own. That is because you're not pushing yourself. Notice that as your breath softens, your stress levels decrease. How does following your breathing change the way you go about your daily chores? Do you notice that you can accomplish just as much, but with less tension? Do you notice that you are more efficient and at the same time calmer?

• **When ready, follow your breathing in more challenging situations.**

Once you can follow your breathing in simple daily activities, start following your breathing in more challenging situations: a difficult conversation with a colleague or family member, working out at the gym, going for an interview. Give yourself time to develop this skill.

Notice how committing yourself to being more balanced in your breathing affects the situations in which you find yourself. How does breath awareness affect your interactions with people? Are you less reactive? How do others respond to you? Do they seem to feel more comfortable with you, or to perceive you in a different way?

Suggested Reading

Herbert Benson, *The Relaxation Response* (New York: Avon Books, 1976). A classic early study by a well-known doctor, on the physiological benefits of meditation.

Thich Nhat Hanh, *The Miracle of Mindfulness* (Boston: Beacon Press, 1975). This easy-to-follow manual on meditation, written by an eminent Vietnamese Buddhist, supports moving into an effortless lifestyle.

chapter 7

Effortlessness: Feeling Our Physical Bodies

To let go of effort, we have to become passionately interested in cultivating a feeling of effortlessness, of being in the flow. Relaxing into our breathing is an important tool for accomplishing this. It gets us in touch with the feeling of ourselves and brings us more into our bodies. The more we get in touch with feeling our bodies through breathing, the more effortless we become. However, becoming truly effortless goes beyond this. It involves relaxing into feeling our bodies as a whole.

If you practiced the meditative exercise from the last chapter, you noticed that before you focused your attention on your breathing, you began by tuning in to the general sensation of your body. This practice of feeling the body is common to many traditions of meditation. One reason is that feeling your body takes your mind off thinking, and meditation aims to give you a calm mind, free of thoughts. But there's another reason for focusing on feeling your body: the practice of exploring bodily sensations in a neutral, detached manner automatically *relaxes you and opens you up*. It's part of getting in touch with who you really are, as opposed to who you think you're supposed to be, or who your mother or father told you you were.

Just as when we explore our breathing in a non-judgmental and curious way we become very relaxed, so too does the same thing happen when we explore any bodily sensation with the same attitude. We experience the resulting relaxation of tension as a softness in our tissues and in ourselves. Softness is our subjective experience of letting go of effort.

Many therapies recognize that learning how to stay with the overall sensation of one's body in a non-judgmental, attentive manner produces deep relaxation. Progressive Relaxation, developed by Edmund Jacobson, trains students to alternately tense and release muscles in all their limbs, and then to focus on absorbing the sensation created by the release. Jacobson developed Progressive Relaxation when he became aware that many people were so out of touch with their bodies that *they could no longer feel themselves*. It's a sad fact but true that most people are so deeply out of touch with themselves that they are neither aware of their lack of awareness nor of the frozen attitude toward life that shuts them down.

Body scans offer another approach to relaxing into experiencing oneself through feeling the body. In doing body scans, people learn to relax by bringing awareness to how different parts of their bodies feel, without trying to change anything. Used widely as a relaxation technique in Yoga and dance classes as well as in holistic medical practices, body scans offer practice in self-awareness.

Here is a simple exercise that will show how *tuning in to your sensations* can help you become *soft*, how becoming softer makes you *effortless*, and how becoming effortless creates greater pleasure, more efficiency, and enhanced self-awareness. Do this exercise now, allowing yourself to pause after each instruction.

Take a pen in your hand and write a few lines on a pad of paper. What you write is not significant. Now put the pen down and rest your hand in your lap. Begin exploring the sensation of your hand, giving yourself plenty of time to do this. Become interested in the feeling of each of the fingers, and then the thumb. Notice the feeling of the wrist and palm. Give them your undivided attention and interest, as though there were nothing in the world that could interest you more.

You will observe the sensation of your hand becoming clearer. You may notice a tingling or warmth, or have the impression that your hand is becoming larger. Now imagine the hand is melting like a puddle. Each finger is becoming softer and softer. Your fingers, thumb, palm and wrist are all melting. Take a moment to absorb these feelings and to let them become part of you. Finally, pick up the pen and write again. While you do this, hold on to that melted feeling in your imagination. Notice what this feels like as you write.

Did you notice that you are writing with less effort than before, yet just as efficiently? Did you discover that when you had been writing earlier, you were using far more effort than necessary? Did you realize that you had been using too much force to write what could be done more pleasurably, with less tension in the fingers? By becoming present to the feeling of your body, you can do whatever you were doing with far less effort.

How is it that when we do not pay attention to the feeling in our bodies, we can pick up a pen and work too hard to write down a few lines? What does this say about our entire lifestyle? What does it say about how present we are to ourselves? What does it say about how we feel about ourselves? It would be easy to answer that the question is not so complex, and that we just grip the pen too tight because we grip the pen too tight. Yet nature made us with incredible economy. It's natural for us to do things the least effortful way, and not in a way that expends excess energy. We see this when we watch infants learn to roll over, crawl, sit and stand. They find out exactly what level of strength they require for the movement. They don't force the issue.

Our Forcing, Frozen Selves

Unlike children, adults do use force. We grip too hard because we are frozen, and we are frozen because we grip too hard. Our bodies are frozen from trying too hard for too long. They are frozen from years of holding on to illusions and demands and from years of holding back on self-expression and authenticity. Eventually, it becomes impossible to perform even the simplest movement without tension. Our frozenness makes it difficult for us to feel our bodies. Rigidity, tension and loss of sensation go hand in hand. Ours is a society of wooden men and women. We have lost the softness that comes from being in touch with ourselves and that gives life its passion, beauty and endless subtlety.

Wilhelm Reich, a founding father of body-centered approaches to psychotherapy, knew about the freezing pattern behind a neurotic civilization. He said personality disorders were identical with tendencies to *armor* the body through muscular contractions. He was the first modern teacher of emotional healing to use bodywork as a guide in helping patients let go of long-standing neurotic emotional patterns. His work focused on releasing the armor that people put up, an armor that is both a personality defense and a tightening of muscular tissue which holds back and deadens feeling.

Alexander Lowen, the founder of Bioenergetics and at one point a student of Reich's, further developed Reich's insights. He elaborated a brilliant and powerful analysis of personalities in which each basic personality type was identified with specific frozen areas in the body—neck, chest, pelvis, etc. He showed how these frozen areas of neuromuscular contraction and rigidity defend a person against feeling the core emotions that rule his life. Today, many body-centered therapies help clients heal by accessing deep emotions concealed under neuromuscular tension. They engage energy blocks in the body, and when the blocks give way, a person frequently recalls significant charged experiences that had been buried in the unconscious. Afterwards, the person usually feels physically lighter and emotionally unburdened.

Other twentieth-century innovators in the field of bodywork have also identified a freezing response underneath physical, emotional and cognitive problems that people face in their lives. Frederick Mathias Alexander, the founder of the Alexander Technique, felt that a bodily freezing that expressed excess tension, loss of sensitivity, and fear of being oneself resulted in problems of epidemic proportions.

Alexander began his explorations when he was a young Australian actor around the turn of the century. He had started suffering from voice problems that medical intervention could not alleviate. Frustrated at his condition, he took to observing himself very carefully in the mirror when he spoke, in order to see if there was anything he was doing that might account for his problem. Through meticulous observation he became aware that whenever he spoke he subtly contracted the muscles in his neck. This contraction triggered a tightening of muscles down the length of the entire spine. By observing what he was doing with his muscles, Alexander discovered that instead of opening up to speak he was closing down. Just as we grip our pen too hard to write, he was gripping in his body in order to talk.

What Alexander observed consciously is something we frequently become aware of unconsciously. Have you ever been turned off by someone when you heard them talk? Did you feel you couldn't quite put your finger on it, but there was something irritating or slightly uncomfortable about the sound of their voice? You might have been picking up the subtle muscular gripping that went along with that person's speaking. This gripping makes you automatically distrust what the person is saying, because that person is not at ease.

What Alexander observed in himself was the startle reflex, the muscular contraction that is part of the fight or flight response and that starts in the eyes and back of the neck and travels down the length of the body. Whenever he spoke, his need to perform fostered a subtle startle reflex, or fight or flight response. Because the reflex was habitual, initially Alexander couldn't feel it. Over time, he did train himself to become aware of and inhibit the tightening response in his body. He eventually cleared his voice problem and began helping other people with voice trouble. His work expanded when he discovered that the bodily freezing he had first noticed in himself was not confined to people with vocal difficulties. It was virtually universal, contributing to anything from anxiety to serious disease and constantly limiting performance in any area of activity.

Alexander realized that everyone he worked with had a habit of contracting or freezing when they focused on a goal they wanted to achieve. They weren't aware of it because they tended to be so intent on their goal that they didn't pay attention to what was happening in their body. Alexander hypothesized that the tendency to ignore body awareness for the sake of getting a result underlay numerous mental and physiological problems and accounted for a general underdevelopment of human potential.

Over the years, Alexander worked with thousands of individuals who were seeking both relief from serious medical problems and enhancement of poise and mental power. He also founded a school of bodywork named after him. Attacked by the medical profession, Alexander nonetheless received widespread recognition for his work, and counted among his students luminaries such as George Bernard Shaw, Aldous Huxley and John Dewey. The philosophies of both Huxley and Dewey were deeply influenced by their contact with Alexander.

Moshe Feldenkrais, who founded another widely acclaimed system of bodywork, also taught people how to let go of deep freezing patterns that alienated them from themselves, and to redevelop a capacity for sensation, self-awareness and pleasure. Like Alexander, Feldenkrais thought that most people had lost the ability to feel, with painful consequences for their emotional life and their health. He trained people to regain lost mobility and vitality by learning to feel their bodies more and more clearly. They did this by exploring how to make simple movements with less and less effort, paying attention to exploring the sensation of the movement.

Feldenkrais said we become frozen because we learn to associate success with effort.

> Our parents and teachers say, "You could be someone if you would only make the effort, if you only wanted. Look, other children make an effort. They sit, and do, and become good pupils—and you are a silly ass. I pay for you, I work and teach you, and what happens? You make no effort." Therefore, unless we make efforts we don't deserve to learn anything, or be able to do anything. We get so used to that that we make efforts when it's not necessary. We make efforts that don't improve our learning; they improve our ability to suffer and expend energy futilely.... It's only when you have learned it on your own body, that you will see that to make a wider choice for yourself, you will have to increase your sensitivity, and reduce the effort.[*]

Thomas Hanna, a student of Feldenkrais and founder of a bodywork method called Somatics, expanded Feldenkrais' insights into an analysis of aging. Hanna saw aging as the inevitable consequence of a progressive development of what he called sensorimotor amnesia. As we grow older, a sedentary lifestyle combined with neuromuscular tension resulting from stress cause us to lose the ability to feel our bodies as clearly as we did as children. Once we can no longer feel clearly, the inevitable happens: we also move less easily. Effort and decreased sensation are partners, just as effortlessness and enhanced sensation are partners. The less we feel ourselves, the more rigid we become. Similarly, the more rigid we become, the less we feel ourselves. The solution? Rejuvenate the body by reawakening our ability to feel ourselves. How do we reawaken the ability to feel? Simple: by practicing feeling!

---

[*] Moshe Feldenkrais, *The Master Moves* (Cupertino, CA: Meta Publications, 1984), p. 27.

Each of these somatic pioneers said that both our bodies and our minds degenerate when we lose the ability to feel ourselves. Each of them said we lose the ability to feel ourselves because we contract and tighten up in the face of life. We contract and tighten up because we lose touch with the fact that our most fundamental journey in life has to be an exploration of ourselves, and not an attempt to live by somebody else's rules. Reich, Lowen, Alexander, Feldenkrais and Hanna all also pointed to the same, simple remedy to the problem: *Practice being with your sensations, and this will lead to self-knowledge, healing, self-transformation, and self-empowerment.*

In our society, people are encouraged to spend thousands of dollars on talking through or thinking about their problems. *But what about the power of just getting in touch with feeling our bodies?* We have a very ambivalent relationship to our bodies, as is shown by the billions of dollars spent on over-the-counter analgesics each year. We would rather not feel. But learning to feel the body is one of the most powerful tools of self-empowerment that we have. When we start feeling, our bodies automatically start correcting what is wrong.

The Healing Power of Sensation

Feeling our bodies in an accepting, non-judgmental and curious way promotes physical health by helping us let go of the unconscious contractions that promote disease. My first experience of this occurred a number of years ago. I woke up in the middle of the night in an agony of abdominal pain and nausea caused by food poisoning. I knew that a drug would only suppress the symptoms without resolving the problem, so I opted against the pharmacological approach. I alternated between lying in bed sweating and moaning and standing over the bathroom toilet groaning. Then it occurred to me that if I joined with the discomfort in my body instead of fighting it, something might shift.

I put my attention on the pain and tried to appreciate what it actually felt like. I tried to get closer to it. That was difficult. At first, the knot of pain in my belly intensified so much that it felt unbearable. Then, just as I was feeling I couldn't stand it any longer, it turned into a ball of energy, shot right through my torso, exploded out through the top of my head and disappeared. My body felt fine. As for me, I cried and cried. Something unusual had definitely just shaken my worldview. How could an intestinal bug pass out the top of my head? If I was going to absorb this, I was going to have to see health and illness through an unconventional paradigm. The experience taught me that the body is really a system of energy. By entering into rather than resisting the pain, I had allowed the knot of trapped energy that was creating the pain to find the most direct route out of my body. That route happened to be out the top of my head.

Since this experience, I have often guided clients through releasing pain by becoming more present to it. A gentleman named Mark came to visit me, complaining of chronic gastric discomfort. He lay down on the bodywork table, and after guiding him into deeper relaxation, I asked him to get in touch with the sensation of the pain. Rather than resisting it, or thinking about how much he disliked it, he was to adopt an attitude of detached interest. As he did this, he felt more clearly what the pain was: a hard round ball about the size of a fist, burning in the middle of his abdomen.

I asked Mark to treat the ball as a part of himself, and to imagine feeling love and acceptance toward it. It took him a while to shift his attitude, and not to think of this just as an intellectual exercise. He was, however, able to make that deeper shift, and as he did, the hard ball softened and then began dissolving and spreading through his body. Mark watched and felt the ball melting, until it turned into what he described as streamers of light that were very pleasurable.

Mark had learned how to join with instead of fighting a knot of his own energy, and this had allowed the energy to release harmlessly. He realized then that it was his attitude toward his sensations that had created the chronic pain. His tendency to judge and fight his own sensations had put him at war with himself. It was when he tried to control or reject those sensations that they turned into the enemy. He healed himself by replacing fear of his body with acceptance.

There are many levels of acceptance and many lessons along the way of learning acceptance. I once developed a fairly serious case of poison ivy. Anyone who has had the experience of prolonged uncontrollable itching knows that it can drive you absolutely mad. The poison ivy had spread from my hands and arms to my thighs and belly, and it was getting worse by the day.

One evening, rather than either wishing the poison ivy itch would go away or trying to distract myself from the itching, I let myself become interested in exploring the feeling of the itch. After all, what's the use of fighting with something that is so close? I got interested in breaking down the sensation into its component parts, feeling exactly where it had spread, and what an itch actually was made up of. Then I spoke to the itch as if it had its own intelligence. At that moment I was able to say with genuine sincerity, "Okay, it's your ball game. Do whatever you need to do, I won't resist." I stayed with my intention, and the rest of the night, even though I was aware of intense itching, it was as though the itching were not mine. It didn't bother me at all. I was that detached. The next day proved a turning point, and the itching lessened rapidly.

This experience reminded me of a comment by the well-known sensitive, Jack Schwarz. Schwarz could put nails straight through his arms, piercing the flesh on both sides, without this affecting his vital signs. When he was hooked up to monitors at the Menninger Foundation, his heart beat and brain waves would register absolutely no reaction. When asked how he accomplished this remarkable feat, Jack said that he had developed the art of seeing what was happening to his body as if it were happening to someone else. He was so removed that he not only felt no pain, his body also had no reaction to the trauma, and would heal within minutes of removing the nails from his body. Jack was extremely detached. It was a small taste of that detachment that I experienced briefly with my poison ivy.

Allowing ourselves to feel sensations non-judgmentally opens up the body and allows for a freer flow of energy, and that supports healing. Many illnesses are due to bodily contractions that shut us down. These contractions can exist on an energetic or neuromuscular level, or both. If we got in touch with them and learned how to release them, we would have a lot more control over our health than we do today. This requires being willing to get in touch with our sensations.

Unfortunately, many people are either afraid of their sensations or don't know how to get in touch with them. As a result, they are sicker than they might be, and more powerless as well. Our fear of our own sensations, our lack of familiarity with our own bodies, and our neurotic need to have someone else decide our fate drive us into the arms of medical experts. Yet we could often solve our problems much more easily ourselves.

We do not need experts anywhere near as much as we think we do. The answers we need to find can be found closer at hand and are more common sense than we think. What we need to do is to look for what is right in front of our eyes, patterned into the body. That is something that medical practitioners, with their excessive reliance on fancy equipment, can sometimes be inept at doing.

Jim's story provides an example of how medical care can overlook the obvious. Jim was carrying a stress pattern in his body that should have been easy to diagnose and that too many doctors failed to pick up. He came into my office because he had been suffering from chronic, debilitating headaches for two years. He had been through MRIs, X-rays, blood tests, acupuncture, just about everything you could imagine. I was his last resort.

Jim's headaches had started after a vigorous game of tennis in which he had pulled a shoulder muscle. As it turned out, that pull had been one stress too many on a body that was already under stress. Part of the tension came from poor breathing patterns. The rest came from the way he moved his feet and carried his head. His feet were so duck-footed that they caused his pelvis to drop forward, creating a sway back. The sway back cost him the structural support his spine was supposed to give his torso. He was like a building whose main vertical beams are bent rather than straight. Since he was lacking his central support, the muscles of his upper body, including his neck, had to work extra hard to hold up the rest of his torso. The tension this caused in his neck was radiating upwards into his head and causing the headaches.

Jim needed to rediscover the support of his spine and bones so that his muscles could relax and stop doing so much work. I had him explore realigning his feet so that they pointed forward and his spine straightened out a bit, lessening the impact of the swayback. Jim immediately felt a release of pressure in his neck. We continued to work in this way, showing Jim how he could change movement patterns to release tension. Eight sessions later he was completely free of headaches.

Jim didn't need an MRI or X-rays. He needed to explore how

changing the way he used his body changed his stress levels. He needed to use his own feedback system more effectively. How many doctors teach us how to do that? It should be obvious that our health depends on our ability to respond constructively to the feedback our body gives us. Yet teaching people to explore how different ways of standing, sitting and walking affect their bodies and create relaxation or pain seems to be a lost art. And most doctors would rather give an MRI or an X-ray than use their eyes to observe a person's patterns of movement.

I once worked with a fifty-year-old woman who had been suffering from severe headaches from the age of fifteen and who lived on painkillers. The first time I met her I saw enormous tension in her eyes. I asked her if she had any problems with her eyes and she told me that at the age of twelve she had had surgery to correct a wandering eye. Surgeries like this, which are basically cosmetic, can wreak havoc on our feedback system. Ever since that surgery, Ann's eyes had been struggling to readapt, creating extreme tension in her extra-ocular muscles. This tension had radiated to the back of her neck and down her spine, causing chronic headaches as well as an irritable disposition.

In all the years that Ann had been visiting doctors, no one had ever noticed the stress around her eyes or found any significance in the fact that Ann had started suffering from severe headaches three years after her surgery. It doesn't take much knowledge of the body to know that the functioning of the eyes (which give us our sense of space) and of the neuromuscular system (which enables us to move through space) are closely related. Yet apparently the compartmentalization that results from medical specialization, combined with poor observation skills, obscured this fact from view among the many experts Ann visited. Ann's work in becoming aware of and releasing tension from the muscles around her eyes freed her from headaches, from dependence on drug therapy, and from the disempowerment of living in a recalcitrant body.

Physical Release and Emotional Healing

Feeling the body more clearly and with less tension induces emotional as well as physical healing. I was working with a client who had been suffering from back pain resulting from an automobile accident several years before. Suzanne had gone through surgery, but the results were mixed. We were using a combination of relaxation techniques and movement patterns to help strengthen her body. On this particular day, we began playing with an image to help her get in touch with and release deep tension.

Suzanne lay on the floor, imagining her body to be a container filled with water. As she moved slowly from side to side, she felt the internal contents of her body moving like liquid, flowing into different parts of her torso. Where her body was relaxed, the liquid flowed freely. Where there was tension, she had trouble feeling that place and letting the water flow through. The area instead would feel heavy, insensitive or dense. Each time we hit a dense part of Suzanne's body we slowed down and stayed with that area until it opened up.

We were working with the left side of the pelvis when Suzanne suddenly burst into tears. When she stopped crying, Suzanne told me that as soon as she started focusing her awareness on the left pelvis she realized in a flash that she had suppressed her sexuality after the automobile accident because her husband had been cold and unsympathetic about her disability. She had unconsciously frozen in her pelvis in order to close the door to sexual intimacy. But this hurt her more than it hurt her husband. She needed to reclaim her sexuality rather than cut herself off from it. It was part of her. While she might not be able to heal the issues with her husband, it was inappropriate for her to deal with the situation by cutting out her own ability to feel herself as a woman. In coming to this realization, Suzanne had released an energy block—a frozen area—that was tied up with blocked sexual energy. She had done this by imagining the frozen part of her body becoming more liquid.

The more tension we carry, the less we can feel our bodies and the more out of touch we are with our emotions. Many of my clients discover tensions in their bodies that they had no idea existed. That discovery in turn leads to emotional realizations.

A Yoga teacher named Terri who came to work with me had already done quite a bit of work on herself, but she needed to go to a deeper level. As we were talking she commented casually how life always seemed for her to be a struggle. My hunch was that this comment reflected deep-seated tension. I noticed that the left side of Terri's jaw was slightly askew and asked if she had ever been hit as a child. It turned out that she had been hit repeatedly on the left side of the face. Terri's left eye also pulled to the right, and it got tired when she was reading. She also mentioned that she had a tendency to grind her teeth at night. The blows on the face, the visual problems and the teeth grinding all indicated intense facial constriction. Emotions were buried under that constriction.

I guided Terri through some gentle movements of the jaw and eyes to loosen up muscles in her face. She performed these movements the way most people do when they are out of touch with themselves: she pushed her jaw and eyes back and forth until they virtually ached from the strain. Terri was out of touch with how delicately the body can move, and she thought that more meant better. She needed to be reminded, as Lao Tse said, that, "The soft overcomes the hard, the slow overcomes the fast."[*]

Slow, gentle and easy movement reaches far deeper into the body than aggressive movement. It invites the body's resistance to give way. I suggested to Terri that she slow down the movements and focus on making them softer. Even tiny movements were fine, so long as they were increasingly gentle and effortless.

Terri noticed an uncomfortable tension on the left side of her face that she said she had never felt before. Since the exercises were releasing frozen areas, her sensitivity was improving, and she was able to feel what was going on in parts of her face with which she had completely lost touch. Terri didn't want to feel the discomfort that had always been there but that had been unconscious. She associated discomfort with things being unpleasant, and if she had been alone, she would have stopped the exercises right then and there. Instead, I encouraged her to continue gently releasing the tension. Soon, the uncomfortable sensations decreased and she felt better.

Terri's experience shows that opening up requires overcoming resistance. That resistance usually takes the form of pain. The pain is there as a signal that we need to find a way to release held energy rather than avoid or repress it. Every time we release pain, we open up our bodies to more life energy. And if we are going to continue opening and expanding our capacity to handle vital energy, we may have to go through further discomfort down the road as our bodies try to accommodate to higher and higher levels of energy.

---

[*] Stephen Mitchell trans., Tao Te Ching (New York: Harper and Row, 1988), #36.

During one stage of own my battle with chronic pain, I worked on opening up my pelvis, breathing into and softening that area. As I opened up my pelvis and connected to it more fully, the pain in my body gradually dissipated, and for quite a while I was free of pain. I didn't know at the time that what I had accomplished had set the stage for the next level of work. A number of months later I developed intense, viselike sensations in my neck. By opening up my lower torso I had enhanced the energy flow through my body. That energy was now causing pain at the next bottleneck in my torso: my neck. What seemed like a step backward was actually a step forward.

It was important for me to realize that the pain was not bad, and it was neither a sign of failure nor a new disease. Instead, it indicated an increasing life force that was trying to find its way through me. Realizing this helped me work productively with releasing the pain in my neck.

When people come to me in pain, they are frequently experiencing the body's attempt to try to open up rather than shut down. In being born, a baby goes through pain in the birthing canal as part of coming into a new life. The baby's participation in the experience of pain is quite active, since it helps push its way through the uterus. If it avoided pain, it could not be born. Pain during life, as in birth, can serve the purpose of shifting us to the next level of existence. But if we do not see it that way, we don't work our way through it. Instead, we fight it or suppress it, refuse the change it brings, and sometimes bring on chronic illness.

When Terri worked through her pain by focusing on letting go of chronic tension in her jaw and eyes, she relaxed into a new level of ease. After the brief uncomfortable period, she discovered that she felt better than she had in years. She also started being much more outspoken with her husband. Her emotional expressiveness was a direct consequence of the movement work with her jaw and eyes.

When Terri had been struck as a child, she had learned to shut up by clamping down her jaw to keep from saying anything. She had also learned to look away from people in order to avoid confrontation. These two patterns started as a childhood defense but eventually ossified into chronic jaw tension that blocked her vocal self-expression, and into visual pulling to the right that blocked her ability to confront life straight on. Life felt difficult and effortful because her body was locked into struggle, and she was perpetually clenched. When Terri released the physical pattern that underlay her existential stance, she began relaxing, standing up for herself more clearly and speaking her truth.

The Sensation-Focus Connection

Feeling our bodies or being present to sensations promotes physical and emotional healing. It also improves focus and performance. This is most obvious in the performing arts and in athletics.

If you are a pianist and are studying a difficult passage of music, you might be tempted to continue pounding away at that passage, trying to get it right. But if instead you have the patience to play that passage very slowly, paying attention to the gentle shifts of sensation as your fingers move across the keys, your performance will improve much more rapidly. By focusing your awareness on how the fingers feel on the keys, and on how lightly you can play, you are improving your feedback.

Similarly, if you play tennis or golf, you will improve far more rapidly by exploring feeling your body as you play, instead of thinking about your next shot or criticizing yourself for your last one. As you tune in to feeling your body, it also helps if you can remember that less is more, and explore where you can apply less force to achieving your goals more effectively.

I once worked with a golf pro who complained both of performance anxiety and of a tendency to lose his balance. His performance anxiety was actually making his body rigid and unbalanced, and his rigidity was then worsening his game. In order to improve his performance, I had him let go of thinking about the score he wanted or about how he was going to hit the ball. Instead, we spent an hour during which he explored the sensation of his feet as he swung the club.

I asked the golf pro to rate the level of tension in his feet between a minimum of one and a maximum of five. Each time he swung the club he reported to me where the tension level was in his feet, on a scale of one to five. When he started, the tension level in his feet was up at four or five. By the end of the hour, he was fairly consistently able to keep the tension level low, at one or two. Both his control over the club and his sense of balance had improved markedly. He had been paying attention to his sensations, working on being more relaxed in his body, rather than focusing his attention exclusively on the club and ball. When he brought his new body awareness into his game, and consistently focused on keeping his body relaxed, his playing improved dramatically.

Sports and music show us that concentration is identical with body awareness and relaxation. This holds true for all areas of endeavor, and is well recognized by esoteric disciplines. Eastern spiritual traditions are based on the principle that *intense concentration is identical with deep bodily presence and ease*, and that bodily presence and ease happen when we let go, *occupying our body instead of controlling it.*

Buddhism, Zen, Tai Chi and Yoga all teach bodily awareness as a tool for achieving highly focused powers of concentration. The spiritual teacher G. I. Gurdjieff, who drew from many esoteric traditions, oriented much of his training for building mental power around developing bodily presence. One aspect of this training is a simple exercise in "self-remembering" that is a form of body scan. Here's how to do it.

1) Center and calm yourself by following the breath as in meditation, simply resting your attention on appreciating the feeling of the breath coming in and out of your body. Do this for a minute or so, until you find your mind beginning to get quieter.

2) Now let your attention rest on the sensation of each part of your body, gradually including more and more of the felt sensation of yourself. Start by focusing your awareness on the feeling of your right foot. Once the feeling of your right foot is clear to you, expand your awareness to include your right calf.

3) Once you are fully present to the sensation of both your right foot and your calf, expand your awareness to include your right thigh along with the foot and calf.

4) Then do the same with the left leg, starting with the foot.

5) Proceed in this way throughout the entire body.

By the end of the exercise your sense of yourself, and your ability to feel exactly where and how you are in space, will be enhanced. You will feel yourself more clearly. Since you'll be more in touch with yourself, your feedback system will also be enhanced. The ultimate goal is to develop this kind of awareness in everyday activity, so that you are completely present to your body in everything you do. This is in itself great training in concentration, since most people have difficulty staying with anything for very long, let alone their bodies. And since "self-remembering" centers a person at very deep levels, it improves focus in anything you do.

Summary

We live in our bodies, and they are constantly sending us messages. We are meant to receive those messages. If you think of the mind-body loop as an electrical circuit, it will be obvious that the more easily information flows through that loop, the more effectively the system will function. Unfortunately, somewhere along the way we have learned to be afraid of our bodies because we are afraid to be ourselves. We are also afraid of our bodies because we cling to fear instead of to pleasure.

What we are afraid of we try to control. But whenever we try to control, we stop listening. We stop listening to and responding to our bodies. Physical and emotional health depend on our listening to our bodies rather than controlling them. And listening comes down to feeling ourselves more clearly. That's the simple message of the preceding pages.

We have to stop controlling ourselves so much, and stop being afraid. We have to practice appreciating the feeling of ourselves instead. This is the teaching encoded in some of the most powerful transformational disciplines of world history: the ancient disciplines of Yoga, Tai Chi, Qi Gong and other esoteric arts. If we tune in to our bodies, we can learn how to be more effortless. When we learn how to be more effortless, we become more ourselves. We stop putting up defenses against being ourselves.

Learning to feel our bodies teaches us how to let go of being frozen. It's because we are frozen that we get sick, unhappy, and mentally constricted. Practicing feeling our bodies improves physical health, emotional health and concentration. Of course, the discipline and fascination of becoming more present to the body can absorb a lifetime, but the basic methodology is simple.

All of the Suggestions for Practice that follow are about letting go. Each one presents a slightly different way to approach a simple goal: feeling your body. Feeling your body essentially means being curious about it, relaxing into enjoying it, exploring it, and listening to it. Take any one exercise and play with it. Use the ones that appeal to you most. You'll find that each exercise does the same thing, but in a different way: it extends the idea introduced in Chapter 6, of finding effortlessness through your breathing, into finding effortlessness through appreciating the feelings of your body.

If you are not already very familiar with body-awareness work, the *Effortless Practice* cassettes referred to in the Suggestions for Practice are especially recommended. They provide experiential training in learning to feel your body at deeper levels. Getting in touch with your body, like getting in touch with your breathing, is an ongoing process that is a key ingredient in effortless living, and using cassettes can speed that process along while giving you plenty of enjoyment.

*Suggestions for Practice*_____

1. Enjoy Your Body's Sensations. 📼

This practice teaches you the pleasurable and deeply relaxing art of getting more in touch with your body. Explore the first suggestion at night when you go to bed, or at any time of the day when you want to take a break from tension. Then explore the second one at odd moments during the day. Use the exercise (20 minutes) on Cassette 2 of Effortless Practice *or follow the text below.*

• Tune in to the sensations of your body.

Sit or lie down and take a few minutes to absorb the sensations of your body. Start with the toes of your left foot and move through the foot, up the ankles, up the knee and to the thigh. Take enough time to get deeply in touch with and appreciate how your foot and leg feel. Then do the same thing with your right foot and leg. Continue this process, appreciating the sensations of your pelvis, torso, arms, hands and fingers, neck and head. Your whole body is one giant pattern of sensations. Get acquainted with it.

Avoid judging as you feel your body. Enjoy picking up the information your body sends you. Forget about thinking you have to do something about that information. Notice any temptation you may have to label a sensation as bad or worrisome. If you feel pain or discomfort, allow yourself to register that without judgment. This allows the sensation to pass through and dissipate. It's negative thoughts about our sensations that alienate us from our bodies, and that's where the trouble begins.

Notice how the feeling of your body changes as you pay attention to it. Does it become more tingly? Lighter? Heavier? Register these impressions with curiosity. Notice the increasing feeling of relaxation that happens naturally when you just allow yourself to feel.

• Tune in to your body while doing things.

Once you can tune in to your body's sensations when you're sitting or lying down, try tuning in while you're doing something: watching your favorite television program or reading a book. Practice feeling your body while having a conversation or sitting at your desk. Feeling your body is naturally enjoyable, so let yourself be a hedonist and get into it.

Notice how it relaxes you when you allow yourself simply to be in touch with your physical sensations. Notice how pleasurable this is. Finally, notice that when you can be more present to your body, you start picking up tension before it becomes a problem and are able to let go more.

2. Do Whatever You Do with Less Effort. 🔲

This practice teaches you how to eliminate constant and unconscious tension from your daily life. Use the exercise (10 minutes) on Cassette 2 of Effortless Practice *or follow the text below.*

• Bring less effort into all your activities.

Lighten your touch at the computer. Soften your grip on the steering wheel when driving. See how lightly you can walk across a room, or how little effort you can apply to opening a door. Lift weights with relaxed easy breathing. Hold a tennis racket or golf club with a lighter grip. Feel your ankles and feet floppy and relaxed as you run. Do whatever you do with less.

Notice what happens when you apply less effort. Become aware of the impact of trying to do things with less effort. Do things become easier? More pleasurable? More focused? Do you notice yourself letting go of tension? Do you notice that you had tension that you weren't even aware of until you consciously worked on letting go? You are letting go of unnecessary fear- and stress-based tension.

3. Explore Your Own Flow and Inner Feel. 🔲

When we live too much "on the outside," or are preoccupied with how other people see us, we tend to see our bodies from the outside. We tuck our bellies in so that we look good to others, put on crippling heels or uncomfortable suits for the sake of appearances, and generally torture ourselves in the name of appearance. All of this makes us rigid. It also takes us away from contacting our natural inner sense of grace. Take a risk and start living from the inside. You'll like it because you are infinitely interesting inside. Follow the suggestions below, or use the related exercise (15 minutes) on Cassette 2 of Effortless Practice.

• Start living from the inside instead of the outside.

A simple way to begin living from the inside is to notice the difference between what it feels like to walk down a street focused on how other people see you, and what it feels like to walk down the same street focused on your own internal sensations: the swish of your arms, bounce of your feet, etc.

Notice how doing the first makes you more and more uptight. Doing the second makes you more and more free because there's no one judging. There's just you experiencing yourself.

• Explore your own flow through movement.

Since most of us are quite out of touch with how we feel on the inside, getting in touch can take some practice. Go into a room by yourself, close your eyes, hold out your arm, and then move it in graceful, flowing motions. By closing your eyes, you enhance your ability to be present to the feel of your movements.

See if you can let the movements become more and more fluid. To do this, you will have to slow down, become attentive to the feeling of your arm, and be very gentle with your gestures. Don't be discouraged if at first you feel stiff or uncoordinated. Learning to feel your sensations by moving slowly will reawaken your inner flow. Just slow the movement down, and explore what it would be like to make it softer. You're discovering how to let go of tension and rediscover your natural grace.

When you have explored the feeling of flow in one arm for a while, add the other arm, and then gradually begin to move your whole body fluidly. Keep your attention on finding a way to allow all the movements to become increasingly slow and soft. If you like, put on a favorite piece of music, and let yourself move rhythmically with the music. Imagine being a graceful animal that appeals to you, a cheetah or a swan. Play at having flow, and you will find it.

Notice how different it feels to have your attention inside you, focused on the feelings of your body, instead of thinking about others. It's a revelation to let go of everything around you and go inside. It's profoundly satisfying. After a while, you'll have that easy, fluid feeling in your life with your eyes open, on the street, in the lecture hall, and at the negotiating table. You'll be learning to live from the inside, shedding the painful habit of living from the outside.

4. Be a Friend to Your Discomfort.

• Explore yourself when you feel uncomfortable.

When you feel uncomfortable, go inside your body and find the place of discomfort. Instead of being afraid of it, bring to it an attitude of loving, accepting attention. Imagine that the pain is part of you trying to communicate itself. Feel it, listen to it, appreciate it. Don't try to change it or react to it.

Notice how appreciating the sensation of pain without judgment often allows it to change, and sometimes even eliminates it.

5. Explore Bodywork Resources.

• Seek support in finding out about your body.

Let a professional bodyworker help you find and release your body tensions. Find a teacher of the Alexander Technique, the Feldenkrais Method, Tai Chi, Qi Gong, or Yoga, and explore what that teacher can show you about your body. For information on Alexander Technique teachers in your area, contact the American Society for the Alexander Technique at 1-800-473-0620 or at www.alexandertech.org. For Feldenkrais practitioners, contact the Feldenkrais Guild, in Albany, Oregon, at 1-800-775-2118. Tai Chi, Qi Gong and Yoga instructors can be found through local fitness clubs and directories.

• **Visit your bodywork professional for problems.**

Many physical problems are a direct result of being out of touch with our bodies. When you have pain or discomfort, consider the possibility that there is unconscious tension at the root of the pain. Visit a bodywork professional and see if she can tell you something that your doctor can't. She may be able to help you to help yourself in a way that goes beyond conventional medicine's current capabilities. Finding a way to empower yourself and change your relationship to your body—instead of just giving your body over to someone else to fix—can change your life in dramatic ways.

Suggested Reading

Michael Gelb, *Body Learning* (New York: Henry Holt, 1987). One of the best and most entertaining books written on the Alexander Technique. Also an excellent study of how we defeat ourselves through holding on to unnecessary and unconscious tension.

Eugen Herrigel, *Zen in the Art of Archery* (New York: Random House, 1989). An early and classic study of the discipline of effortlessness pursued through the martial arts, by a professor who lived in Japan after World War II.

Thomas Hanna, *Somatics* (New York: Addison Wesley, 1988). Excellent study, by a pioneer bodyworker, on reawakening the mind's control of movement, flexibility and health.

chapter 8

Feeling Our Emotional Bodies

Ours may be a society addicted to emotional drama, but it is not a society that cherishes authentic feeling. Authentic feeling came up when Rachel (Chapter 6), who came to me to study meditation, breathed so easily that she let down into her tenderness and vulnerability and began to cry for joy. She experienced a part of her feeling self that had been repressed and rejected by many years of achieving and caretaking. Authentic feeling also came up for Terri (Chapter 7), who worked with me on releasing her eyes and jaw. As she did this, she began to express her own truth freely instead of accommodating to what she thought she was supposed to be like.

The stories of Rachel and Terri show that the more we get in touch with our bodies, the more we get in touch with our emotional lives. And that's not surprising. Our emotions are nothing but energy moving through our bodies, as the etymology of the word *emotion*, which means to "move out," so aptly expresses. Emotions or feelings are visceral sensations that express our organic reactions to the world. The depth of our feeling life measures the depth of our life force, and if we judge, contain, or repress our feelings we repress our life force.

There's no way to avoid repressing our feelings if we identify ourselves with how successful we are and how we appear to others.

And that's what we do when we focus on doing. We put our own feelings in jeopardy by fostering conflict between ourselves and our masks.

If the feelings we have are out of line with the persona we are trying to project, then we can no longer express ourselves straightforwardly. Eventually, if we stop expressing ourselves spontaneously, we also stop knowing what we truly feel. A jazz musician knows what he wants to say by entering into the flow of his music, and we know what we feel by exploring our feelings through expression. But if we put restrictions around what feelings we think we're supposed to have, when we're supposed to have them, where and with whom, we end up being pretty confused. That's why the normal state in our culture is a state of diminished feeling. We make up for that lack of real feeling by craving superficial intensity.

A World of Confused Feelings

Our lifestyle and our cultural values teach us we are not supposed to feel what we feel. Here are stories of some of my clients, and how they suffered from being out of touch with feelings they repressed as unacceptable.

Jeanette

Jeanette had chronic fatigue that started two years after her marriage and a year after she gave birth to a baby girl. Prior to her marriage, she had loved the freedom of life as a single woman. She had not expected to get pregnant so quickly after being married, and while she and her husband wanted their baby, this made for big changes in her life. Suddenly her time was not her own. She felt angry about this but was unable to express her anger because she also felt guilty about feeling that way. She thought that she couldn't possibly be a decent mother if she was angry about the constraints that constant mothering put on her life!

Jeanette also had trouble expressing any strong feeling directly, especially if it was a feeling that someone else might not like. As a child, whenever her emotions had gotten the upper hand, her parents had promptly sent her to the basement to work things out by herself until she could behave, be a good girl and rejoin the family circle. Now Jeanette had to learn that feelings were feelings, with no right or wrong about them, and that she did not have to banish them to an emotional basement. Once she could do this, she could move toward dealing with the conflicts in her life constructively, finding out how to manage both being a mother and having greater autonomy. Dealing with those conflicts was for her a big part of letting go of chronic fatigue.

Margaret

Margaret has been married for thirty-five years and has three grown children, all of whom have done well for themselves. At the age of sixty, Margaret is confronting the emptiness of her marriage. She and her husband have few interests in common. Her husband is uncommunicative and a workaholic to boot, and he confines his comments on what needs changing in their relationship to instructions about how his wife should change.

Margaret is lonely. She wishes that she and her husband could find more rapport for the last years of their lives. She has set up numerous couple therapy sessions, most of which her husband attends grudgingly. She has tried repeatedly to find points of contact with him and has been consistently rebuffed. She feels angry and rejected. But instead of taking in the message of her feelings—that she needs to acknowledge the dead end that exists in the marriage and move toward creating more of her own life— Margaret questions her feelings. She feels that she should be more unconditional, more loving, more accepting, because that is what the spiritual books she reads talk about. She interprets the nature of unconditional love through the lens of her own self-demeaning co-dependency. She feels that because she's not unconditionally loving she must be failing at being the person she should be. She thinks that if she really loved unconditionally, then she wouldn't be hurt!

By telling herself that there is something wrong with her feelings, Margaret stays on the merry-go-round of taking sole responsibility for trying to make her marriage work, getting hurt and angry, and then getting upset with herself for being unloving. In order to change the situation, the first thing she has to do is to accept that her feelings are legitimate, if for no other reason than that they are hers. That doesn't mean her husband should change to meet her needs. The fact that we are unhappy about what someone else is doing doesn't give us any rights over them. But if Margaret can fully absorb her feelings instead of criticizing them, she will move toward resolving them. She might do that in any number of ways. She could let go of her expectations. She could make clear to her husband that his behavior toward her means that she will inevitably pull away from him, just as he has pulled away from her. She could develop more inner and outer independence. Or she could leave her husband. What specific solution she finds is not as important as the fact that she needs to take how she feels seriously.

Kitty

We make a mistake when we think we're supposed to have certain feelings and not others, and we can't help doing that if our sense of ourselves depends on how others see us. We're supposed to have exactly the feelings we have because our feelings are who we are. If we tell ourselves we can't have our feelings, we end up being deeply disconnected. One woman who came to see me was excruciatingly aware of this sense of disconnectedness. Kitty was in training to become a healer. Her outer appearance was extremely calm, but something else was going on beneath the surface. Kitty's expression was almost flat, and her voice had no rise and fall, no energy. It was as though she were speaking from a shell, and her real self were a long distance away.

As we talked, Kitty revealed that she felt a terrible gap between herself on the inside and the persona she presented to the outside world. When I asked her to tune in to her body, she felt tension and jitteriness. She said she had to separate from these sensations in order to let the tension subside. I asked her instead to get in touch with the jittery feeling, which she identified as fear, and then to go back in her imagination to the first time she could remember feeling that way. She returned to being five years old in kindergarten, and to her painful experience of terror at the chaos of a room full of noisy children.

As soon as Kitty was back in her early experience she burst into tears, and in exploring how she behaved as a child, we found the root of her adult problem. Her childhood reaction to her feelings of terror at the chaos around her had been to hide her fear by retreating and going off by herself. This had saved her from the chaos, but at the cost of isolation. Others could neither perceive nor acknowledge where she was emotionally.

All her life, Kitty had used the same tactic to deal with her fear and loneliness, burying them inside and putting on a semblance of calm that isolated her. Whenever she felt threatened, she withdrew into a false presentation of calm. She also assumed that it wouldn't help her if she shared what she felt. She walked around in the world feeling terrified and looking peaceful, at least to the casual observer. Kitty couldn't have her emotions—any emotions—in front of other people. If she had found out that it was possible to have emotions in front of others without collapsing or dying, she could have begun to transcend her painful isolation.

In our session together, I encouraged Kitty to have her feelings in front of me. Unfortunately, although it was an obvious relief for her to let down in front of me, she also went into a defense that she must have employed hundreds if not thousands of times in her own mind. Even as she was crying she said to me, "I don't know if this is doing any good." She wanted to have her feelings openly because she knew that if she didn't she would be false. But then she told herself (and me) that expressing her feelings wouldn't help her. This was that same attitude that had led her as a five-year-old child to retreat into a corner rather than cry on a teacher's lap and find the consolation of a sympathetic fellow human. Kitty never came back after that first session. She was not willing to own her emotions in front of others.

The Importance of Feelings

Feelings give us energy, passion and vitality. If we want to throw ourselves fully into living instead of constantly putting up walls, we have to start by taking the simple step of owning and experiencing our feelings or emotions. We are afraid of our emotions because we repress them, not because they are bad in and of themselves.

Unfortunately, we've been saddled with an intellectualist tradition that says that emotions are irrational drives and that only the intellect is capable of guiding us. This tradition originated with the philosopher Descartes, who in the late sixteenth century separated mind from matter, included emotions in the world of matter, and then proclaimed that the mind or intellect is the only part of us capable of freedom and higher values. But Descartes was wrong. Mind divorced from feeling is not a good guide for living.

Emotions, far from being irrational and uncontrollable, are a necessary foundation for meaningful commitment. This truth is beautifully documented by neurologist Antonio Damasio in his literary and scientific masterpiece entitled *Descartes' Error*. Damasio presents a fascinating case study of a gentleman named Elliot, a successful businessman and head of a stable and happy family, who had undergone surgery to remove a brain tumor that was endangering his life. After the brain surgery, tests and in-depth personal interviews demonstrated that Elliot had all the faculties that would normally be considered necessary and sufficient for rational behavior. In fact, he had a superlative IQ, a flawless memory, was coherent and well informed, had good attention, memory, perceptual ability and language. But despite the fact that surgery left Elliot's intellectual functions intact, his life began to disintegrate. This financially successful head of a thriving family began making terrible business decisions that eventually led to bankruptcy, divorce, remarriage, and another divorce.

The problem was that the operation had affected Elliot's ability to feel emotions. He could know, but he couldn't feel. He could think and talk about choices in a rational manner, including discussing the probable merits and drawbacks of different lines of action. He was the perfect intellectual and would have performed brilliantly in a classroom, analyzing, debating, memorizing and attending along with the best of students. But he couldn't decide what mattered to him; he lacked a sense of purpose. He would go first one way and then the other. He couldn't care deeply about anything, and he couldn't develop the consistency of behavior and direction that comes from caring. He was unable to act in a way that demonstrated a sense of responsibility toward himself and others.

From the study of Elliot and research into similar cases, Dr. Damasio concludes that the ability to care deeply is an integral part of the machinery of effective reasoning. He argues that the absence of emotion is damaging to the ability to reason well as human beings in situations that involve personal and social survival and benefit. If we cannot feel deeply, we cannot make responsible decisions, no matter how high our IQ.

Caring deeply enables us to put our hearts on the line, to buck the tide of other people's opinions, the restrictive demands of a job, or the rush of events, and to chart our own direction through the unknown waters of life. Our world is in a mess because too many of us have lost touch with the art of caring. We need to learn how to care, and there is only one way to begin doing that: to practice experiencing our feelings. We do that by feeling how we feel where feeling happens: in our bodies.

Feeling Our Feelings

Learning to feel how we feel involves turning our attention away from our minds, with all their endless thoughts, and toward our bodily sensations. Here are a few examples of what people can learn about themselves when they do this.

Richard

Richard came to work with me because of tensions and anxieties related to a painful divorce as well as the failure of a year-long relationship that had begun after the break-up of his marriage. He said that in both relationships he had done everything he could to make things work. In both cases, however, his wife and then his girlfriend had stretched the limits of his tolerance to the breaking point and then walked out on him.

Richard was a very responsible person, and if anything he bent over backwards for other people. That was his problem: the more he bent over backwards, the more people took advantage of him. As I sat and listened to Richard, I was struck by the tension in his voice and by his lack of affect. There was so much pain in him, but he didn't know how to reach in and let it up. He was reporting about his life, but he wasn't in it. There was a big gap between how Richard actually felt inside and what he was able to express. And if that gap was showing itself in our session, then it had to be part of his everyday life as well. He probably encouraged people to treat him poorly by being so unexpressive and burdened in his demeanor.

I asked Richard to forget for the moment about giving me all the facts of his life, and instead just to tune in to how he felt. His first reaction was to start telling me how he *thought* he felt. I interrupted and asked him again not to *think* about how he felt, but to *feel* how he felt. I suggested that if he directed his attention into his body, how he felt would become clearer to him. Since we have our feelings in our gut, chest, throat and so on, appreciating how he felt in those places might get him in touch with his emotions.

I told Richard to take as long as he wanted, to forget about me, and just get in touch with himself. This helped him let go of being overly responsible toward me, just as he was overly responsible toward everyone else. His job for the moment was to be present to how he felt in his body.

After a while, Richard said he felt very tired and weighed down. I asked him where that weighed-down sensation was in his body, and he said in his chest. I asked him to stay with that sensation and see how it felt. After a few more moments, Richard became uncomfortable and wanted to stop. I redirected him again toward staying with the sensation, saying that however he felt was fine. That was when Richard said, "I feel angry. I feel so angry! How could anyone treat me that way?" He was finally beginning to feel what he felt.

Part of Richard's difficulty in his relationships had been that he always blocked how he felt. But since he blocked his feelings, he didn't participate fully in his relationships, and the women he lived with used him to their advantage, resented him without understanding why, got tired of him and dumped him. Richard had to practice getting in touch with his feelings, and at each session we did this in the same way. When I sensed that he was in his head too much and was just reporting, I would stop him and ask him to tune in to his body, take his time, and tell me how he felt in his body. He was learning that our emotions are in our bodies, not our heads, and if we want to get in touch with them, that's where we have to go.

Maria

When Maria first walked into my office, her demeanor was completely different from Richard. She was a bundle of energy. Maria was rebuilding her life after her divorce a year earlier. She came to me because she was interested in meditation training. She was a petite, slightly overweight and very dynamic fifty-eight-year-old. She talked and talked and talked, filling me in on all the details of her life.

Halfway through the session, I asked Maria to stop. As with Richard, I asked her just to close her eyes for a moment, and then to let herself feel how she felt on the inside, in her body. Maria fidgeted around for a bit, and I brought her gently back to herself a few times, reminding her that she didn't have to tell me anything, and all I wanted her to explore was being with herself on the inside. I suggested that she might tune in to her chest or her belly, or whatever else drew her attention. After a little while Maria started crying. Underneath all that chatter, she felt lonely and afraid. Like Richard, Maria needed to stop defending against her feelings so much. She was dancing around like crazy, being entertaining and dynamic in order not to feel. She needed to allow herself to be more authentic instead of putting so much energy into avoidance.

How Easily We Do or Don't Feel

Women supposedly find it easy to talk about their feelings. They get together for coffee or lunch or call each other on the phone, all in order to talk about their feelings. But most of the time, they are reporting on the feelings that they have had—about a lover or spouse, children, an experience at work—and that's very different from being with your feelings as you feel them in the moment.

It's easy to talk about feelings we have had, but not so easy to be vulnerable enough to be in our feelings, sharing them as we are having them. Talking about our feelings is reporting on life, but being in our feelings is living life. In order to feel our feelings, we have to stop spinning on our endless merry-go-round of activities, including the gabbing about feelings that can be a substitute for feeling them. We have to pause and wait, and take the time to let the feeling emerge, whether it is from our chest, our throat, our belly or some other part of ourselves. We have to stop performing and just be.

Because we keep on moving, we're not used to feeling our feelings completely. The first reaction to letting ourselves feel can be to contact profound sadness, fear, anger, or deep loneliness and vulnerability. Most of us are afraid of feeling how vulnerable we really are. We need to know that if we own our buried feelings of anger, fear, grief or shame, these feelings give way to deeper peace and a sense of well being. We're meant to experience our feelings so we can let them go. We're meant to experience them so that we learn that there is nothing inside of us that we have to fear. We're also meant to experience them so that we can share them genuinely with others instead of hiding from the people we care for.

The place where we all have most trouble owning our feelings is in front of other people. It's one thing to get in touch with how we feel in the privacy of our own room, on a walk by ourselves or lying in bed at night. But feeling how we feel in front of others is different.

A friend of mine who was quite distraught came over to talk to me one evening. At first she just burst into tears and we held hands for a few moments. But then she started giving me her interpretation of what was going on in her life, and as soon as she did that, her face lost its softness. She was explaining instead of experiencing. I told her she didn't have to explain anything and she didn't have to talk. After a while, she settled down into being real. When she needed to talk because of what she was feeling, she talked. Otherwise, she stopped. We accepted the silences that came up between us instead of filling them up with words.

In my group sessions, I sometimes engage students in an exercise that can be quite uncomfortable but that also demonstrates very effectively how hard it is for most of us simply to be ourselves in the presence of others. I have people pair off and sit with each other, looking into each other's eyes without talking for several minutes. Most people find this extremely difficult, even with people they know quite well. If we don't talk while we're looking at someone else, we may become aware of feeling fidgety, embarrassed or tense. Of course, the reason for the exercise is not to create tension, but to become aware of the fact that we become tense as soon as we are refused permission to speak, and to explore why we have that tension, what it is about, and how it may motivate our behavior every day without our conscious awareness.

That tension comes from performance anxiety, from feeling we have to do something in front of the other person: entertain them, be a good listener, take care of them, be taken care of, etc. The feeling of tension becomes conscious when we are silent in the face of another person because we refuse ourselves permission to entertain, take care of, etc. We refuse ourselves permission to perform. But that tension is always there: it is the reason we feel compelled to perform. Something deep inside tells us that if we don't perform, we are no good.

The problem with having to perform is that we're constantly driven by a subtle anxiety in the presence of other people. When we look at each other without talking, we become aware of the anxiety that triggers us into talking. If we inhibit ourselves from going into our compulsive talk reaction, eventually the anxiety dissipates. That's where real feeling and real communication begin to be possible.

Here's another suggestion I make to clients to help them practice being more authentic with others, being with their feelings instead of reacting to performance anxiety. I tell them, when they walk into a room with other people or come home to their family at night, to do exactly what they would do if they could let go of all sense of obligation and there were no expectations of them. I tell them to avoid doing what they think is expected. It is surprising what a challenge this can be, even when the actions involved are very simple.

One of my clients automatically goes to greet her husband watching television in the living room if she comes home late after a meeting. The greeting is usually perfunctory: she is doing it because she thinks it is the right thing to do. As for him, though he expects her greeting, he is involved in his program and doesn't want to talk. So no real contact is made. What interested my client was the fact that when she thought of *not* going in to greet her husband, she felt waves of fear! If she failed to make this simple gesture, her conscience told her she was a terrible person and she panicked over whether her husband would feel angry and rejected. Fear, masked in the language of duty, was the driving force in this woman's behavior. When we let this kind of motivation drive us, contact becomes perfunctory at best and real communication dies.

But isn't it real communication that makes for good relationships? This is not to say that we shouldn't be nice or polite, but rather that if we focus too much on being nice or polite we may lose the ability to be genuine. It's only when we're genuine that intimacy has a chance of developing. After this woman explored her motivations, she began to make a point of doing what she was sure she wanted to do, instead of what she thought she was supposed to do and was afraid of not doing. She became a lot more interesting, and while she wasn't always so available for her husband, he appreciated her a lot more!

Letting Discomfort Be Our Teacher

Emotions are visceral sensations, and we often feel uncomfortable when these come to the surface. Compulsive behavior involves avoiding the discomfort of an emotion struggling to become conscious. We eat, drink, clean house obsessively, talk compulsively or turn on the television, all to avoid the discomfort that accompanies feelings emerging. But if we want to become our own persons instead of conforming to someone else's concept of how we should be, and if we want to own our own truths, then it's important to learn how not to avoid that discomfort. We have to stay with our physical feelings of discomfort so that we can come to grips with what is going on inside. So long as we don't try to get away from our discomfort, we eventually gain insight and freedom.

I remember the first time I practiced staying with a feeling of physical tension in my body until it disclosed what it was there to tell me. One evening, I decided to break off a relationship with a close friend. She had several times broken appointments, I was hurt and angry, and I felt that she was unreliable. The morning after making the decision to stop seeing her, I woke up with a sensation of tension in my chest. Earlier in my life, I had dealt with tension like this by becoming hyperactive. I would go into motion and achieve, achieve, achieve, all from a place of restlessness. This time, I decided to approach how I felt differently. I didn't talk to anyone about my discomfort and I didn't try to analyze it. But I did stay present to the feeling.

All day, as I went through the usual round of meetings, appointments and phone calls, I would tune in and acknowledge the heavy tension in my chest. I didn't worry about it and I didn't try to push it away. I treated it as a friend or as something that was there for a reason. The sensation persisted.

At five o'clock that evening, I was driving down a street on the way to pick up groceries and I came to a stop sign at an intersection. As I paused, I felt a rush of emotion welling up in my chest and tears came to my eyes. Simultaneously, my attention was drawn to the friend I had decided to stop seeing, and I realized instantly that I cared for her too much to say good-bye. It didn't matter what she had done. As the tears flooded down my cheeks, the pressure in my chest dissolved. I had learned what it was there to tell me: that I had made a decision about my friend that didn't match my heart's needs. My anger at my friend was less important than my love for her.

We often believe that we have to think about how we feel. But we don't. We just have to stay with how we feel until it becomes clear. I came to understand how I felt about my friendship neither by analyzing it nor by thinking about it. I didn't even know that I had made a decision that didn't match my needs. All I knew was that my chest felt uncomfortable. It was by assuming that the feeling was there for a reason and maintaining a neutral presence to it that I gave my deeper emotions a chance to surface. When they did, I knew I had discovered the right direction for myself because my body felt so much better.

A client came to see me after spending a weekend at her mother's house. Even though this woman experienced her mother as belittling and demanding, she maintained a close relationship with her. She had felt a lot of tension with her mother that weekend, and we began to explore what had happened.

My client remembered arriving at the door of her mother's house and thinking, as her mother opened the door, that she should kiss her mother. But as soon as she had that thought, she felt her abdomen tightening up. Her body was saying to her mother, "I hate you," and, "I don't want to kiss you," because she had gone through so many years of feeling put down. At the same time, her mind was telling her, "You are a bad girl if you don't kiss your mother."

My client's conscious mind, a faithful representative of filial duty, was in conflict with her unconscious needs, which reflected the pain of years of emotional abuse. Her body knew how she felt unconsciously and was telling her that she was angry and hurt. Her mind, however, was keeping her in the victim stance by telling her she was mean-spirited if she didn't act warmly. This woman needed to be more authentic by tuning in to her body and admitting to herself how she felt. It wasn't appropriate to be unkind to her mother. But it also wasn't appropriate to accept her mother's behavior, pretend that nothing was bothering her, and be unkind to herself. When she learned to take her body's discomfort as a sign that she had to be more true to herself instead of belittling herself, she worked on sharing some of her perceptions with her mother in a way that her mother could hear. Over time, they developed a more equal relationship.

If we can stay with our emotional bodies and treat their discomforts as a form of visceral intelligence that is trying to communicate with us, we will become a lot more honest with ourselves and with other people. The cost of not slowing down enough to listen to our discomfort and respect it as a friend is high. The more we avoid our discomfort—by any kind of obsessive action, from compulsive performing to substance abuse—the more we avoid our deeper needs. The more we avoid our deeper needs, the less effectively we make decisions about our lives and the more dysfunctional our relationships become. The ultimate cost of suppressed discomfort is chronic illness. That illness is the price we pay for repressing our life force: our feelings.

Expressing Our Emotions Full Throttle

One piece of my own physical healing from chronic illness came from letting up deeply buried feelings that I had, feelings of pain and rage. I had successfully avoided these feelings for years by channeling my energies and tensions into becoming an academic star. Unconsciously I made the decision at an early age to become the daughter I thought my father wanted me to be, not the person I needed to be. Without the slightest understanding of my deeper motivations, I began at the age of ten to drive myself harder and harder in my academic work, in an unconscious quest to gain the love from my father that I felt I lost when my parents had divorced.

I was ten when my father remarried and began to build a new life with a second wife and family, leaving the children of his first marriage with deep feelings of abandonment. He never spoke to me about this decision or shared his personal grief. He locked his conflicts up inside himself, defending himself against his own regrets by becoming ever more critical of the children he had left behind. As for me, I single-mindedly pursued and achieved intellectual stardom. My intellectual life was my one guaranteed point of connection with my father. He had found success in life through his intellectually brilliant contributions as a world-renowned mathematician. Perhaps if I could succeed in my intellectual line of endeavor, he would see in me a daughter worthy of love.

It was also only through intellectual pursuits that I could find a way to communicate with my father. Communication on other levels was taboo. Since he could not divulge his own pain around leaving his first wife and children, I could not share or even admit to mine. And so when my birthday would come around each year, my father forgot it, but I said it didn't matter. Unfortunately, my father was not even available to celebrate with me my intellectual achievements. When I graduated first in my class at college, my father failed to attend the graduation, but I told myself it didn't matter. When I received a fellowship to study at Cambridge University in England, he hardly congratulated me. But I kept on saying to myself that he loved me. I kept on telling myself I loved him. And I kept on struggling to achieve in an unconscious attempt to ensure that my illusion wouldn't break down.

I lived with my inner contradictions about my father until the week after he died. By that time, I had been through the worst of my own illness, had left my marriage and was working full-time. Even though I still had bouts of weakness and pain from my long illness, I seemed to be well on my way to mending.

A few days after my father's death, I attended the funeral service in New York City, spent the afternoon and evening with his second family and then came home. The only feeling I was conscious of at that time, as during the last weeks of my father's life, was deep grief. But the day after the funeral, I had a recurrence of physical symptoms from my illness, including burning sensations throughout my body and crippling back pain. I was in bed for a week.

I couldn't understand what had happened. Where did this come from? It wasn't until the end of that week, during a conversation with a young friend of the family visiting from Europe, that I began to have insight. Perhaps it was because she was so young and so far removed from my life that I found myself expressing to her feelings that I had never even expressed to myself. Perhaps it was that now that my father was gone, I could let my inner charade collapse. And so the feelings came out: my anger that my father had never been there for me; my fear of his critical gaze; my pain at how he could never tell me he loved me; my pain that I

could never ask him to come out of his shell. All of this poured out
and poured out in a conversation with a woman so young that she
hardly understood what I was saying, even though she did her
best to be attentive. The next day I felt markedly better and I
began to learn a hard lesson: *when your body collapses, assume
that there are emotions there that need to be acknowledged.*

Emotions are powerful energy. The more we repress them, the
more explosive that energy becomes. I needed to do a lot more
than just admit my feelings in a conversation. I needed to let out
years of pent-up rage and grief. Over the months that followed, I
had intense imaginary dialogues with my father. I told him in no
uncertain terms how I felt about his behavior, and I was definitely not ladylike about it. I used every curse word I could think of!
When I felt weak or when symptoms reoccurred, I would pace up
and down the road outside my house, stomping my feet and hiss-
ing at him: how dare he treat me that way! I announced to him
sometimes in intense whispers and sometimes in shouts that I
was not going to be his good little girl anymore. I hit the rage and
grief out of me by beating pillows into submission. I lay on the
floor pounding my arms and legs against the floor like a three-
year-old having a tantrum until I could pound no more. I cried and
begged and wept. I did not act rational. But I did let it out. I let
out all the energy of that withheld rage and pain, so that I could
be done with it and move on in my life.

When I was finally done, I was surprised at a new turn of
events: I could come back and tell my father I loved him. Now I
knew I really meant it. I was no longer using a claim of love to
deny the pain I felt inside. By this time, I also realized that my
father loved me, both while living and in spirit. He simply had
been in too much inner pain to transcend his own fears. Today, my
inner bond with my father's spirit is a positive force in my life.

I make it a practice to give myself permission to discharge the
energy of pent-up emotions whenever it builds up and needs
release. I encourage my clients to do the same. This energy can
build up because of painful, long-buried experiences. But it can
also build up through the stress of dealing with daily life and
because of the sometimes very dishonest and manipulative practices of people living in a world that knows far too little straightforward, decent honesty. The hardest part of finding release is

first, to let yourself admit how strongly you feel and then, to let yourself go *full throttle*. It's hard because we are so unused to doing this. We are all so polite! But we're not meant to be polite. We're meant to be *alive*. And we have too few spaces for finding permission to be alive.

Traditional cultures recognized the importance of giving space to emotional release by incorporating rituals into daily living. Many of those rituals centered on healing and invoked special forces, both demonic and divine, in the dynamics of the healing process. Other rituals centered around rites of passage: into adulthood, marriage, birthing or dying. Rituals set apart a time and place to celebrate our right to profound, cathartic emotion, emotion that is hard to express in the dynamics of daily living. Feeling those emotions allows us to let go and move on.

Healing rituals are returning into the fringes of our society, instinctively called into being by people seeking a deeper contact with the life force. As a professional healer I partake in such rituals. For example, I occasionally meet for as much as a week at a time with other healers, all of whom are seeking to find greater contact with their emotional source. Doing this always requires courage, always involves embracing powerful life forces, and always means entering into the dark places inside ourselves.

I remember working together with a group of other healers, assisting one of them who was a former marine. He was lying on a bodywork table with a number of us enclosing him in a circle. With our support, and through the energy of our hands, he began to access the deep rage he felt over the treatment he had both received and given while he had been in the military. He was angry enough to kill and shamed enough to die.

As this marine expressed his feelings, it took the strength of five people to hold him down enough so that he could scream and flail and twist his agony out of his body. I had never in my life seen such volcanic power or such an outright expression of violent rage. He needed to let it out in order to be at peace with himself. And with our support he let it out harmlessly. His eyes were gentler when it was over, and he was more in his heart. As for the rest of us, we were downright joyful. It is incredibly liberating to witness someone else being authentic, especially about difficult emotions and especially if it is not hurtful. We realize then that anger is like a cloudburst in the sky. There is neither right nor wrong in a cloudburst. It just is. Can we allow our own anger just to be, as well?

When we feel conflict, rage, pain or grief in our lives, we need to let it out. We need to beat pillows, scream in our car, pound the floor, do what we need to do to feel release. The bigger the range of emotions we can express, the healthier we are. The more we let these emotions move through us, the less we need to resort to this cathartic form of expression as time goes by. Our bodies will have less blockage. The blockage is our own fear of ourselves. When we learn not to fear our life force, it eventually becomes a beautiful, exotic friend instead of a fearful foe.

When we release feelings, we stop acting them out on other people. We acknowledge how we feel and give our life force its full play *without hurting others*. If we feel deeply frustrated with how other people are treating us or with what we feel to be an injustice in our lives, and if we release the tension of those feelings privately, we can then cope with the situation we are dealing with more realistically and less reactively. Instead of blowing up or withdrawing from the people who hurt us, we find it easier to tell them matter of factly where we stand, or even to walk away from the situation without a residue of rancor or resentment.

If I am angry at someone and the anger boils inside, I know that I will make a mess of communicating with that person if I do not first take care of releasing the anger on my own. But if I release the tension of the anger first, I can come back and tell him or her what bothered me without bringing in that edge of resentment or rage that makes for dysfunctional communication.

Living well is about keeping the lines of communication open. This can only happen when we neither stuff our emotions nor make other people responsible for them. Instead, we learn to have full access to our feelings in the appropriate way and at the appropriate time, without splattering them on others. We also learn to share with others the content of our feelings in such a way that they can hear us rather than becoming defensive.

The more we enjoy giving ourselves the freedom to feel our emotions full force in our own space or in the healing company of witnesses, the more easily we are able to communicate with people how we really feel, without that edge that makes everything fall apart. Then they understand that they can do the same with us, and together we begin to find more genuine sharing.

Summary

Learning to feel our emotional bodies helps us become physically and emotionally healthy and authentic. We learn to feel our emotional bodies quite easily and naturally by getting in touch with and listening to the feelings of our bodies without judgment. While we have already looked at how to get in touch with the body and its needs through exploring breath awareness in Chapter 6, and bodily sensation in Chapter 7, this chapter has focused specifically on getting in touch with and expressing the bodily feelings called emotions. We have looked at how to feel our feelings, at why we should not avoid the discomfort of our feelings, and at how we can learn to express our feelings full throttle.

Feeling our feelings is simple. After all, they are ours! But it's also hard, because when we focus too much on how we should be, and on what we think our emotions should be, we get out of touch with them. The mind comes in and wants to decide, and the mind is a control-freak. It tries to judge and direct how we feel. If we are going to be healthy, we have to want to feel our feelings no matter what they are, and we have to avoid judging them. The Suggestions for Practice that follow offer tools for learning to feel how you feel more clearly.

Suggestions for Practice

1. Feel Your Feelings.

These practices do exactly what they say: they teach you how to feel your feelings. Since feelings are bodily sensations, you learn how to feel your feelings by attending to your body. You also learn how to stop avoiding feeling your feelings, whether by thinking too much or talking too much.

• Feel your feelings in your body.

In order to be more in touch with your emotional life, make a regular practice of settling down quietly somewhere and bringing your awareness into the feeling of your body. What does it feel like in your gut? When you focus on your gut, stay with the sensation long enough to really absorb it, and to let it grow or change. Do the same with your pelvis, your chest, your throat, and any other part of your body that draws your attention.

Avoid thinking about your feelings. Thinking about your feelings is different from feeling them. When you think about how you feel, you stop feeling and start judging. You leave your feelings behind and start getting into control. Notice if you are thinking instead of feeling. What are you thinking? See if you can come back to just feeling, simply absorbing your visceral sensations.

Don't run away from discomfort. When you tune in to your body, if it feels uncomfortable, let yourself stay with the feeling instead of running from it. Don't try to change it. Instead, accept it and view it as a way your body has of trying to tell you something important that you are not yet aware of. Allow the feeling to be there and honor it. If you do this, you may be surprised to feel grief or anger coming up. If the discomfort simply persists, allow it to do this for as long as it wishes. Eventually, it will reveal its meaning.

Notice how you become more conscious of your real feelings when you just allow yourself to sit with your body sensations without judgment. Notice how your body sensations change and grow. Are you discovering unexpected feelings of sadness, grief, anger, or even joy? Do you notice that it takes time to feel your feelings, and that sitting quietly with yourself helps you to do so?

• **Stop talking and start feeling.**

Play a game with a friend. That friend will talk to you for three minutes, and you will just listen. Let the subject be anything from what your friend ate for breakfast to his or her latest romance. The topic isn't important. What is important is to become aware of how easy or hard it is for you simply to be present without talking. Your friend's goal is to become aware of what it feels like to talk without having the listener interrupt. Then change roles. Have your friend listen to you for three minutes while you talk.

Notice your reactions to having to play the role of the listener without talking. Are you learning something about what motivates you to talk? Do you find yourself wanting to interrupt to make a point, or to explain something to the other person? Does it make you nervous not to be able to talk? Do you think you may sometimes resort to talking when you are anxious, to avoid empty spaces in conversation, to prove that you're listening to someone, to take care of them, or to show that you have something to say?

How does refraining from talking affect your listening skills? Do you notice that you can really hear what the other person is saying when you don't have to think about what you should say back? Do you become a better listener? Do you become more relaxed because there is no pressure on you to say something, to be brilliant, or to take care of the other person? What about when you change roles, and you become the talker while your partner listens? Does it make you nervous to have the other person listen without responding? Or do you find that after a while, you feel like you have truly been heard? Most people find this exercise very difficult at first, and at the same time transformative and healing. What have you learned that you can include in your daily practice?

2. Release Your Feelings Full Throttle

This practice is about honoring your right to feel your feelings, no matter what they are, and no matter what you or anyone else might think about them. Life is full of frustration and disappointment, yet we suppress our anger and pain because we think they are unacceptable. Suppressed feelings, however, only lead to bottled-up rancor and rage, and often to illness. Feelings are feelings, and they have to be released in appropriate ways.

• Give yourself permission to express your feelings fully.

If you go through an experience that leaves you hurt or angry, or harboring other difficult feelings, release those feelings: beat pillows, stomp up and down, or lie on the floor and have a tantrum.

Avoid judging your feelings. When you release your feelings fully in private, by yelling, stomping, beating pillows or whatever works for you, you'll be healthier and more alive. You'll also recognize the difference between appropriate and inappropriate release. Appropriate release involves taking responsibility for letting your feelings out. Inappropriate release means venting your feelings on someone else.

Notice how releasing your feelings changes you. Are you more able to acknowledge how you really feel? Does this help you become calmer inside? Do you notice that when you release your feelings by yourself, instead of venting them on someone else, you are better able to express how you feel to others in a way that they can hear?

• **Give others permission to express their feelings fully.**

When someone you know is going through a hard time, consider suggesting to that person to try some of the expressive work that you are exploring for yourself.

Notice if you are able to give permission to someone else to express his or her pain or anger or sadness, without feeling either that this is an imposition on you or that you have to take care of that person. Can you go into neutral, recognize that someone else needs to release, and that it's not your job either to judge or to fix that person? How does this affect the way you deal with people?

Suggested Reading

Eugene Gendlin, *Focusing* (New York: Bantam, 1981). Written by a psychotherapist, this book describes how to contact feelings by focusing inside your body.

Gay and Kathlyn Hendricks, *At the Speed of Life* (New York: Bantam, 1993). An excellent exploration of personal change through body-centered therapy.

Arnold Mindell, *Working with the Dreaming Body* (London: Routledge and Kegan Paul, 1985). An eminent Jungian psychologist explores how the body reveals a person's life story and charts directions for change.

chapter 9

Grieving Our Emotional Bodies

When Jason came to see me, he was working as a computer systems manager at a big corporation. At the age of forty-four, Jason was aware that even though he was quite successful, he was hampered by fear in his relationships with other people. We worked with breathing and body awareness to help him go into a deeper state of relaxation. Then I invited him to go back in his imagination to one of his early memories of feeling fear.

I gently guided Jason back in time, and he found himself standing in the yard of his family's suburban home at seven years of age. He was looking at his house with a desperate desire to escape. When I asked that little boy why he needed to flee so badly, he said his parents were constantly criticizing him. He could feel a cold sweat on his hands and a clenching in his gut, feelings that he now recalled were all too common in his childhood. Jason was overwhelmed at the strength of this simple yet painful experience. He hadn't realized how alienated he had felt as a child. As he said, "It's hard to admit what really happened to me." Yet acknowledging the pain he had gone through as a child somehow helped him to be less fearful and less critical of himself. That didn't happen by *remembering* his childhood experiences. It happened as a result of *reliving* them.

Reliving Our Emotional Past

Just as inner growth requires that we be willing to experience honestly whatever our emotions are today, it also requires us to experience honestly what our emotions were in the past so that we can clear our personal history. It's through reliving and letting go of unacknowledged feelings from the past that we get beyond chronic fear, anger and pain.

One of my clients who was a clinical psychologist had a tendency toward low back pain. She was also aware that she was dissociated from her pelvic area. Diane admitted she didn't want to feel her pelvis because it felt like there was anger there. It was difficult for her to reconcile her desire to be a good person and her reputation for kindness with this angry aspect of herself. She felt as if part of her were living a lie.

Because Diane wanted to move on in her life, we worked together on contacting the feeling in her pelvis. Diane realized that she was holding on to childhood rage against her father. Her father had regularly beaten Diane's sister when they were children. Diane went back in time to what it felt like to hear the blows and listen to her older sister crying while she hid as a small child in her room. She had avoided her father's beatings by being docile and quiet. Night after night she had felt the helpless rage of a trapped creature. In her sessions with me, Diane took permission to express her rage, to act it out and let it go. Once she owned the appropriateness of her anger, she no longer lived split in two: good on the outside and angry on the inside.

In growing up, we protect ourselves from our pain by denying its reality. Emotional wholeness, however, depends on recognizing the *illusions* we have created around our lives. Jason denied his pain by saying, "This didn't really happen to me." He pretended his parents weren't as critical as he knew they really were. Diane denied her pain by saying, "I don't really feel this way." She suppressed her anger as a child because she couldn't do anything about it. When we recognize our own illusions, it's appropriate to express our real feelings and then to mourn our lives. We stop pretending that we had some kind of special protection and that bad things didn't really happen to us. We feel the grief of being ordinary human beings suffering in the way human beings suffer. Then we can leave our pain behind.

If we can't appreciate the truth of what we felt as children, we can't own what we feel now. That makes it impossible to act from a place of strength and integrity. We become too accustomed to lying to ourselves. A woman named Kristin provides a good example of this dilemma. She was constantly getting herself tangled up in asymmetrical relationships in which she did three quarters of the work of maintaining her relationships instead of sharing fifty-fifty. Kristin was a caretaker. She resented this, but then criticized herself for her own resentment and kept on doing too much for the people close to her. Why did she keep on defeating herself?

When we explored Kristin's childhood, she recalled having her diapers changed by her mother. She could remember her mother carelessly and even brutally poking and picking at her. She was a tiny, soft and infinitely frail baby. The one person she depended on most was rough, insensitive and even malicious with her. Like any small creature, she was both terrified and enraged at this. Yet even as she was recalling the experience, Kristin found an excuse for her mother's behavior. She told me her mother had done the best she could, so how could she blame her? If her mother was not loving and soft, that was because she didn't know how to be.

There was truth in Kristin's perception. But it was also true that even as an infant, she had taken responsibility for her mother's weaknesses. Because she was dependent and couldn't object to her mother's behavior, she had rationalized it. Because she rationalized it, she accepted her mother's uncaring behavior as appropriate, and couldn't accept her own legitimate infant rage. She told herself that since her mother loved her, then she was in the wrong for feeling upset! But who was taking care of whom here? Was Kristin's mother taking care of her, or was Kristin really taking care of her mother? Just as she had taken care of her mother even as an infant, Kristin as an adult continued to take care of all the other people who demanded too much of her and gave too little.

Once Kristin could let the infant she had been own her anger, she got things in better perspective. It *is* appropriate for an infant to receive real love, and it *is* appropriate to feel pain and anger when this is not the case. As Kristin recognized this, she became better at dealing with her resentment and anger as an adult. She could say straightforwardly to people that she didn't want to have relationships that gave her too little.

The illusion that Kristin lived with as a child was that her mother really loved her. This illusion was soothing on one level because it's nice to think things are wonderful. But it was a form of denial and it forbade Kristin from feeling the pain that she had had as an unloved child. When she owned that pain, she became capable of acting more genuinely on her feelings.

Kristin also went through a transformation that shattered a second illusion. While the first illusion had involved an overblown perception of her mother, the second illusion involved an overblown perception of herself. Kristin began to see that her tendency to be overly responsible with her friends gave her permission to be irritated at them all the time. In her own way, she poked and pinched at her friends because she felt they were failing her. And who wants a friend like that? She tended to feel that she was being abandoned by her friends, but now Kristin began to see that she was partly responsible for driving them away when she did too much for them and then held it against them. In order to shift this pattern, she had to change her relationships in two ways. First, she had to give herself permission not to do so much for others that she became resentful. Second, she had to give up her own cherished habit of being angry and unconsciously demanding.

The first step in healing our emotional past is to experience the truth of how much we have suffered, including at other people's hands. The second step is to realize the suffering we have unwittingly caused others. We don't take the second step fully until we have taken the first step, because it is feeling our own pain that allows us to empathize with the pain others feel. It is also feeling our own fears that allows us to see how we hurt other people through protecting our own vulnerability. When Kristin took the second step toward emotional healing, she saw how the needs she had toward others sometimes made her unkind. She let go of some illusions about herself.

I remember undoing some of my own illusions in working through my relationship with my father. As I have already mentioned, when my parents divorced and my father remarried, I hid from my feelings of betrayal by creating a fiction of love between my father and myself. After my father died, and I came to grips with how deep my pain was, I decided to speak to my stepmother and half-sisters about this. I needed to share how much I still felt like a second-class citizen in my father's second family.

It was difficult for me to broach this subject. Yet when I spoke with my stepmother and sisters, I was surprised at how quickly they appreciated my experience. They were very receptive to talking with me about my feelings. That night, we stayed up late sharing our different perspectives on the family history. I felt welcomed into my second family in a way I never had before. And something else happened that I hadn't expected. When I saw how easy it was to share feelings I had hidden away for years, I realized that I was partly responsible for all my loneliness.

I had spent a long time locking myself away, creating a wall between myself and my second family. I had also contributed to making communication with my father difficult and had overridden and rejected some of my father's attempts to reach me. Just as I had been rejected, I had also been rejecting. It was true that my father had failed me in many ways, but it was also true that I had withdrawn from my father. I began to lose my own overblown perception of what a great person I was, and to care more genuinely about other people.

Feeling the pain of our lives leads us not into celebrating our victimhood but rather out of needing to be victims. If we fully experience what we have been through, we let go of holding on to our pain. When we have the courage to feel the truth of our childhood pain and to mourn it, we also mature into mourning the pain we have unwittingly caused other people. This step is a natural result of learning to love ourselves. Loving ourselves enables us to love others. That happens spontaneously out of seeing that we're all in the same soup. We all suffer. We all unknowingly cause suffering. At bottom, everyone really is the same.

When we hold on to our pain and fear, that allows us to separate ourselves from other people and somehow make ourselves special. Separateness is the fundamental evil, and there is only one result of holding on to our sense of separateness: we cause other people pain, in exactly the same way that pain is inflicted on us.

Energy: The Common Link between Physiology and Emotions

Jason couldn't release himself from fear, and Diane and Kristin couldn't release themselves from anger, until they acknowledged the childhood experiences that imprinted that fear and anger in their bodies. For all three, this acknowledgement also made them healthier. Jason's stomach settled down; Diane's back bothered her less frequently; and Kristin moved more rapidly toward letting go of her fibromyalgia. They got healthier because they acknowledged their emotional traumas. Unacknowledged emotional trauma causes energetic contractions in the body. The feelings generated during the traumas persist, and the contractions lead to blockages that eventually create disease.

Just as emotional trauma creates energy blockages that produce physical imbalances, physical trauma also disturbs the energy field of the body. Physical trauma can cause energetic imbalances that remain for years and that have painful emotional consequences. The common reality underlying both our physical and our emotional realities is *energy*. Deep emotional change, being energetic, also generates physical changes. Deep physical change, being energetic, creates emotional change.

Trauma freezes our body's energy patterns in time. What should be fluid is immobilized. It's as though we can't move forward. We are stuck in a repetition compulsion until the trauma is released. I had the opportunity to witness this freezing very vividly when a woman of about forty came into my office eight years after an accident in which she was hit by a truck and thrown to the ground while crossing a busy street in New York City. The accident had ended her career as a dancer. Her body was twisted out of shape. She had difficulty with her vision, with balance and movement, and she suffered constant headaches. She couldn't think straight and was emotionally distraught. I asked her to describe the accident as she remembered it, and to show me how she remembered striking the pavement after being hit by the truck. When she lay down on the floor and showed me how she had landed when she took her brutal fall, I realized that her entire body was still stuck in the exact pattern of her fall. The way she stood and moved carried the imprint of that fall. The shock had been so intense that it locked her into its pattern. She had not been able to dissipate the intense experience of shock by releasing it and having it pass through her body. If she had had proper support at the time of the accident, she might have been able to let go of the emotional and physical trauma. Instead she lived in a time warp.

It is essential to release emotional or physical trauma as soon as possible after it happens. About a year after meeting the woman who had been struck by a truck, I was in a bad car accident in which a bus tore the door off my car on the driver's side and crushed the entire left front side of the automobile. By a miracle my body did not receive a direct blow. Immediately after the collision, however, I was temporarily unable to speak or move.

The first policeman to come to my assistance took one look at my face and said, "Don't cry!" Luckily, I was in no condition to pay attention to his advice. A friend took me to her home which was close by, and I lay down on a bed and cried and trembled for well over an hour, feeling the force of the blow ebbing out of my body. When my body finally felt quiet I got up, and by the afternoon I was back at business as usual, with no signs of trauma. As it turned out, spending that hour letting myself feel the full force of my reaction to the accident saved me from both whiplash and residual fear.

Emotions are a form of energy, and the body, too, is an energy system. The distinction our culture makes between the emotions and the physical body is one hundred percent fictional. People will give up that fiction when they learn to experience themselves as energy systems. I came to appreciate the reality of energy, and of the unity of emotional and physical life, through experiences that took me into releasing energy blocks that had frozen my body at deep levels. It all started when I began exploring Craniosacral Therapy.

Craniosacral Therapy, Past Trauma and Energy Release

Craniosacral Therapy has its origins early in the twentieth century in the explorations of an osteopath named William Sutherland. Since 1970, the scope and methodology of craniosacral work have been greatly elaborated through the work of osteopath Dr. John Upledger D.O., who is internationally recognized as the world's preeminent authority on that form of healing. Today, Craniosacral Therapy is one of the fastest growing alternative therapies in the United States. It incorporates many different facets of bodywork, all of which involve subtle, non-invasive touch. Sometimes it has a purely physical impact, releasing muscular constrictions and realigning bones. At other times, it induces a deeply altered state. It can also act as a vehicle for releasing suppressed memories.

When I first began exploring craniosacral work, I had no idea that a practitioner's touch could trigger a client into reliving buried memories, bringing them to consciousness so vividly that you often feel as though you are right back in the original experience. One day, I had gone to a physical therapist who was also a practitioner of Craniosacral Therapy, to deal with some muscular tension I was experiencing. I was lying on a bodywork table while she did some gentle hands-on work. Suddenly I was in my mother's womb. I did not ask or plan to go there. It just happened. Like most genuine experiences, this one wasn't premeditated. I also did not wonder whether or not it was true that I was in my mother's womb. The experience was so vivid that I had no question as to whether it was happening. This was real!

There I was in my mother's uterus, and I desperately needed space. My twin sister was in there with me, and I was the smaller and weaker one. Through no fault of my sister's, it was a real struggle for me to get my survival needs met. I wanted to kick and scream and get more space.

Lying on the bodywork table, I gave myself permission to do exactly what I had not been able to do in real life. I kicked and I kicked and I kicked. I screamed and I screamed. And I felt enormous relief. I was speeding along my own healing by reconstructing my early traumatic experience with a more favorable outcome. All my life I had felt crowded in by people, and now I knew one reason why! At the very beginning of my life, I had had no space. Later I also realized that my prolonged illness in my thirties was connected to a deep sense of internal cramping that had begun prior to birth. Subconsciously, cramping was the only way I knew to be in my body, and when I became ill, my body went into a deep cramp that lasted three years.

Two weeks after this first experience, I relived my own birth in another Craniosacral Therapy session. My twin sister and I were born five weeks premature. Our nervous systems were raw and unformed, and throughout my life this created in me a tendency toward excessive sensitivity. For me, the birth was also excruciatingly painful. My sister was the first of the two twins to be delivered, and she came out headfirst. My birth was a delayed breech birth. As I went through the birth canal, my body twisted and turned in agony. Something wasn't right. I was trying and trying to straighten myself out, to find space and to move through the uterus. My entire spine felt bent out of shape, and I was struggling to straighten the spine, to let the energy flow through my central canal.

From this experience, I realized why I had been born with scoliosis. The birthing left an imprint of twisting, or scoliosis, in my body because my body torqued severely in the process of being pulled out of the womb. I was so premature that my neuromuscular system could not recover from this shock. That torque stayed with my body until I completed my own healing.

The night after this rebirthing experience, I felt a headache coming on. I could tell that it was connected to tension in the muscles on the left side of my head. I decided to let my body go in the direction of least resistance and let my head turn toward the left, following the tension. Before I knew it, I wasn't initiating the movement anymore. Instead, some force was moving through me. I ended up twisted to the left, lying on my bed in a pattern that looked like an extreme version of my scoliosis, and sobbing.

When the sobbing abated, my body took over again with its pattern of spontaneous movement. This time my head twisted to the right as I wept. A flood of pain and grief traveled through my head, chest and right arm, and then the whole right side of my body felt intensely alive and full. I fell asleep, exhausted and relieved.

The next morning when I sat down to meditate, my head wanted to twist to the right, so I let myself go with the movement. Soon I was propelled up onto my feet. It felt like I was being moved by an energy circuit in my spine. Without thinking about it, I began spontaneously assuming some Hatha Yoga positions. I realized later that these ancient practices were simply ways of letting energy move from the core of the body outwards.

For about an hour, my body followed the spontaneous pattern of movement, and I could feel my spine clear, fluid and sinuous, exactly like the *kundalini* snake described in Yoga traditions. Energy ran freely all the way up my spine for the first time in my life. By allowing myself to stay with the feeling of the energy and to put aside any conscious attempt at control, I was correcting the damage my body had experienced years before. When I stopped, it felt like the core of my body was a clear channel, while my outer structure, which had for years held together a twisted spine, was confused and out of place. Instead of my inner core adjusting to the demands of my outer armature, now my outer body had to adapt to my inner core.

For months after that, I felt currents of energy moving through my spine. My body would twist and turn, sometimes even going into contortions. My early trauma had led me to hold on so tight that when I finally let go, the energy flooded through my entire system. My job in healing from this trauma was to let the energy do what it wanted to do. I learned to welcome the strange experiences that were flushing through my body, no matter how peculiar they felt. The more I did this, the more I began to feel comfortable in my own skin in a way that had I never before experienced. I corrected most of my scoliosis and gained a new sense of vitality. I also began to find a space within myself that I knew was home.

The beneficial impact of these experiences was so profound that I was unequivocally convinced of the value of craniosacral work, the therapeutic modality that had triggered my own ability to relive past trauma. I trained in Craniosacral Therapy at the renowned Upledger Institute founded by Dr. John Upledger, and have since incorporated many craniosacral techniques into my own practice. I have witnessed hundreds of people moving forward in their lives through releasing the energy of emotional and physical trauma trapped in their bodies.

When I was first exploring the power of early memories, I wanted to share experiences like my own rebirthing and the energetic unwinding of my spine that Yoga traditions describe as "*kundalini* rising." But since even today concepts like rebirthing or *kundalini* remain the province of the esoteric, most people would look at me askance, as if something were wrong with me. I received the distinct impression that they thought I was inventing something or being overly dramatic. I had to get to the point where I was confident of what I knew, regardless of what other people thought.

What I learned through these experiences is only common sense. Our entire life histories are encoded in our body memories, and because of this those histories are available to all of us. A great deal of what keeps us from accessing our early experiences and our subtler nature is our own cultural belief system. We believe we cannot remember, and so we do not. We think we are mind and matter rather than energy, so we miss the energetic component. Beliefs are very powerful. They can open us to a reality or they can hide it from us. If you are interested in becoming more transparent to yourself, in knowing who you are and reclaiming your life, it is important to work with people who have let go of restraining beliefs and opened up the doors of their own memories. They will give you permission to do the same with yourself.

It can be life transforming to relive our pasts because this process helps us confront illusions about ourselves. We will not remember unless we want to find our truth. But the truth *does* set us free. It helps us understand who we are. It helps us let go of emotional patterns that don't work for us. It supports our health. And most of all, it develops in us the habit of authenticity. It is authenticity that has been buried in a world focused on appearance and driven by fear. And it is through learning authenticity that we begin to discover and follow a path that is truly meaningful for us.

Learning Detachment

When I explored my own rebirthing and other sometimes traumatic experiences from infancy, I began to notice something very interesting. On one level, I was going through extremely intense experiences. But on another level, I was very detached. At the same time that I was back in time, living out some event exactly as it happened, I was also observing myself in the experience. Some part of me was separate and was saying, "Okay, let's do what we need to do in order to help Ingrid out here, so that she can move on with her life."

I was discovering the quality of detachment, the ability to somehow both be in an experience and observe myself undergoing that experience. In meditative traditions, this quality of detachment is described in terms of a "witness consciousness" that remains centered and unaffected as we undergo an experience. By developing the ability to witness what happens to us, we mitigate the tendency we all have to be overwhelmed by the intensity and immediacy of our reactions to events.

Detachment is a critical ingredient in learning to love ourselves. The idea of loving ourselves implies a relationship between the person to be loved or healed (ourselves) and the person who is doing the loving or healing (also ourselves). The more detachment we have about ourselves, the more we can both see what can help us and marshal the appropriate resources for accomplishing that goal.

I remember the first time I experienced this sense of detachment and was able to bring a healing presence into my own life. I was lying in bed, feeling fairly wound up after a demanding day at work. Then something happened and I was floating above myself, looking down at the person in the bed. I was both in the bed and above the bed looking down. The part of me that was floating above me saw immediately what the other part needed. In my imagination I gave myself a long hug and felt much better.

In detachment, we stop identifying with our internal states and simply observe them. The importance of letting go of identification, or of practicing detachment, is recognized by virtually every psychological and spiritual tradition. It's through detachment that we begin to develop the ability to choose who we want to be at very deep levels.

Detachment allows us to become creative about our lives instead of either overly self-centered or overly self-critical. One way I teach detachment is by asking clients to imagine that as they are doing something, they are also standing in another part of the room, watching themselves. Simple as this technique is, it helps people to develop a greater sense of objectivity about themselves. It can shift their perspective in surprising ways, teaching them how to see themselves in a way that is both neutral and compassionate, but not self-protective.

A man I was working with practiced watching himself in his imagination when he was talking with his children at breakfast. He pretended he was standing at the doorway of the kitchen observing himself. He was surprised to find that from the outside he looked as if he was being bossy and abrupt. He hadn't been aware of this until he adopted a third-person viewpoint on himself and began to see himself as others might see him. He was embarrassed by what he saw but also mature enough to recognize that he was better off if he could see what he was doing more clearly and could correct whatever was necessary. He changed his style to align his outer behavior with his inner intention of being supportive and loving with his children.

Patterns dominate us when we cannot see them. Becoming conscious of them can help us release them if that is appropriate. When we can see ourselves from the outside we can also direct ourselves to change in beneficial ways. We increase our options.

The more detached we can be, the more our self-exploration becomes a fascinating journey of sometimes mythical proportions. I once sat with a friend as she did some work with herself. She lay down, focused her attention on how she felt inside, and noticed a tension in her lower abdomen. She was drawn to dig at that part of her body with her hands. Soon it felt as if she had gotten something in her hands that needed to pass out of her body. It moved up into her chest and lungs and she began to make sweeping motions across her chest with her hands. She continued to make these sweeping and caressing motions and started crying deeply at the same time. This went on for about ten minutes until there were no more tears, and my friend opened her eyes. Despite the long weeping fit, she looked radiant. Why? Because of the detachment she had experienced throughout the process. She was the person who had been crying deeply. She was also the person who had been taking care of someone else—herself—who needed to cry. The detached part of herself had been helping out the part of herself that was in pain by washing the tears out of her body.

My friend experienced the grief of her tears, but she also experienced those tears in another way. To the detached part of her, it felt as though there had been water in her chest and that this water needed to be cleared out. As the healer healing herself she was able to sweep the water out of her system with her hands, encouraging the tears to flow out of her body until her chest felt completely dry. I pointed out to my friend that she had uncovered through her own process one of the truths of Chinese traditions of acupuncture. In acupuncture, the lungs are associated both with the water element and with grief. My friend had been washing water, which also manifested as tears of grief, from her lungs.

The combination of detachment, deep listening, and creative power that we can bring into our own relationship with ourselves sets a model for our relationships with other people. We learn to accept, love and engage our own feelings. That creates integrity—another word for oneness—within ourselves, instead of the conflict that we experience when we are driven to live up to an external standard. When we can feel oneness with ourselves, it's no longer frightening to be ourselves with others. If we have nothing to hide from ourselves we have nothing to hide from others. In fact, we can give a lot more to others because we give ourselves.

By learning detachment we use our self-awareness to heal what needs healing. Because we're more self-sufficient, we can just let other people be themselves instead of needing something from them. Because we heal ourselves, we don't need to be healed by them. Because we heal ourselves, we also respect other people's abilities to take care of themselves and we hold them up to that standard. Relationships then begin to have creative potential instead of getting mired in conflict, fear, need and subtle struggles for power. Once we can feel confident in being ourselves, whoever we are, we can let go of masks and share. We can also support others as they do the same.

Summary

In order to heal our emotional bodies, we have to grieve our illusions about our past, illusions that keep us in self-denial. This means acknowledging the depth of anger, pain and fear that are part of our life's inheritance. Acknowledging the reality of our past is emotionally and physically healing because 1) our emotions are a form of energy, 2) blocked energy creates physical and emotional distress, and 3) it is through releasing energy that we can find greater physical and emotional health and enhanced personal authenticity.

The Suggestions for Practice offered below represent three fundamental ways in which we can heal from the grief of our past, grief that we all experience simply in the process of being human. The first is to seek to become conscious of the illusions that we cherish as a way of protecting ourselves from admitting where we hurt. The second is to actively reawaken and relive buried memories, freeing ourselves from the impact they have had on our lives. The third is to practice the development of detachment, an art which is identical with the ability to love and nourish ourselves so as to maximize our creative potential.

Through healing our emotional bodies, we bring a new dimension into our lives: the dimension of spiritual self-creation. We let vision rather than fear determine who we are. We become creative rather than driven. We develop an inner sense of higher calling and personal destiny rather than finding the rules for our lives in external standards. We nurture relationships based on that sense of higher calling rather than on fear and power struggles.

The spiritual dimension is an integral part of the art of effortless living because only when we align ourselves with a sense of our own higher potential does life unfold meaningfully rather than stressfully. All the events of our lives become vehicles for personal self-enrichment. Our own deeper values begin to find their reflection in outer circumstances. Developing a spiritual commitment to higher values is the subject of Part III.

Suggestions for Practice _____

1. Grieve Your Past.

Grieving your past involves not so much specific exercises as it does making a commitment to learn about yourself and who you have been. Assume that much of yourself is unknown to you. Assume that you do not know what has actually shaped you. Then be open to discovery.

• Explore your Illusions.

Take some time to think about the most important relationships you have had: with your parents, siblings, close friends, etc. How do you characterize these relationships? What have been the good points and the bad points? Then ask yourself if there were some sorrow or anger here for you, or some sense of betrayal that you are not admitting to, what would it be? Ask yourself the opposite as well: if there were some sorrow or pain for the other person that you have not been aware of, what might it be? You might also take advantage of the safe company of a close friend to explore these issues, since a third party can often bring clear perception into the panorama of your life.

Notice whether feelings of pain that you find it hard to admit to come up. Notice that these feelings are different from the "poor me" feelings that we can all indulge in. Previously unacknowledged pain is pain we need to feel. Pain that we have acknowledged a million times—as in the "poor me" syndrome—is pain we need to let go of. Notice also whether you begin to see that some of the people in your life may themselves have suffered in ways you never before perceived. Notice how these realizations change your perception of yourself and of the people in your life.

• Relive your past.

Consider visiting a craniosacral therapist as a possible vehicle for contacting buried memories that need to be released. Most Craniosacral therapists have licenses in either massage therapy, physical therapy or movement therapy, and many are listed in local or regional holistic directories. Consider calling the Upledger Institute in Palm Beach Gardens, Florida, (Tel: 561-622-4706) and asking for a recommendation for a craniosacral therapist in your area. You can also call the International Alliance of Healthcare Practitioners at 1-800-311-9204, ask them for a copy of their national directory of bodyworkers, and look for bodyworkers in your area who have trained in Craniosacral Therapy. Finally, you might consider exploring hypnotherapy, as many hypnotherapists practice emotional regression work.

You will probably be more successful in identifying critical incidents from your past if you let a therapy session decide what is important to remember, rather than going in with your own ideas about what you want to learn. Bear in mind that reconnecting to what is buried is part of a larger process of being open to unconscious guidance, instead of needing to control the show.

2. Explore the Art of Detachment.

Learning detachment is a lifelong process. The two exercises below offer ways to begin thinking about detachment by developing a form of witness consciousness that is separate from your everyday consciousness, and that can begin to guide and direct you.

• Practice developing a witness consciousness.

One way to practice developing a witness consciousness is to set aside some time to go into deep relaxation, through meditation and following your breathing. Then imagine that a part of you, let's call it Self 1, is leaving your body, which we will call Self 2. Self 1 (your detached, floating self) now looks at Self 2 (your body) and observes what kind of state your body is in. Let Self 1 decide what Self 2 needs and give it to Self 2. Experience

Self 2 receiving and absorbing the gift.

Notice that if you can detach from your body, and have Self 1 look at Self 2, you may discover something about yourself that you didn't know. Do you see yourself in a new light? Do you perceive any tension in your body that you weren't aware of before? Or are you perhaps more aware of how you feel, now that you can see yourself from the outside? Notice that once you are more aware of what is going on for you, your detached Self (Self 1) can help you. What do you need to do for yourself? Give yourself a hug? Talk to yourself? Notice that you are learning the art of self-nurturance.

• Be your own loving and objective teacher.

As you go through the day, periodically imagine that you are watching yourself as though from another part of the room. Appreciate your experiences as though they were someone else's, with a bit of distance. As you do this, ask yourself what you can give the person you are watching (who is yourself) so as to help that person feel safer, more loved. How can you help that person to improve their life?

Notice that when you practice detachment, you are your own objective and loving teacher. You become the person who heals yourself, by taking your experiences less personally than you might, and seeing how you can creatively shift them toward a better outcome.

Suggested Reading

Barbara Brennan, *Hands of Light* (New York: Bantam, 1987). Written by a well-known healer, this book explores healing and self-healing through bodywork and contacting the energy field of the body.

John Upledger, *Your Inner Physician and You* (Berkeley CA: North Atlantic Books, 1991). A fascinating study of the development of contemporary Craniosacral Therapy, by the most influential person in the field.

part III

The Power of a Higher Life: From Effortlessness to Self-Creation

chapter **10**

Developing Our Higher Selves

Evolving a higher sense of vision that we rely on to guide our lives moves us out of fear and into purposeful self-creation. One way to connect to our higher sense of vision is to pay attention to the spontaneous images that can develop when we go into a deeper state of relaxation. Amy was lying on the bodywork table in my office with her eyes closed. I had guided her into an altered state, encouraging her to let her attention move inward. As she moved into self-hypnosis, a spontaneous visualization formed and we decided to follow it.

Amy's visualization started with an incongruous image of autumn leaves lying on the ground. Hands appeared and scratched away the leaves, exposing a long dark tunnel underneath. Amy crawled into the tunnel. The farther she went, the narrower it got, and although she was scared she pushed on.

Just when the tunnel was about to become too narrow for Amy to continue, it opened onto an arid, gray landscape full of boulders and dust. The scenery was utterly desolate. Amy crawled out of the tunnel and began walking through this desertscape, absorbing the emptiness of her surroundings and the weight of her aloneness. The forbidding terrain stretched on and on, and she walked and walked and walked. Nothing disturbed the silence. No animals emerged from out of the rocks and no people approached to greet her. Amy kept on trudging.

After what felt like a long time, an almost imperceptible shift began to take place. Small blades of grass appeared by the side of the road. The colors of the rocks became softer and more inviting. The path seemed less dusty and Amy's feet less tired. Then what had begun as a quiet intimation of better things to come flowered into a full, lush countryside. Green fields stretched on either side with blue and yellow wildflowers hugging the road. Off in the distance, purple mountains rose caressed by pink clouds and the soft light of a late afternoon. People began to appear on the periphery of Amy's vision. They joined her at first in ones and twos and then in crowds. They fell in step around and behind her, laughing and chatting happily. It was as though she had created this beautiful space through her pilgrimage, and now that the lonesome part was over, people were coming from all over. They were grateful to participate in the beauty she had found.

As Amy's waking dream came to a close, her heart was filled with joy. What had begun as a difficult, solitary journey through a dark tunnel and desert landscape ended in communion and fellowship in a beautiful valley ringed with mountains reaching toward heaven.

Amy's waking dream represented the archetypal journey into the self. It's a journey into the soul—a journey that leads out of role-playing and out of dependence on a social persona into becoming fully oneself, embracing one's inner destiny. We can't make this trip into ourselves, we can't find our own inner integrity, and we can't see the reflection of our newfound strength in our outer circumstances until we are *willing to be alone*.

Amy's visualization represented her own readiness to go it alone if necessary. It also held an important message for her: if she was willing to embrace the solitude of her personal pilgrimage, then she would eventually find rich companionship. People would want to be with her because of the person she was. But she had to accept her aloneness before the companions would appear.

The Journey into Aloneness

There's no inherent value in being alone. But as long as we are afraid of being alone, we keep ourselves from doing whatever is necessary to embrace our own path. We stick with someone else's version of the truth and someone else's notion of right and wrong, and deep down we feel cheated, though we may not understand why. Willingness to be alone is the personal price we have to pay for finding the unique gifts that we are meant to share with the rest of the world.

When we can accept aloneness, we say to ourselves, "It's okay if nobody else understands this. I have to do it anyway." Getting to that place requires going through a barren landscape because it challenges us to let go of the part of ourselves that is dependent on cultural values and that is scared of the unique individuality of our journey.

In the early days of my personal journey into healing, I had to accept being alone in two obvious ways. I had to let go of my marriage, including the financial and social security it offered and the sense of companionship I gained through it. I also had to let go of the security of a professional identity as a professor of philosophy, and set out to create my own tailor-made profession. That was not easy for me. Far from it. In the end, I only accepted being alone because the cost of not doing so was too high.

My fear of being alone—of being my own person—was part of what made me sick. I clung to the security that I got from my marriage and from an academically recognized professional status. I felt as if I wouldn't know who I was if I let go of these. But the security I had was also a roadblock that kept me from figuring out who I needed to be for myself. Holding on made my life more comfortable on some levels, but at the cost of illness and—even more seriously—of internal stagnation.

My personal desert encompassed the long period of my healing, during which I struggled through prolonged periods of feeling like an outcast as I tried to uncover how to be true to myself. Through that time, I was repeatedly forced to confront the difference between the persona I had grown up as and the person I needed to be. I had to do battle with my need to be needed, my need to be approved, my emotional demands, and my intellectual defensiveness. Most of the time, I did this kicking and screaming. A good part of me was decidedly not on the side of my growth. It took me a long time to get to the point of risking losing connection with others in order to find myself. I had to learn that in going through the desert, we must leave other people's perceptions behind in order to find and live by what is true for us.

All creative, self-determining people face the need to be alone at some point, whether literally or metaphorically, as the price of becoming the source of their own lives. Sometimes they welcome that journey and sometimes they do not. But it is always challenging.

A casual glance at some of history's great figures quickly reveals that people who take on exceptional challenges also accept being alone. Albert Schweitzer, for example, is recognized as one of the extraordinary luminaries of the first half of the twentieth century. An ordained minister and doctor who stood everything to gain from living in the sophisticated European culture of his birth, Schweitzer felt deeply alienated by the modern world of his times—a world that professed progress yet created two world wars during his lifetime. He left the security and familiarity of Europe to live for decades in the depths of Africa, building hospitals and caring for native populations. He often survived for years with only the company of his wife and the Africans he worked with. While Schweitzer was eventually internationally recognized for his work, he withstood great physical aloneness and hardship for the sake of his ideals.

Another traveler into lonely territory, less well known than Albert Schweitzer but equally brave in her own way, was Charlotte Perkins Gilman. A prominent feminist and journalist at the turn of the century, Gilman suffered a nervous breakdown and hospitalization during a personal, inner journey in which she rejected the Victorian chains that surrounded women. Eventually that experience became the foundation for her powerful short story, *The Yellow Wallpaper*, which tells of a woman who goes mad under the constraining influence of a culture and family that deny the validity of women's perceptions.

Gilman braved her own temporary insanity in the process of a personal struggle that led her to create an independent career as a writer and advocate of women's rights. She supported herself as a single woman at a time when women's careers were confined primarily to teaching and domestic positions and when being a single female carried a great social stigma. When Gilman finally embraced her right to be different, she left her own flirtation with insanity behind.

Tolerating aloneness and countering the tide of the way things are done can take subtler forms. It doesn't necessarily mean being physically alone and it doesn't necessarily mean being eccentric in society's terms. What it does mean is getting clear about doing things the way you are doing them because you need to do them that way for yourself and because you treasure what you are creating in your own life.

Frances is a highly successful manager at a major corporation who came to me initially because of physical problems. With her soft curly black hair and large violet eyes, Frances's natural look was the look of an angel, but she had that well camouflaged since angels don't make good corporate material. Frances had learned to put on a tough veneer, and she responded to negative behavior from other people by saying to herself, "I can take that!" and setting out to prove how much she could handle. It had become part of her identity to prove her worth in the face of hostility, a common enough reality in the corporate environment. Even at home, she responded to negativity in a similar way. Instead of rejecting her husband's attempts to control her through legislating what she could spend her money on and when she should come home, she went about tolerating this while saying to herself that that was okay, she could handle that too.

Things changed as Frances went through healing. She came to grips with the fact that she was always proving herself to other people and that on a subtle level she was inviting her superiors to be demanding, her colleagues to be competitive, and her husband to be controlling. She had also taken on materialistic values and moved in a crowd whose main interests were making money. There's nothing wrong with making money, but the people Frances spent time with weren't giving much support to the part of her that wanted to be soft, receptive, vulnerable and compassionate.

When Frances began to recognize that being a tough survivor was costing her her natural self, she went through an inner crisis. She came into my office one day saying she wondered if she was crazy. When I asked her why, she said that she could no longer accept the turf-building at work. The truth was that underneath the veneer of politeness, people clawed at each other. Each person saw the other person's gain as their own loss. This no longer made any sense to Frances. Her own motivation to join in the dog-eat-dog atmosphere was vanishing as she recognized that underneath her colleagues' polish of competency they were really motivated by fear and pain. She wanted to address that fear and pain rather than contribute to it by being yet another anxiety-driven performer.

Frances was also having trouble at home. Her insecure self asked how she could possibly object to her husband's controlling behavior. After all, he was doing so many things for them, fixing the roof, putting in a new driveway and so on. But she didn't care about this so much anymore. She wished that they could just talk together. She didn't care about his being a financially successful head of household if that came at the cost of losing a loving partner.

Frances felt crazy because everything that she had accepted for so long no longer made sense to her. Her first reaction to this was to wonder if the problem was with the people around her or with her. And the old part of her, the frightened part, was saying, "If you stop playing by the rules you'll get in trouble!" But she decided to reject this frightened part of herself as unhealthy.

Frances went through a period of feeling profoundly alienated from her colleagues as she tried to readjust to being softer, kinder, more supportive and collaborative. She didn't complain about the competitiveness and hostility of the work environment. That's easy to do and many people do it. Instead, Frances changed herself even while living in that hostile environment, so that her behavior wouldn't contribute to its negative ethos. Doing that took strength.

Frances had to let go of feeling pressured by her boss' tendency to put her down. She had to avoid proving herself to him and concentrate instead on what she thought was doing a good job, regardless of what he said. She had to stand up for herself firmly but calmly. She had to sidestep the anxious atmosphere at work and bring her own values of balance, peacefulness and kindness into her office. Instead of spending her time complaining about how mean other people were at work, she became the kind of person she thought a good person was. And of course, changing ourselves is the most efficient way to change our environment. Over time, Frances's internal change transformed the atmosphere in her office, showing people that they could collaborate and support each other in order to produce. Her husband also appreciated her softer style and began to soften himself.

Frances was willing to run the risk of not fitting in and of other people misperceiving her. In this sense she was willing to be alone.

Wherever we are afraid to be alone or afraid to be different, that is where our edge is. That is where we need to work on ourselves and own ourselves more fully. Addressing our fear of being alone doesn't mean we have to end up being alone. But it does mean that the fear of being alone should not guide our behavior. That fear makes us compromise. Compromise makes us untrue to ourselves. And being untrue to ourselves makes us unfulfilled.

Finding Inner Guidance

Being willing to be alone doesn't just mean being different from others or being solitary. The real meaning of being willing to be alone is deeper. It is about learning to take the journey into contact with an inner rather than an external source of guidance. The art of effortless living is about finding inner guidance because that is the only way we can live without conflict.

We have to withdraw into ourselves in order to become ourselves more completely and in order to give genuinely to others. The inner journey is well-represented by two of the archetypal cards embodied in the ancient system of symbolism called the Tarot. One card is the Hanged Man. In the Universal Waite pictorial version of the Tarot, the Hanged Man is suspended upside down with one leg attached to a tree branch, his hands behind his back and a serene look on his face. The Hanged Man represents that time in our lives when everything gets inwardly turned upside down. We no longer know what works for us. We have to go through a fallow period to discover how we are going to move forward authentically. During this time outworn perspectives are shed, and in the ensuing emptiness the Hanged Man *waits and listens* to find guidance. There is no other way to proceed because nothing yet fills the space occupied by outdated ways of seeing things.

The second Tarot card representing the inner journey is the Hermit. The Hermit is a cloaked, bearded person carrying a lantern before him as he stands in deep *contemplation*. He is the part of us that retreats into inner self-awareness in order to work on self-development.

Waiting, listening and contemplation: as the Tarot shows, these are the keys to finding inner guidance. These practices have nothing to do with doing and performing. They are about becoming quiet and receiving. It's our receptivity that allows us to take in new nourishment. It's our receptivity that connects us to something larger than ourselves and that teaches us that we are not isolated. It's our receptivity that cultivates an inner attitude of trust instead of fear, because when we learn to receive we learn to be supported instead of having to prove ourselves. It's our receptivity that connects us to our inner wellspring. Receptivity is a profoundly feminine, *yin* virtue. It's the ballast for meaningful action and *yang* energy.

Finding inner guidance is a lost art in our society because we don't value receptivity. We spend most of our time acting and very little time receiving. It's also a lost art because receptivity is a right-brain function and ours is a left-brain culture. To be receptive and find inner guidance we have to cultivate our right brain. We have to develop our ability to let things come up without having either to control the show or to analyze what's happening.

Inner guidance comes from the unconscious. Our conscious mind is made up of culturally accepted perceptions. It tells us that the way things have been seen and done in the past is the way they must be seen and done now. In contrast, our unconscious mind holds our creative potential for the future. One reason we don't hear the unconscious is, quite literally, that we don't listen to it. If somebody came into your room and started talking to you and you didn't pay attention, eventually that person would leave. It's the same with our unconscious mind and with the inner guidance that comes from the unconscious. It stops talking and leaves us alone because we don't listen.

Most of us pay virtually no attention to the exceedingly powerful dimension of our lives that is represented by our unconscious wisdom. We don't take the time to stop and receive, and we don't train ourselves in receptivity. Even our dreams, which are readily available to us as a source of knowledge, get blasted out of our heads by alarm clocks insisting on our return to the daily frenzy. We pay the price. Our inner guidance leaves us, and we end up trusting ourselves so little that the only path we know how to follow is the one already set down by social convention.

In order to develop personal power and authenticity, we have to learn to value unconscious guidance. We have to practice opening the doorway between the conscious and the unconscious minds. We have to develop a relationship between the conscious mind and the unconscious part of ourselves that houses our higher self.

Having a relationship with our inner guidance or higher self is having a relationship with a source that feels both like part of us and at the same time different from us. A person who has found inner guidance feels as though there is some being inside himself that is also separate from him and taking care of him. This being feels separate because it's not part of the conscious mind. But it also feels connected because it is internal. The higher self is like a voice in our ear or an angel on our shoulder.

Opening the door to our unconscious, higher self is the most important thing we can do in our lives. In order to do that we have to believe that this higher self is available to us and we have to ask it to speak to us. Disbelief slams the door shut. Belief opens that door.

Since receptivity to our higher self is a right-brain capacity, imagination plays an important role in nurturing a relationship with it. When I first began seeking inner guidance, I spent some time every evening having imaginary conversations with my higher self before I went to sleep. I didn't know exactly where or who she was, but I decided to trust her implicitly and to speak with her as if she were the most intimate of friends. I would close my eyes as I lay in bed and talk to her, telling her everything. I would describe for her how I felt about the events of the day. I would tell her how my body felt. I would ask for advice about anything that was bothering me. Then I would close my imaginary conversation by thanking her for listening and asking her to give me whatever guidance seemed appropriate.

Sometimes after talking to my higher self, nothing happened. At other times I would find that a problem resolved itself without my knowing quite why. Sometimes I had sudden flashbacks or vivid images. And sometimes my dreams revealed important information to me. When this started happening, I expanded my explorations, and each evening I would ask my higher self to provide specific guidance for me on particular issues through my dreams.

I kept pencil and paper by my bed and jotted down whatever I remembered of my dreams when I woke up. Usually answers came through in cryptographic, symbolic form, but I kept notes anyway, trusting that over time the meanings of my dreams would become more evident. And that is what happened. For example, I once asked my higher self for guidance in dealing with a friendship that was causing me anxiety. That night, I had a dream in which a voice spoke to me saying, "The answer to your question lies in the meaning of the name Michael." I was puzzled by these words, and then it occurred to me that Michael is one of the oldest names of the Judeo-Christian tradition, and that the archangel Michael had fought with his angels against Satan. I looked up the meaning of the name, and found that it meant "beloved of God," or "one who is like God." As soon as I read these words, I felt an immediate sensation of recognition and relief—typical signs of tapping into the subjective truth of the dream, or its unique meaning for me. I realized I would feel better if I relied less on my relationships for a sense of well-being, and more on my connection to an inner source. This realization helped me deal productively with my friendship—another indication that I had read the meaning of the dream appropriately.

Through talking to my higher self, I developed a new orientation to life that placed less emphasis on planning and control and more on receiving and being in the current of things. This led to a number of very profound changes. The first was that while I had begun by imagining that I had a higher self, over time it became quite clear to me that there was a real presence guiding me and that I was not alone. I had opened up a channel between my conscious and limited ego self and my larger and wiser unconscious self. The conviction of a guiding presence gradually became the most important force in my life, far more important than the perceptions of people around me. I could let go of my need for external reassurance and support without struggle because this other source was stronger, clearer, and more reliable. The second change that happened was an expansion of my right-brain creative potential.

Higher Guidance and Right-Brain Creativity

As a culture, in our schooling and in our approach to work, we place far too little emphasis on the potential of the right brain. Yet many geniuses have consciously exploited the development of right-brain power. Thomas Edison, for example, approached his own research very largely through his right brain. When he wanted to solve a scientific puzzle or develop ideas about a new invention, he would sit down with little balls in his hand, close his eyes, and roll the balls back and forth in a rhythmic motion to put himself into a hypnotic state. If he fell asleep, the balls would drop into a metal tray beneath him, making a noise that woke him up. Then he would return to the pre-sleep state that is characteristic of self-hypnosis and that is a fertile source of imagination. Edison trained himself to use self-hypnosis to stimulate passive creative visualization on the scientific questions that intrigued him.

Edison was also well known for putting his hand to his ear and listening for an answer when someone asked him a scientific question. He was adopting a stance of receptivity and waiting for the answer to come from a source outside his conscious control. Interestingly, Edison was an active participant in the Theosophical Society, an influential spiritually-based organization founded toward the end of the nineteenth century. The Theosophical Society promoted the integration of esoteric knowledge from ancient spiritual traditions, the development of clairvoyant skills which they felt accessed this knowledge, and futuristic scientific work. Like many other scientists of his era, and unlike many people in the scientific establishment today, Edison believed that the development of the higher self and scientific discovery went hand in hand.

When we use our right brain to create, we become aware of something that is there but that is not available to ordinary, accepted perception. In my healing work using mind-body techniques and subtle touch, activating my right brain opened up my capacities for extended sense perception. Initially this happened sporadically. I could occasionally "see" problems that my clients were suffering from: for example a bladder problem, congested arteries, or a subluxation in the spine. I gradually learned to trust these perceptions by sharing them and receiving confirmation from my clients or having them visit a doctor for further corroboration.

I also began to know the general outlines of events in clients' pasts, again without being told. For example, one of the first times this happened, I knew that a man who came to work with me had been sexually shamed as a boy. I knew this before we began talking. This knowledge was in the atmosphere surrounding the man and didn't need to be solicited through information-gathering and discussion. Over time, I began to take it for granted that one could know a great deal about a person, including even specific events in their lives, without having to search these things out through conversation.

In addition, I began to experience numerous precognitive episodes. I would get a sense of what a new client looked like before she appeared at my office, or I would see in my mind the face of a total stranger whom I would then meet a few hours later. I began to use this precognitive skill—essentially a form of intuition free of the constraints of space and time—to focus on my clients before an appointment, so as to get a sense of how I might best help them. The information I received was always specific to ways in which, given my profession, I might be able to help them.

Over time, as I began to trust these kinds of experiences, they became more regular and reliable. Today, I regularly use high-sense perception—also called extrasensory perception—to tap into psychic knowledge about my clients that can be useful for their healing. I work as a medical intuitive to diagnose physical, emotional and spiritual problems clients confront. I can with confidence say that the information I receive through psychic impressions is at least as accurate and often far more informative than those I obtain through ordinary sense perception.

Psychic knowledge or extended sensory perception was for me a natural consequence of training myself into a state of receptivity. The more receptive I became and the more willing I was to let go of prejudgment, the more information spontaneously poured in. The more I relied on my ability both to diagnose and treat people through respecting psychically perceived information, the more successful I became in receiving this information and in using it effectively.

I believe that psychic perception is a completely normal ability. The regular practice of all the lifestyle approaches detailed in this book will spontaneously open up or enhance a person's psychic abilities and inner guidance. I also believe that psychic perception will become increasingly commonplace over the next few decades, both because of growing cultural acceptance of the psychic dimension and because the development of high-speed technology is breaking down the mental commitment to linear space and time. It is this commitment that makes us think extrasensory perception is weird or imaginary.

Psychic perception seems natural and normal when we recognize that we are all like radio transmitters. Our brains are complex systems of electrical circuitry designed to receive and transmit an infinite amount of information. If our conscious, planning and directing minds are too active, we cannot receive or transmit very effectively because there is too much static on our channel. But if we eliminate the static—the mental over-thinking and emotional turbulence—then we become receptive to information. We become more highly attuned in our five senses, and at the same time we pick up frequencies that extend beyond normal five-sensory perception. As a culture we have just begun to tap the potential of the right brain. The key in doing this is to practice letting go of control and focusing the attention on letting in or receiving.

Receptivity: A Necessity for Planetary Survival

A number of years ago I was attending a week-long conference in the Rocky Mountains west of Denver, Colorado. It was early summer, and every morning I would get up at dawn and hike for a few hours before the meetings of the day began. This was an old practice of mine that I had developed during my long period of recuperation from illness. I had discovered that I could not get in touch with what was important to me, or with anything that would be useful to communicate to someone else, unless I found a way to spend long periods of time in silence. Hiking by myself was one way to accomplish that goal. It also exposed me to uplifting natural scenery.

One morning I paused by a trailhead at the edge of a rushing torrent. I looked past the grassy lowlands and the timbers to the tall, snow-laced mountains in the distance. A soft cloud hugged one of the rocky peaks, draping over it like a lover caressing its beloved. It enveloped that peak so softly that it touched it delicately and completely. A touch like that from a human hand could invite a person into ecstasy.

After a while the cloud detached itself from its rocky mate lingeringly, easily, and without haste. I watched as the two forces, the cloud made of water and air and the mountain built of earth and stone, parted ways. After such intense intimacy, they once more stood separately. That slow-motion movie seemed an extraordinary teaching beyond words on what personal relationships could be like. Perhaps we should look more closely to nature to understand ourselves and receive guidance on how to be with one another.

I hiked up the trail, passing through a whispering grove of aspen trees, and after an hour came to an outcropping overlooking the valley. I sat there, taking in the pattern of clouds and mountains off in the distance. Within a minute, a large bird flew right in front of me and settled on the limb of a nearby scruffy pine. He hopped back and forth, seeming to inspect me. He took the opportunity to fly right by me several more times, seemingly wishing either to engage my attention or to observe me further. I enjoyed the company.

As I stood up to leave, another bird flew very close to me and then accompanied me a short distance down the trail. I was touched by the power of our communion. I headed down the trail, and at one point I looked to my left and saw a deer standing at the edge of a clearing observing me. I stopped and talked to him with my eyes. After a little while, he moved farther into the clearing, then paused again to observe me. I took a few steps, waited, and connected with him again. We continued this way with each other until the deer was content to enter and graze in the clearing while I walked slowly past.

I entered the aspen grove I had passed on the way up the trail. The energy of the trees was emanating palpably through the rustling of leaves, and it filled the atmosphere. At the same time, underneath the rustling and the singing of the birds an enormous silence throbbed through everything. I felt how very small I was in an awesome universe whose pulse permeated every tree and plant, the air around me, the rain and the wind.

As I blended into the landscape and the landscape blended into me, I became a part of this life force expressing itself through the play of changing colors and the melody of nature's sounds. Reverence filled me. In the face of such vastness, it's impossible not to let go of the petty opinions and needs that fill our all-too-human lives. I was being given a gift of the insistent silence, power and beauty of things that are not man-made. The animals, trees, clouds and mountains fed me enormously because I was blessed enough on that day to be there to receive them.

In all my hikes through the mountains during that week, I came across only one other person who journeyed in silence. I ran into numerous couples and groups who tromped over the rocks and through the woods, talking about computer programs, business deals, what he said and what she said. It saddened me to see how people cut themselves off from their own source.

Nature is an incredible teacher. We are meant to revere her, to listen to her in awe and to become part of her. Every flower is a sacred lesson, every bird call another interpretation of reality, every animal a unique expression of the energy that floods the universe. If we cannot let go of our own concerns long enough to let nature in, it is impossible to receive the abundance of her nurturance. When we stand in nature's kingdom and allow ourselves to receive, we immediately feel the profundity and ineffable beauty of things as they are. This calls us to a higher purpose within ourselves. Nature teaches us nobility and profundity. But if we do not open ourselves to her, then we cannot learn from her.

It is one of the tragedies of our age that we are so oblivious of the grandeur that surrounds us. Through our obliviousness we both destroy our teacher and decimate the source of our own livelihood. Even so-called nature lovers rarely allow themselves to enter her fully. I know this from personal experience, because while I have since childhood sought out nature as a source of pleasure, it is only recently that I have begun to enter more fully into the experience of her power and magnitude.

Many of us say we love nature, but how much do we really recognize what she is? Do many people in our contemporary world have an idea of what it meant to the Native American Indian to perceive nature as his mother? When we look at nature through the windows of a car, we see a pretty picture. But we do not feel the tangible force that fills the universe. And if we stand in nature yet busy ourselves with our own thoughts, we also miss the truth. We don't get to share space with other animals and recognize their inherent wisdom. We don't get to feel our connectedness with life. We see nature as cosmetic and become careless with her. That carelessness can ultimately lead only to our own destruction since we desecrate our own foundation. And we lose out in a deeper sense. We fail to get in touch with the fact that we are part of something vast. That experience is the most transformative one there is, and it is right there in front of us, waiting to be had. It helps us trust that there is a higher force guiding our lives. It helps us become receptive to what enfolds us.

Receptivity and Non-Resistance

Receptivity is about letting go of planning and forcing, allowing ourselves instead to be guided. That's what makes it so effortless. By working on cultivating a relationship to a higher self, we
get out of our own way and let the deeper intelligence that is within us direct our lives. We recognize that the conscious mind is really not the master of the situation, and align ourselves with our
unconscious wisdom so as to avoid thwarting its intelligence.

William James, who devoted much of his life to exploring the
psychology of spiritual growth, felt that so long as we allied ourselves exclusively with our conscious mind we would repeatedly
feel derailed and frustrated by life, because it will serve us up
experiences different from the ones our conscious mind intends.

> A man's conscious wit and will are aiming at something only
> dimly and inaccurately imagined. Yet all the while the forces of
> mere organic ripening within him are going on to their own
> prefigured result, and his conscious strainings are letting loose
> subconscious allies behind the scenes which in their way work
> toward rearrangement, and the rearrangement toward which
> all these deeper forces tend is pretty surely definite, and defi-
> nitely different from what he consciously conceives and deter-
> mines. [*]

In order to avoid the frustration that follows from thinking life
should flow the way we want it to flow, we need to practice receptivity. Yet letting go into receptivity usually involves a crisis of
trust. How can we let something else run the show if we're used to
thinking our security depends on keeping our hands on the reins
of control?

When we're in control, we plan where we're going to go and
then we direct ourselves there. But think about this: how many
times do we plan something, arrive where we wanted to
go and discover that we didn't get what we really wanted?
When we practice receptivity we play by different rules.
Instead of planning so much, we let life plan. We practice letting the experiences that we have teach us instead of deciding
what we're going to do. We take the attitude that what we are

---

* quoted in John Dewey, *Art as Experience* (New York: G. P. Putnam's Sons,
1958), p. 72.

learning in the process of living takes us where we are meant to go, instead of deciding where we are going to go and shutting down on anything that doesn't match our expectations.

A client of mine had a dream which perfectly expressed his own changing experience of life and his growing receptivity. He dreamt that he was in a strange town attending a "conference for learning." The conference was packed and as part of the learning experience participants were supposed to explore the town. In his dream, my client went off into town by himself. There was a lot of ocean (a classical symbol of the unconscious) around him, and he didn't know where he was, but he felt he was in the right place.

After a while, he found his way back to the meeting hall, although he didn't know how. Then he set out on another learning experience. This time he went much farther into the town than on his first adventure. He began to be concerned that he was lost. He didn't know how to get back to where he had started from, and he didn't know how to go forward. He was relieved when some other conference members turned up.

Unfortunately, however, they were also lost. The whole group was in a quandary. They decided to risk pressing forward into the strange town, even though they knew that this would take them farther and farther away from their starting point. They let themselves get even more lost. Lo and behold, they ended up exactly where they were supposed to be: in a conference room with a seminar coordinator who was waiting for them. They had reached their destination without knowing where it was or how to get there.

For my client this dream told him that life is a journey, and that the journey is identical with the learning we do along the way. So long as he accepted the journey, he would learn what he needed to learn. That meant he had to give up on knowing the answers beforehand or directing the show too strongly. Instead, he had to be available for whatever the journey had to teach him. He had to be more receptive.

The shift that happens when we become more receptive and open-ended is enormous. For me, the signs of this shift are clearest in my work with clients. There was a time when, if a client came through my door, I would have a theory about what was wrong and would direct the show with a plan of action. That was an important period of my own growth. But now, the theories and plans have receded into the background. It would be unfair of me, and a loss to both my clients and myself, if I put them in boxes and labeled them. I try to be more open-ended. I am at my best when I have a gut feeling that my client and I are going in the right direction even though we are not entirely sure where we're going. As an analogy, it is well known that dogs and cats that are by accident separated from their owners can sometimes find their way home even though they may be miles away. These animals have a radar sense that directs them home far more accurately than following directions on a map. Yet obviously they don't know where home is or how to get there in any usual sense of the term to "know." They just know that they are going there! Faith is something like that. We don't know exactly where we're going but we do know that we are going and that the direction in which we are going is a good one.

We become more receptive as we develop trust in the life process, and this means letting go of resistance to the way our lives unfold. One way that I practice non-resistance is to assume that whatever is happening is what is meant to happen or that it is happening for the best reason possible. If someone doesn't behave the way I would like him to behave, I try to let go of anger or irritation and instead assume that there is an opportunity for learning here that is for my benefit. If I am scheduled to give a seminar and it falls through, instead of being upset at things not going the way I had planned, I ask myself what the unexpected change of events opens up for me. Perhaps now I can spend time seeing friends I haven't seen in a long time, or reading up on a subject that interests me. When we practice non-resistance, we stop trying to make life turn out the way we want it to. Instead, we notice the way things are and ask ourselves how we can grow from that.

Summary

Developing our higher selves requires the courage to be alone when it is appropriate to be alone. Through our willingness to be alone, we develop the commitment to a deeply personal truth that guides us through life's experiences. Developing our higher selves also requires that we call on and be receptive to inner guidance. Once we increase our receptivity to our higher selves by calling on inner guidance, we begin to see ourselves as parts of a larger being. This includes beginning to love and honor nature, and to revere her presence in our lives as something that can teach us values extending far beyond the human concerns of our everyday lives. Finally, becoming receptive through seeking inner guidance entails learning to practice non-resistance in the face of life's endless and often unexpected changes. We learn to see whatever happens to us as a gift, and to let go of the frustration and anger that attend experiences when things don't turn out the way we think they should.

The Suggestions for Practice incorporated below all involve ways of learning to develop the skills integral to connecting with our higher selves.

*Suggestions for Practice*_____

1. Explore Your Feelings about Being Alone.

If you are afraid of being alone, you are dependent on others for your sense of self, and if you are dependent on others, you block your receptivity to inner guidance. Being willing to be alone involves being willing to be different, to have commitments and values that don't blend with any crowd, be they conformist or non-conformist crowds.

• **Ask yourself where you compromise in relationships out of fear of being alone.**

Do you stay in a relationship with a family member or partner because you are afraid of being alone? Do you compromise your own values because you think the people around you won't accept them? Are you ever afraid of saying what you believe because you think you'll be rejected? Look at your significant relationships and ask where you hold back from saying things or from being the way you want to be, out of fear of rejection or of being left alone. Ask yourself where you can challenge your fear. Can you speak or act your own truth more clearly?

Consider the small and large ways that you may manifest your own fear of being alone. Do you socialize so as to feel that you are popular, or are you comfortable with who you are regardless of how many people want to be with you? Do you buy clothes because they're in style or because you like them regardless of whether they're in style? Do you call someone because you think you're supposed to or because you want to? Where do you hold yourself back from something because of how you think it will be perceived?

Notice how often people respond to you positively when you speak your own truth, even though that can feel frightening. Most of us appreciate honesty in others, although we may be afraid of being honest ourselves. Notice how you feel about yourself when you act more from your own values, and worry less about what others think. Do you feel more empowered? Notice how some of your weaker relationships tend to fall away, while relationships that hold real potential get stronger.

2. Develop a relationship with your higher self. 🖭

While developing a relationship with your higher self is an ongoing process that can deepen throughout your lifetime, the key is to open yourself up to listening to inner guidance. Use the exercise (20 minutes) on Cassette 3 of Effortless Practice *for comprehensive training in learning to listen to inner guidance, or follow the suggestions in the text below.*

• Practice speaking to your higher self.

Find a place where you can be alone for up to half an hour. Lie down and begin by relaxing into the meditative state that helps you obtain inner guidance. (See pp. 83, or Cassette 1, for guidance on achieving a meditative state.) Then imagine that you have an inner healer, a loving presence that is close by listening to you. Speak to that loving friend with total sincerity. Speak out loud, as this will help you to avoid drifting off, and will encourage you to articulate your feelings clearly. Describe in detail your emotions of the day, your reactions to events and even your physical sensations. Remember that the more information you give your higher self, the more benefit you will gain from your communications. After you tell your higher self your concerns of the day, ask to receive any guidance, advice or support that seems appropriate. If you like, formulate specific questions. When you are finished, close by thanking your higher self for being there. Repeat this exercise at least several times a week, preferably at night when you go to bed.

Notice that this exercise works best if you remember not to look for or expect any specific response. Adopting the attitude that appropriate guidance will come at the appropriate time is key, because it's your attitude of receptivity that opens the door to inner guidance. Instead of looking for specific results, begin to notice how you feel after you talk to your higher self. Do you feel more relaxed? Do unexpected feelings come up? Do you find yourself having insights more often? Are your dreams more vivid? Are you beginning to get the feeling that there really is some larger presence watching over you?

3. Practice Reverence for Nature.

We all have an inherent love of nature, because we are part of her. This exercise simply stimulates greater receptivity toward nature's gifts. It reminds us that the universe teaches us and loves us.

• Commune with your natural surroundings.

Make your time in nature a pilgrimage, a time to silence your everyday concerns and let in the teachings of the rocks, trees, grasses, clouds and sky, and of the animals around you. Pick a place in nature, go and sit there, and focus on letting go of all your thoughts. Let yourself absorb the scenery. Become one with it. If you go with someone else, agree to make this a time for silence. Spend at least twenty minutes in silence, letting in the universe around you.

Notice how peaceful you become. Notice how, when you become quiet, nature comes alive. Notice how much more you are capable of absorbing when you become still. Notice what emotions come up. Do you feel reverence for creation?

4. Practice Non-resistance.

Non-resistance means developing trust. It's about letting go of your own will in the face of the larger will of the universe. It's part of developing wisdom, and recognizing that whatever happens is meaningful, even though you may not understand that meaning at the moment.

• Incorporate non-resistance into your daily life.

Assume that whatever is happening to you is happening for a good reason, even though your ego might not want to see it that way. Look at every event in your day that causes you stress, irritation, frustration or unhappiness. If someone disappoints you, ask yourself how you can grow from the experience. If things turn out differently from what you would like, look for the hidden benefit in the turn of events. If a seminar you wanted to attend was cancelled, did that give you the opportunity to call old friends who you'd been too busy to connect with? If your child got sick, and you had to cancel plans for an evening out, did that give you the opportunity to spend special moments with your child? How can you interpret every frustrating event in your day so as to see the unexpected opportunity it brings?

Notice how easily frustrated you get when you don't practice non-resistance, when you focus primarily on the disappointment of things not going your way. Notice how much personal energy that disappointment eats up. Notice also how full of opportunity life becomes when you assume that whatever happens, happens for a reason, and that you can benefit from life's daily events in some unexpected way.

Suggested Reading

Machaelle Small Wright, *MAP: The Co-Creative White Brotherhood Medical Assistance Program* (Jeffersonton, VA: Perelandra, 1990). This off-the-beaten-track book includes unusual and detailed methods for developing higher guidance.

chapter **11**

Cultivating Passion

Wouldn't life be easy if we could guide ourselves completely by listening to inner guidance? We wouldn't have to make any decisions ourselves. We'd just abandon ourselves to letting our higher selves take the reins, knowing that we could rest in the certainty of going in the right direction. We'd be totally surrendered.

In real life, however, surrender is not so easy. Most of us would rather stay in the illusion of control even if that makes our lives harder. We'd rather pretend that if we can just keep on deciding how things are going to go, then life will turn out better. But control is an illusion. It's when we try to control the outcomes of our relationships that we find frustration and disappointment, when we try to control our bodies that we get sick, when we try to control other nations that we end up in wars that destroy us all. Part of living effortlessly is accepting that trying to control puts us out of control, and then learning to move through the river of life flowing with the current instead of arrogantly fighting it.

There's another reason that surrender and receptivity, which are the opposite of control, are difficult virtues to cultivate. They are about letting inner guidance run the show, but inner guidance doesn't come into our lives consistently until we have thoroughly demonstrated our sincerity and commitment to listening to our higher selves. It's as if our higher selves were saying, "Let's see whether they really mean what they say when they tell us they want our guidance. If they can prove through their own behavior how committed they are, then we'll step in and give them a hand."

A classic story of Eastern spiritual traditions tells about an aspiring young man who visits a renowned master in hopes of becoming his disciple. He is fascinated by the master's special powers and wants to develop them as well. Instead of taking him right in or showing him his bag of tricks, the master sets him to work doing menial jobs: chopping wood, washing dishes, cleaning house, tending the garden. If the student is sincere about wanting to study with the master, he does this for a year, two years or three years. Exactly how long doesn't matter. What does matter is that it's a long time, and it takes considerably more patience than the average person would demonstrate. It's only once the student has proven his patience and sincerity that one day he receives the overt blessings and guidance of his master. He has shown that he has an unquenchable passion for the wisdom held by his teacher and that nothing will keep him from pursuing this wisdom. And without knowing it, he has already gone a long way toward developing the special capacities for which he had come in search. He has built the inner strength of character that is the foundation for higher levels of attainment.

Character As Key

Translating this story into contemporary terms is easy. We all want to develop our full potential, including accessing the guidance of our unconscious wisdom. We would all like to become everything that we can be, to rise above the boredom of everyday life, and to let go of petty concerns. But accessing our potential and receiving support from the storehouse of power each of us holds inside takes sincerity and discipline. To get the rewards we're looking for we have to develop commitment.

Commitment depends on character, and character includes such qualities as poise, forbearance, kindness, patience, courage and more. We aren't born with these traits. If we have them, it's because we cultivate them. Cultivating them takes focus and perseverance. It's because it's so easy to get distracted by daily events and pressures that so many of us don't develop character to a

point where it can bring deep rewards. One day we commit ourselves to a grand vision of what we want to do with our lives, and
the next day we're seduced by a tempting financial offer that takes
our life down another, less visionary road. One moment we're sure
we want to go our own way, and the next moment we succumb to
the pressure of family or friends who disagree with us. One
moment we commit ourselves to being loving, and the next
moment we forget all about that because someone on the street
behaves rudely to us. One moment we're all for living with high
ideals, and the next moment we're complaining to friends about
how awful the world is. What we're actually doing in that moment
is contributing to the general negativity of the world. We're filling
the atmosphere with the depression and cynicism we've imbibed
from the negative images that pass for news in the media and that
fill most people's consciousness.

In order to be able to listen to our own higher selves, we have
to become like rocks inside. We have to develop consistency, commitment and sincerity. As the story of the disciple and his master
shows, we have to refuse to let outside events get us down. We
have to develop an interest in genuine nobility and an attitude
that says it's never okay to blame our lapses in becoming everything we want to be on other people or on events around us. Our
primary focus has to be on identifying and pursuing being everything we can be regardless of circumstances. Strength of character
is about having inspiring ideals, and pursuing those ideals is what
makes life an act of passion.

Many years ago I saw a film called *Swept Away* in which two
individuals are consumed by a passionate, torrid, and rather
destructive relationship. That film was about passion in exactly
the opposite sense of what I mean here. It was about a tidal wave
hitting two people, with the result that both of them lose their
bearings and slide down a long slippery slope toward mutual misery. Real passion is not about being swept away by somebody else
or even by something else outside us. That kind of passion is what
we look for when we're bored or dissatisfied with our lives because
we don't have our own lodestar. Real passion is about being swept
away by our own inner vision. It's about cultivating a power of
commitment in our lives that becomes so strong that it takes us
through the worst situations with an unswerving directive. It's
about creating standards and beliefs for ourselves and living by

them instead of looking to someone else's standards. Passion is not something that happens to us. It is a way of living that we develop.

If we want passion, we have to focus our attention on what lifts us higher. Things that lift us higher are the only things that can hold our attention over the long term. They cultivate our capacity for commitment.

Some of the best examples of true passion are to be found in the lives of great spiritual teachers—Christ, Buddha, Mohammed and others. Such teachers were driven by a longing to find an ideal that was so inspiring that it would enable them to live a totally committed life. They fell in love with vision and wanted to be consumed by it. They gave their lives over to the service of their visions, so that nothing else mattered. Most of us are not meant to live the lives of spiritually extraordinary individuals, but we can learn from their lives about how to develop passion and override the everyday grind.

The travails of the greatest spiritual leaders of the past are to some extent buried in history, and so we may not always fully appreciate the depth of personal struggle that accompanied their search. Detailed descriptions of the experiences of more contemporary spiritual luminaries are illuminating. I remember being fascinated by the story of the Indian saint Ramakrishna who lived in the second half of the nineteenth century and who is widely recognized as one of the greatest spiritual figures of India. Ramakrishna was consumed by a desire to experience God. He drove himself relentlessly in pursuit of this experience. He prayed, meditated and engaged in numerous spiritual practices for as much as twenty-four hours a day. He hardly slept for six years in the stage of his life prior to achieving what his chroniclers have described as God-realization. That experience launched him into an almost constant state of ecstasy. Once he began collecting disciples around him, it was typical for him to teach as many as twenty hours a day, seeking to open the door of ecstasy for those who wished to learn from him.

It wasn't easy for Ramakrishna to achieve his personal connection to God. His practice of devotion was so intense that nothing less than the total experience was good enough for him. He couldn't think of anything else. It was the torture of longing for absorption in his ideal that drove him.

Today, Ramakrishna is viewed by many peoples of the world as the equivalent of a Christ or a Buddha. Yet he achieved spiritual height not just because he was gifted but also because he struggled ceaselessly to identify himself with a vision that he wanted to embody. Once he proved his devotion to that vision, it became the regulatory force in his life.

Ramakrishna's foremost disciple was a man named Vivekenanda, whose story has also been extensively chronicled. A tireless seeker, brilliant teacher, and charismatic speaker, Vivekenanda is responsible for expanding Ramakrishna's teachings from the province of a small band of disciples to a spiritual approach whose influence radiated throughout the world.

It was Vivekenanda who first brought Indian Vedantic spiritual traditions to the West. A fiery Indian monk, Vivekananda arrived as a total unknown at the World Parliament of Religions in Chicago in 1893. He managed to obtain permission to address the audience toward the end of one of its daily meetings and promptly electrified the people there with his message of universal tolerance for all religions. He rapidly developed a large following and laid the foundations in the United States for the growth of interest in eastern spirituality.

While Vivekenanda's teacher, Ramakrishna, was an ecstatic devotee of God abandoned to perpetual bliss, Vivekenanda appears more as the powerfully restless lion relentlessly in search of liberation. Yet they both also knew and taught that personal power and freedom come from ceaselessly cultivating within oneself the yearning for something higher.

Vivekenanda spoke eloquently on the importance of nourishing a focus on high personal ideals and developing indomitable willpower in the pursuit of these ideals. "Fill the brain with high thoughts, highest ideals, place them day and night before you, and out of that will come great work."[*] When we are consumed by a vision, the power of our vision helps us transform obstructions that to another person might seem insuperable into minor irritations that we brush aside in our headlong rush toward union with our ideal.

---

[*] Ed. Ann Myren and Dorothy Madison, *Living at the Source: Yoga Teachings of Vivekananda* (Boston: Shambhala, 1993), p. 85.

The key to a satisfying life lies not in finding something outside ourselves but in cultivating an inner vision that transforms us, shedding its radiance through our own lives and into the world around us. We do not become bigger and better people by wishing to be bigger and better. We become bigger and better by training ourselves to place our attention consistently, intensely and with great sincerity on the inner qualities that we think are valuable. We develop conscious passion.

Developing Conscious Passion

Conscious passion is the practice of cultivating personal vision. In order to develop passion, we have to be willing to nurture three qualities in ourselves: our power of attention, genuine sincerity, and a commitment to inner ideals.

Attention

The power of attention is critical for any meaningful achievement. If we don't have the ability to focus our attention at will, we can accomplish very little. If we do have that ability, we can shape both ourselves and the world through daily, patient perseverance, keeping our attention on doing whatever is necessary day by day and being the person we want to be moment by moment.

I remember working with a client who suffered from attention deficit disorder and who was completely unable to focus his attention at will. As he saw it, he wasn't going to be interested in something unless it was exciting, and he was easily bored. As I saw it, he was unable and unwilling to develop the attention that creates and sustains interest. Things would hypnotize his attention from one moment to the next, but he had no power to focus consciously on staying with something and training himself to become absorbed. At the age of forty-five, this bright individual with creative potential could go no further than showing brief flashes of brilliance. Not surprisingly, he was both jobless and divorced. Instead of deciding that things weren't worth his attention because he couldn't control his focus, he needed to practice training his attention. And through much work, he did in fact begin the slow process of rebuilding his life.

One of the best ways to develop our powers of attention is to focus on something that on the surface looks repetitive and boring.

The very fact that it seems repetitive and boring means that instead of being hypnotized by what we're paying attention to—which is the case with action-packed movies, suspense thrillers, and the like—we have to direct ourselves consciously toward focusing on the object of our attention. Meditation—placing our attention deliberately on observing the sensation of the breath over a period of time—is a good example of a practice that develops our power of attention by having us focus on doing something simple and repetitive. Tai Chi, in which students repeat the same movement forms day after day, month after month and year after year, is also on the surface boring and repetitive. Yet it develops extraordinary powers of attention.

If a person is looking for entertainment, he will avoid inner arts like meditation and Tai Chi. If he needs to have something grab his attention in order to stay focused, he'll go for high impact aerobics with music, suspense-filled television shows, dramatic sports events, or personal crises. Those will be guaranteed to keep his attention. The problem is that if he needs drama to hold his attention and stay focused, then he can't decide what direction he's going to go in. It's what's outside him and not what's inside him that determines his focus. He doesn't have the capacity to pay attention at will.

In a culture like ours, which neglects the inner arts, developing the power of attention is often something we get interested in only when other possibilities fail. I remember a man who came to me for visualization training to deal with an upcoming operation to remove a tumor. He was a very successful businessman, and my first impression was that he was unusually well focused. I wondered how he had come to be this way.

As we talked about his life, this man revealed to me that he had spent sixteen years of a previous marriage living with a woman who was chronically ill and who eventually died. He had loved his wife and he had had to come to grips with the fact that her illness and pain could consume him as well as her. That would have benefited neither of them. He developed an interesting practice that helped him deal successfully for many years with being in this stressful situation. The practice also incidentally improved his focus.

When he went to bed at night, this man would ward off the temptation to worry or go into depression by playing golf in his mind. He was an avid golfer and had played at clubs all over the country. He would pick a club to play at, and then go there in his mind. He would see the scenery in vivid detail, see the imaginary partners he was playing with and hear their comments, as well as play his own golf game.

When he was going through particularly hard times, this man sometimes spent several hours at a time playing golf in his mind. In addition to alleviating the pressures of his involvement with his wife's illness, this nightly practice turned him into an excellent golfer and enhanced his overall concentration in all areas of endeavor. He developed this power of attention because he understood instinctively that his ability to direct his attention away from the pain around him and toward things that sustained him would help him survive and help his wife as well. Had he not been stuck in a situation over which he had little control, he might very well not have developed the sense of focus that then served him well throughout the rest of his life. Naturally, in our work together he very quickly incorporated some new visualization techniques to deal with his cancer operation.

Like this man, who gravitated toward the practice of visualization to help himself in his life, people who have a regular and committed practice of meditation often come to that practice by learning the hard way that developing focus can change our lives in a way that nothing else can. In the 1970s, professor of medicine and author John Kabat-Zinn, who wrote the bestseller *Wherever You Go There You Are*, opened a meditation-based stress-reduction clinic at the University of Massachusetts medical center in Worcester. The patients who came to him were people who had exhausted most of the traditional medical resources available to them. They were victims of cancer, heart disease, chronic pain and anxiety disorders who had tried it all and were still suffering. Since all else failed and nothing that anyone did for them seemed to solve their problems, they were willing to work on themselves by exploring meditation techniques. Kabat-Zinn's six-week stress-reduction program required them to meditate for forty-five minutes a day, six days a week, no excuses accepted.

Most of the patients went crazy the first week. They were totally unused to focusing their attention for so long, let alone focusing it on something as boring as following their breathing. By the second week, however, patients began to feel the benefits of training their attention. They began to discover that focusing their attention at will could help them reduce physical and emotional pain, and that if they could focus deliberately on their breath for minutes at a time, they could also focus on being more relaxed, on thinking positively, on mastering difficult feelings, etc. Once they committed themselves to developing their powers of attention by focusing on something that seemed dull and repetitive, they began to achieve significant results in other parts of their lives as well. Their powers of attention spilled over.

More and more people are coming to realize that developing the ability to control their focus is a key ingredient to successful living. It is partly for this reason that inner arts like meditation, visualization and Tai Chi are growing in popularity. Any activity in which we direct our own attention over a period of time, instead of reacting to the demands of something or someone outside us, contributes to improving our power of focus. But the most powerful tools for developing attention are those that minimize external input and maximize internal input. They ask more of us. They teach us how to block out external stimuli and create our own scenario. That's real power. One of the best exercises I ever read for developing the power of attention was in Brugh Joy's book, *Joy's Way*. It's a demanding visualization exercise. Here it is:

1) Start by going into a relaxed state of mind, spending four or five minutes following your breathing and releasing tension from your body.
2) Now imagine that you can see a large, black curtain in front of you. Below the curtain is a pile of gold numbers ranging from one to one hundred. Each number is large, colored a brilliant gold, and clearly and perfectly shaped.
3) Imagine that you see two hands pick up the first number, a bright clear number one. See the hands pin it onto the curtain with a pin, leave it on the curtain for a minimum of five seconds, then take it down and pick up the next number.
4) Repeat this process until you have seen those hands pin up and take down numbers all the way from one to a hundred.

Accomplishing this exercise requires considerable skill, both because the visualization is extremely detailed and because it asks you to spend a long time creating a precise scene in your imagination while excluding distracting mental and physical stimuli. It may not be too difficult for you to get through seeing up to number ten, or twenty, although even that is quite a feat. But try going to one hundred!

Once you master this visualization process you will have greatly enhanced your overall ability to focus at will. Then you can apply that increased focus toward accomplishing things that are meaningful to you and toward becoming more of the person you want to be. You will be able to override many of the distractions that you encounter and that may sometimes discourage you from following your own path.

Sincerity

Sincerity describes a quality with which we can choose to approach life. When we're sincere, we put ourselves one hundred percent behind what we think, say and do. I once had a housemate who was well-intentioned and probably thought of herself as sincere, but in fact wasn't. Keeping the house tidy was a joint responsibility and she had a tendency to fall short on her end of that responsibility. She would fail to wash her dishes or would leave the bathroom in a mess. If she saw me cleaning up after her she invariably said, "Oh, please don't do that, I'll get to it shortly," but then she wouldn't keep her word. The next day, the dishes would still be in the sink and the bathroom would still be dirty.

My housemate felt guilty when she saw me doing things that she knew she should be doing. She said the first thing that came to mind to alleviate her own guilt. But she didn't take what she said seriously, even though she probably thought she meant what she said. She wasn't deliberately unkind, but she hardly heard herself. She couldn't follow through on what she said she would do. She may not have been intentionally insincere, but insincere she was.

In my ongoing meditation classes, sessions often start with a practice that develops personal sincerity and integrity. Everyone closes their eyes and centers themselves. Then, after some quiet time and personal reflection, we go around the room and each person shares a personal prayer about what they are hoping to create in themselves at the deepest level. As one person speaks, others listen with an attitude of reverence and with the intent of becoming one with the person who is speaking. In a recent class, for example, one participant prayed for the ability to create peace in her life as she went through a difficult divorce and a transition at work. Another prayed for greater strength in standing up for his beliefs without becoming defensive or angry. Class members sat in silence listening attentively until it was their turn to speak.

Making and honoring statements from the heart in this way, in an atmosphere of silence and mutual respect, trains people in expressing themselves with sincerity. It teaches them how to bring their inner life forward and to share its commitments. Invariably people find these practices helpful for a simple reason: we rarely practice real sincerity in our daily lives. It feels like a blessing from heaven to be able to hear other people speak from their hearts, and to be given both the opportunity and the challenge to speak from the heart ourselves. When we do this, we identify what is meaningful for us and strengthen our intention to commit ourselves to what we find meaningful.

The students in my classes practice a type of affirmation. They describe and affirm in front of each other their deep intention to be a certain kind of person. Affirmations can operate as a powerful tool for self-transformation, but their use is often misunderstood. For example, when people practice affirmations like, "My boss is giving me a raise," or, "I win the lottery," all they're doing is expressing wishes. Affirmations should be used as a vehicle for changing ourselves, not for daydreaming or for influencing the outside world. They are a conscious practice of sincerity that then becomes more strongly rooted in our lives. When we affirm to ourselves, "I am being increasingly responsible at my job," we project an intention for our own lives that involves us in raising our personal standards. We are not imagining that our thoughts influence other people to do what we want them to do, although that is how affirmations are often understood.

We should use affirmations to build a commitment to being the kinds of people we want to be. In doing this, we need to approach our practice of affirmations with respect. Simply saying, "I am a peaceful person" will not make us more peaceful if we just mouth these words mechanically. But if we practice making this statement with depth, we invoke a sense of peacefulness within ourselves at the very moment that we affirm this quality. We practice being peaceful, and it's that practice that builds our ability to become the kinds of individuals we intend to be.

Inner Ideals

The last requirement for cultivating conscious passion is a commitment to an inner ideal or inner ideals. *An inner ideal does not involve something we want to do. It represents a way of being that we wish to embody.* The more visionary the inner ideal, and the stronger a force it is in our lives, the more it acts like a personal North Star—it guides us in heading in a direction that we find fulfilling. Without inner ideals, we are rudderless in the turbulent seas of life.

The spiritual teacher Vivekenanda was fond of saying that a person's ability to live a rich life is directly dependent on the existence and force of his ideals.

> If a man with an ideal makes a thousand mistakes, I am sure that the man without an ideal makes fifty thousand. Therefore, it is better to have an ideal. And this ideal we must hear about as much as we can, till it enters into our hearts, into our brains, into our very veins, until it tingles in every drop of our blood and permeates every pore in our body.[*]

The more we align ourselves with an ideal, the more powerfully it directs us to shape our reality in accordance with our intentions while helping us to free ourselves from negative habits. Yet how can we identify what our own inner ideal or inner ideals might be? Three methods for discovering inner ideals are described below. Each of them is also further elaborated in the Suggestions for Practice at the end of the chapter.

1. Identifying an inner ideal through role models. Occasionally we meet someone whom we respect for a particular quality they possess. In this sense, that person becomes a role model for us. The quality we admire is an inner ideal because it expresses a characteristic that we would like to embody.

---

[*] Ed. Ann Myren and Dorothy Madison, *Living at the Source: Yoga Teachings of Vivekenanda* (Boston: Shambhala, 1993), p. 75.

I remember a woman in one of my classes who admired an older colleague for her unstoppable sense of adventure. She had never thought of herself as being at all adventuresome, and her family had encouraged her as a girl to be prudent and careful. When she realized that her admiration for her colleague mirrored her own unconscious need to embrace a more adventuresome life, and that this was one of her inner ideals, she took courage and let go of being hesitant in her life. She worked on releasing the past conditioning that made her excessively cautious and gave herself permission to approach life with a greater sense of fun. By identifying an ideal that had been unconscious, she accelerated her own growth and developed greater self-respect.

One woman I was working with identified Katherine Hepburn, a person of great courage and forthrightness, as her role model. Then she promptly said, "Oh, I can't be like that!" She saw herself as fearful and weak. She didn't recognize that she was drawn to Hepburn because the actress embodied qualities that she longed for herself, and that these qualities were part of her inner ideal. We often refuse to imagine that we could be what we really want to be. To make her inner ideal a reality in her life, this woman had to challenge her own self-demeaning skepticism and begin pretending to be a bit more like Katherine Hepburn. When she did pretend to be Katherine Hepburn, she found herself doing and saying things she normally would be afraid of doing and saying. She also found out that it was easier than she had thought to be more courageous.

2. *Identifying an inner ideal through recalling past experiences.* A second approach to discovering inner ideals is to remember and relive moments in our lives that have been particularly fulfilling. I will never forget coming to the close of my first marathon, in New York City. I had finally overcome my prolonged illness, and finishing the race was my symbolic celebration of that fact. As I came down the last stretch of road and saw the finish line ahead of me, I felt incredibly proud, even indomitable. In that moment, I had conquered so much that earlier in my life I never believed I could conquer. This experience taught me that part of my own personal journey lay in challenging obstacles that my mind told me I could not surmount. I realized that I had a great longing for personal strength, and that I gained strength by overcoming obstacles.

As a result of this realization, I began to make a practice of confronting my inner and outer obstacles by imagining that I embodied the strength I so wished to make a deeper part of my life. When I would feel tired, lost or depressed, I would remember the feeling of exhilaration and power that I had had during the marathon, bring that feeling to the forefront of my consciousness and let the memory become so vivid that it brought a sense of strength right into my present. I used the experience from my past to charge my present. By bringing myself back to that special moment, I would alter my consciousness, erasing the depression, tiredness or loss of focus from which I was suffering. Then I would move forward in my day from this new, stronger place inside myself.

3. Identifying an inner ideal through abstract qualities.

Imitating a role model or projecting ourselves back to a special time in our lives gives us an immediate concrete sense of an inner ideal and of what it would be like to embody that ideal. When we imagine being like someone who models joy for us, we can feel the sense of joy. When we imagine being confident the way we once were, we get a fresh taste of the confidence we once had. We can feel it. Joy or confidence become concrete, lived experiences for us. It's that concreteness that helps us become more like the ideal we want to create in our lives.

Sometimes, however, we can't find role models or experiences from our past that embody inner ideals. Peacefulness or kindness, humor or courage, love or power can all be inner ideals. We may long to make these qualities part of our daily lives yet may not have a role model or past experience that can help us translate those qualities into our experience in the depth that we desire. We may have an intellectual understanding of what words like *peace*, *love*, or *power* mean, but lack a road map to lead us to the experiences for which these words stand.

Many people go adrift just because of this gap between their intellectual understanding of a quality and their lack of real-life experience. It's easy to say that we want to express courage in our lives, but hard to do if we don't have much of an idea of what it feels like to possess that quality. Abstract words like *love*, *joy*, *peace* and *courage* also carry a lot of different meanings, and so long as they remain abstract it's hard even to know what we're looking for. Abstract terms need to be brought down to earth.

Let's say we chose the abstract quality of love as an inner ideal. To make that quality real in our lives, we would have to make it concrete. That means asking ourselves what it would *feel* like to embody love, how we would *move* if we embodied love, what we would *look* like if we embodied love, what our voice would *sound* like if we manifested our inner ideal of love. By exploring these questions we would be *concretizing* our inner ideal of love, teaching ourselves how to become love in the flesh.

Imagery can be very useful in turning abstract qualities that we want to embody into lived experiences. I remember realizing at one point that I had a tendency toward depression that I wanted to release. I asked myself what would be the opposite of depression, and the answer that came back to me was total radiance. The most radiant thing I could think of was the sun. I started keeping the image of the sun in the back of my mind as I went through my day's routine.

This exercise in imagination helped me to counteract moments of declining energy, depression and withdrawal. I noticed that in some situations, my habit was to let my energy radiate, while in others, I held it back. My mind wanted to blame my loss of energy on a boring situation or a demanding environment. But if I put my attention on feeling like the sun, the environment didn't affect me as much, and I regained my power.

The more I committed myself to my inner ideal of radiance, the more positively my energy affected not only me but also the people around me. Before I began using imagery to transform my consciousness, I might have just told myself that I should show a sunnier disposition, without feeling what that might be like. That would have made me forced, and nowhere near as effective, because words don't show you how to go where you want to go. Images do. By using a concrete image of the sun, I changed my physiology directly instead of telling myself that I should be radiant.

Cultivating an inner ideal involves creatively influencing who we *are* as opposed to what we *do*. A lot of people have a very strong desire to be good or caring people, but their ideal of loving kindness gets them in trouble. Why? Because they interpret their ideal of loving kindness in terms of what they do for people instead of what they feel like inside. Then they take on more and more responsibilities, get resentful because they are carrying too much, and end up hating themselves and everyone else. Their dispositions turn sour, and they add to the general poison of the world even while they think they are trying to be good.

It's important to remember that an inner ideal is first and foremost about our inner gardens. It's about how we experience ourselves on the inside and not about what we do. Over time, as we work on embodying our ideals, this has a powerful and healing external influence, an influence that flows naturally from who we are. That influence is pure and deep. As we become people who cherish beautiful qualities on the inside, the appropriate external actions come about naturally and almost without thought.

Manifesting Our Inner Ideals in Daily Life

Life is very short. Conscious passion assists us in making use of the time we have available. It helps us focus our attention sincerely on achieving our inner ideals, changing the world through changing ourselves. If we want to make our ideals real in our lives, we have to make them practical. We have to live them every day. Otherwise, our inner ideals stay at the level of fantasy. The whole point of conscious passion is to change the directive force of our lives. When we live with conscious passion, we decide that instead of life's events shaping us day by day, our inner ideals will shape us. We make a choice for freedom, and that choice is also a responsibility.

Manifesting ideals is a moment by moment affair. We can manifest them alone or with other people, at work or at home, in our professional lives or in play. Let's say one of our inner ideals is to develop greater peacefulness. If we feel anxious or harried while we're sitting at our desks facing a pile of paperwork, we can bring to mind the concrete image of peacefulness that embodies our ideal, and focus our attention on absorbing that image so as to help us to become more still. If we are dealing with a difficult colleague who raises our hackles, we can move toward our inner ideal by focusing on the sense of inner peace embodied in that ideal the next time we see that colleague. We use the focus on our ideal to offset the negative pull of other aspects of our personalities and of events.

Whenever we direct our attention to an inner ideal, we foster a creative conflict between our daily habits or negative patterns, and our aspirations for ourselves. We can give in to the habits, and succumb to arguing or restlessness, or we can use our focus on our ideal to release the compulsive hold of those habits. If we don't have an ideal to focus on, we're likely to stay in the rut of our own negativity. If, on the other hand, we are committed to an ideal, we give ourselves some energy for changing ourselves. We motivate ourselves to break addictive patterns that limit us.

The more we focus on using our ideals to influence specific situations in our lives, the more conscious passion we develop and the more quickly we become the people we want to be. We can also strengthen our commitment to an inner ideal by developing a clear, long-term view of what we will be like in the future, and then letting that vision draw us forward. If we can see ourselves clearly as we would like to be a few years from now, then we can utilize the energy of that perception to change ourselves day by day.

Consciously or unconsciously, we are always projecting images of our future. For many of us, these images are filled with worry and fear. We tend not to take responsibility for the power these images have. When things frequently turn out badly for us, we don't see how our negative expectations influence reality. Instead, we assume the world is against us. By learning how to project an inner ideal, we replace destructive programming with self-empowering programming and allow a vision of life's possibilities to pull us forward.

Attuning life to an inner ideal means accepting change and risk. It involves fostering a creative discomfort in our lives, a requirement that we be more than we are right now, that we stretch ourselves beyond our limits. The higher the ideal, the more tension there is between who we are and who we want to be, and the more welcome the discomfort is. It's the gap between who we are and who we want to be that gives us leverage.

The essence of right living lies in believing that our lives are so important and have so much promise that we ask more of ourselves than anyone else would ask of us. We do this not because we want to prove ourselves to anyone but because we want to be everything that we really can be.

Developing conscious passion means becoming creative artists with our lives. The artist knows that there is no right and wrong, but only life lived more or less fully. The artist never holds back because she knows that the world is as she creates it. She knows that the ultimate gift she can give to the world is herself, so she struggles to be herself as fully, openly, grandly and freely as possible. That can manifest itself in the way she walks down the street, sings a song, shows her love for the people she holds dear, or addresses an audience of ten thousand. It doesn't really matter what the setting is. What matters is that she always refuses to limit herself or to see herself as a victim. She sees herself as a creator. She also knows that creativity doesn't happen just in those special moments of splashing paint on canvas or singing a smash hit for the first time in front of a standing-room-only audience. It happens every day of our lives, and, most especially, in the small events of our lives.

Summary

In order to live passionately, we must begin by strengthening our powers of attention, since it is through our attention that we can control what we focus on. We must also develop sincerity, the capacity to mean what we say, both to ourselves and to others. With a strengthened power of attention and deep sincerity, we can then identify our inner ideals and shape ourselves into who we want to be.

The Suggestions for Practice below provide concrete tools for developing attention, sincerity, and inner ideals. By following them, you can move toward becoming the artist of your life and mastering your creative potential.

*Suggestions for Practice*_____

1. Develop Your Power of Attention. 💾

Cultivating a passionate life involves an unswerving focus on manifesting personal vision, regardless of obstacles. To develop focus is to develop attention. You cultivate attention by practicing an inner art, a discipline that strengthens the power of the mind. Follow the suggestions below, or use the visualization exercise (15 minutes) on Cassette 3 of Effortless Practice.

• To develop your attention, practice inner arts.

Try practicing any inner art in such a way that your mind is fully present to the experience. Meditate, following your breathing with profound interest; practice Tai Chi, being fully present to its graceful repetitive movements; visualize, imagining the scenes you create in great detail.

Notice how doing something simple and repetitive with total absorption increases your power of focus. Notice how inner arts ask you to eliminate from your mind the hypnotic seduction of external stimuli: personal dramas, constant activity, movies, etc. Notice how, when you can follow your breathing for minutes at a time, or absorb yourself in a martial art form, or visualize at will, you have developed a power of attention that you can then transfer to achieving anything you want to achieve. You have developed the power of your mind.

2. Practice Sincerity. 🔲

Being sincere means putting yourself one hundred percent into what you say and do. It is one of the most important abilities you can develop. Follow the suggestions below, or use the related exercise (10 minutes) on Cassette 4 of Effortless Practice.

• Use affirmations to practice sincerity.

To develop your sincerity, begin by using meditative breathing to go into a deep state of relaxation. This eliminates superficial distractions and helps you focus on meaning what you say when you say it. Then, from your quiet and centered state, bring to mind your deepest wish for the kind of person you would like to be, and express that as an affirmation. Examples might be, "I am strong and determined," or, "I am peaceful and loving." As you say the words of your affirmation, feel their truth in your heart. Imagine being the person you describe, and make a secret contract with yourself to be that way throughout the day. During the day, recall your affirmation and your contract with yourself. Seek to be the person your affirmation describes.

Notice that the more you cherish the wish you express in your affirmation, the more likely it is to become a reality.

3. Develop Inner Ideals. 🔲

An inner ideal is not about what you want to do. It is about how you want to be. By focusing on an inner ideal, you strengthen your ability to become the person you want to be, and to influence others through the quality of your character. To develop inner ideals, begin by exploring one or several of the exercises below, or use the related exercises (20 minutes) on Cassette 4 of Effortless Practice.

• Identify an inner ideal through role models.

Pick a situation in your life that you would like to deal with more constructively. Then think about how someone you know might deal with that situation in a way that you admire. What is the quality in that person that you admire? In what regard is that person a role model for you? Pretend that you have the quality you respect in that person. How would you behave? Repeat this process in other situations, and allow yourself to choose different role models for different qualities you would like to develop. Imitate the qualities you admire shamelessly.

Notice that people you respect embody qualities that you are consciously or unconsciously seeking to embody in yourself. The particular quality that you admire in someone else represents an inner ideal. Be aware that each time you allow yourself to imitate a quality you admire in someone else, you grow into more of who you really want to be. Notice how imitating the quality you admire in a role model changes the way you feel and act in a situation. Notice how powerful a tool it can be for self-transformation.

• Identify an inner ideal through a past peak experience.

Remember a time or event in your past when you felt especially good—particularly strong, confident, loving, peaceful, etc. Go back to that experience in your mind. What year was it? What were you doing? Who were you with? Close your eyes and relax into your breathing, and when you are fully relaxed, return in your imagination to that peak experience from the past. Project yourself into the scene, so that you can see the things you saw, hear the things you heard, feel the way you felt at the time. Put yourself right back there, as if you were reliving it. What do you see around you? Let the images be vivid, clear and life-size.

Become aware of how you feel in your body. Is it a peaceful feeling? A feeling of strength and self-confidence? Of pride? Let the feeling become clearer and clearer, until it permeates your entire body. This feeling is an inner ideal for you, it represents the way you feel when you feel best. As you open your eyes, see if you can hold on to this feeling. Repeat this exercise regularly, until you can recall at will the special feeling you had during your peak experience. Then practice incorporating this feeling of strength, confidence, love, peacefulness, etc. into your daily activities.

Notice that by going back to peak experiences in your mind, you are developing the ability to remember the way you felt when you were at your best, and to bring that feeling into your present. By revisiting positive past experiences, you cultivate your ability to be at your peak all the time.

• Identify an inner ideal by picking a quality you like and making it concrete.

Identify a quality that you want to manifest in your life: love, joy, abundance, courage, strength, fearlessness, faith, trust, or any other quality that appeals to you. Ask yourself what it would *feel* like to embody the quality you have chosen. Trust whatever feeling responses come up. They tell you what your inner ideal is like on a feeling level. Ask yourself how you would *move* if you expressed the quality you have chosen. Close your eyes and move or dance around the room in a way that expresses the quality you have chosen. Ask yourself what you would *look* like if you embodied the quality you have chosen. Stand in front of a mirror, and let yourself express the quality you have chosen through your eyes, your expression, your gestures. Ask yourself what your voice would *sound* like if you embodied your inner ideal. Play with letting your voice express the quality you have chosen as your ideal. Commit yourself to feeling, moving, looking and sounding like the quality you have explored, as you go through your day.

Notice that as you explore your ideal in this way, you are concretizing it, teaching yourself how to embody the quality you love in the flesh. When you devote your attention to creating your inner ideal, you invoke the way of feeling, moving, sounding and looking that this ideal embodies, and you make these part of your life.

4. Manifest Your Inner Ideals in Daily Life. 📼

To turn your ideals from vision into reality, practice making them concrete. Follow the suggestions below, or use the related exercise (10 minutes) on Cassette 4 of Effortless Practice.

• Use your inner ideals deliberately to influence specific situations.

Sit down every morning for a few minutes, to preview your day. First relax yourself through following your breathing. Then affirm slowly and sincerely your intention to manifest the inner ideal that is currently important for you. Cherish that inner ideal in your heart. Then imagine the events of the day ahead, picturing what will happen as the day unfolds. As you do this, vividly see yourself manifesting your inner ideal during the events of the day. Go through scene by scene, so that you imagine quite clearly what will happen with specific individuals and situations. Feel how you will feel, see what you will see, hear what you will hear, as you go about being the kind of person you want to be.

Close by affirming to yourself that you will make real what you have imagined. Then, as you go through the day, periodically bring to mind how you imagined yourself being. Keep it in the back of your mind to inspire you. At the end of the day, review what actually happened.

Notice how, if you commit yourself to a visualization of how you want to be, you change the way you deal with situations. Are you gentler, stronger, more courageous, or more fun-loving? Notice to what extent you are able during the day to let your inner ideal help and guide you. Are you able to move yourself out of some negative patterns more easily than you might have otherwise? Notice the impact you have on other people when you commit yourself to living by your inner ideals.

Suggested Reading

Charles Garfield, *Peak Performance* (New York: Warner, 1984). An excellent book on mental training techniques utilized by world-class athletes. The book includes detailed exploration of how to use visualization to improve focus.

George Leonard, *Mastery* (New York: Penguin, 1992). Extremely readable study on how to develop the steadiness of purpose that leads to mastery of living.

Henry Reed, *Edgar Cayce on Channeling Your Higher Self* (New York: Warner, 1989). One of the best, most straightforward and least pretentious books ever written on how to cultivate inner ideals.

chapter 12

Creativity and Shifting Perspective

It wasn't an unusual day, and it wasn't a great day. It was one of those typical days that were all too familiar to me years ago. I was no longer sick in bed. I was back at work, but my back bothered me constantly. Every time I stood up from a chair I hurt, and I had to pause to loosen up before going into motion. I felt discouraged. I had done plenty of physical therapy and movement therapy and was on a super healthy diet, but things weren't exactly improving rapidly. I was so tired of the pain.

As I sat at my desk, I found myself thinking wistfully about the actress Audrey Hepburn, a woman who for me has always been the epitome of grace and lightness. No one could move as ethereally as Audrey Hepburn. Then the idea popped into my head that I might imagine what it was like to be her. She was so different from me, especially at this point of my life! In my imagination, I saw that beautiful, angelic creature sitting on a chair with her eagerly childlike body and radiant smile. Then I imagined her rising gracefully and effortlessly out of the chair, and as she did so, I also rose out of my own chair—*painlessly*! I was stunned. It was the first time in months that I had stood up free of pain. What had happened? This was an experiment I had to try again!

And so I did try it again—about thirty times that day. I sat down in my chair, imagined Audrey Hepburn sitting in her chair, and at the very moment that I saw her getting up in her light and gracious manner, I also stood up. Sometimes my own pain disappeared when I did this. Sometimes it didn't. What was the difference between one experience and the other? As I explored, I realized that the times I got up painlessly were times that I forgot about my own body completely and was totally involved in the image of Audrey Hepburn. It was when I let go of myself and saw the actress vividly and continuously in my mind that my body went to another level and felt freer.

I had just discovered that focusing intensely on an image of how you want to be in your body can produce astonishing effects. I started pretending to be Audrey Hepburn at every moment of the day. I couldn't do it tentatively if I wanted to get results. I had to do it all the way. I really had to be Audrey Hepburn, ridiculous as that seemed.

I also started experimenting with other visualizations. I bought videotapes of dancers and Yoga teachers—people who moved powerfully, freely and gracefully. I watched the tapes, absorbing the movements and imagining what it must feel like to be those people. I held in my own mind an image of a dancer moving when I walked down the street or went from room to room in my house, and I imagined feeling and looking as she must feel and look. I saturated myself with the visual and physical feel of strong, healthy and free people. I was trying to override the familiar program that I had held in my mind for years, a program that identified my body with restriction, limitation and pain. By changing my program I changed my body.

I learned some important lessons from these early experiments with using imagination for self-healing. The biggest lesson was that *our imaginations can affect our physiology and biology far more profoundly than any act of conscious will*. I might decide with my mind that I wanted to move freely, but that decision wouldn't necessarily get me there. I could do exercises, try to move correctly in ways that physical therapists had told me to move, but still the results were limited. Conscious intention and effort were important, but they didn't open the door wide enough.

Imagination, however, brought a whole new dimension of power into my life. The images I held in my mind taught my body how to move effectively in a way that I could never teach myself. My unconscious mind took in the information encoded in the images of graceful movement and transformed that information into physiological and biochemical input.

My experiments also taught me that the more vividly and continuously I kept images in my mind, the more they would help me. It wasn't enough to use an image once or twice, or to spend fifteen minutes a day visualizing what I wanted. My images of healing had to be intense and ongoing because that was the only way they could replace the images that I held unconsciously and that committed me to pain. It was when I discovered that I could shift my perspective, imagining a better reality, that I also realized I had unwittingly cherished a vision of myself as incapacitated. Shifting perspective brought to light my unconscious program.

When we develop the ability to shift perspective we can approach our lives as creative artists. If we can't shift perspective, we can't identify the boundary between what we're causing in our lives and what is beyond our control. It gets too easy to assume that something external is causing the difficulty, or that we aren't contributing to creating whatever we are suffering from.

Learning how to shift perspective helps people to identify where their responsibility and power are. By shifting perspective, they change the way they respond internally to a situation. That means changing the way they picture themselves in that situation, changing the way they feel inside their bodies, changing the way they talk to themselves, etc. They imagine being different, and then observe how that changes things inside and around them. Imagination expands the options. It helps people to let go of unconscious patterns that are not life supporting and to embrace patterns that empower them.

Imagination and Self-Healing

A colleague of mine named Mitchell May once shared a dramatic story about his own use of imagery for healing. Mitchell entered the field of alternative healing as a result of a prolonged crisis in his own life. In 1972, at the age of twenty-one, he sustained devastating injuries in a head-on car collision. Although he was pronounced dead on arrival at the local hospital, the emergency medical squad managed to get his heart working again. He remained in a coma for a week. His left leg was broken in six places. His right leg had endured forty fractures. The knee and ankle joints of his right leg were destroyed, he had lost several inches of bone, and most of the muscle and nerve tissue of the lower legs was gone. After consultation, the doctors agreed that there was no way to save the right leg, and that it had to be amputated. Mitchell refused the amputation.

Over the next several months, Mitchell stayed in intensive care, hovering in and out of consciousness while over forty doctors from numerous hospitals concurred on the need for amputation and sought to persuade him to give his assent. Despite massive infection that was eating away at his internal organs, Mitchell still refused. Even though he was close to death, he felt that something was telling him that he had suffered this injury in order to learn from it.

In despair, Mitchell's parents sought help outside the traditional medical profession. They contacted a healer named Jack Gray, who was on the staff of the parapsychology research laboratory at the University of California in Los Angeles. The first evening that Jack visited Mitchell, he worked on the patient's body using his deep understanding of healing energy. Mitchell had been in unrelenting pain since his accident months before. The pain had been so great that drugs were not able to alleviate it. That night, however, he experienced temporary relief for the first time. Mitchell recounts that one of the first things Jack told him was that he possessed within himself all the resources necessary for his own healing. For just a moment, he fully understood and accepted what the healer was telling him. Jack visited Mitchell daily after that and the patient's healing process began.

Over the next four years, Mitchell recovered the full use of both legs, something that all the doctors involved in the case had said was impossible. His recovery was described as a medical miracle. While Jack employed many techniques with Mitchell, he did not heal him so much as teach him how to heal himself. According to Mitchell, this teaching essentially involved him in learning how to release his identification with his trauma and to change his life story. If he identified with the wounded part of himself, then all he had access to was fear, pain and doubt. If he identified with his larger self, then he could tap into limitless creativity and healing power.

Mitchell worked on imagining how he wanted to be. For example, when he was unable to walk and wore casts the length of his legs, he played "kick the can"—a sport from childhood—in his imagination. He imagined not only seeing himself playing but feeling the sensation of kicking the can. He utilized his kinesthetic imagination to counter the atrophy that was setting into his legs. He overrode reality with his imagination. After his own recovery and a number of years apprenticing with Jack Gray, Mitchell became a healer in his own right.

Imagining something with all our hearts and souls is a precondition for achieving it. The opposite is also true: not being able to imagine having what we want may guarantee that we don't get it. I had a client with neurological problems whose health was slowly improving through our sessions. After we had been working together for a number of months, Jim came in one day, saying that he was feeling exceptionally well, and that our work was giving him greater control over his own life. The next week, however, he came in with a different story. He said he was feeling poorly, as bad as ever if not worse. Jim wondered if he would ever get well.

I was curious to see that just after Jim had reached the point where he felt better than he had in years, he plummeted to feeling worse. Had he sabotaged himself? I asked him if he had a vision of being well—of what he would look and feel like when he was healthy. Jim said no, he had never thought of that. He did say, however, that he *wished* and *hoped* he would get well. Wishing and hoping, however, presuppose doubt, and doubt implies defeat.

As we talked, I realized that Jim demonstrated his doubt every morning. He would wake up and check himself to see if he was feeling better or worse, moving more easily or less easily. I know what it's like to check yourself, especially if you have had health problems and are nervous about your health. I used to check myself all the time. But when we do this, we're acting from a place of fear, and that fear affects how we feel. We also assume that we have no control over how we feel, that how we feel is something that just happens to us. And that's not true. In order to get well, people have to commit their minds very actively to their health. They have to see what they want, and embrace it as though it were already theirs, coaxing their bodies to follow suit.

Instead of embracing where he wanted to go—a state of full health—Jim was fearful that he wouldn't get there. He was mentally sabotaging himself. Merely hoping that his health would improve was a little like getting into the car to drive to a destination without a map for getting there, and hoping that the road he was on was going in the right direction. It was inefficient.

Jim needed to see himself where he wanted to be. He needed an image of what health might be like, and then he had to take responsibility for aligning himself with that image. He had to use his mind as a tool for guiding his body to total health, and to be healthy in his imagination as a precondition for being healthy in reality. His best option for doing that was to identify with positive experiences that made him feel alive.

Jim and I explored what experiences he could use that might help him identify himself with radiant health. Jim had a picture of himself with his son from years earlier. It had been a good time in his life, and in the picture Jim looked fit and healthy. He decided to recall how he felt back then and to identify with the sense of vitality that came up. Jim also had a special love for the ocean, which gave him a feeling of energy and power. He instinctively went to the ocean to be calmed, strengthened and revitalized. In our session, he reaccessed the feelings the ocean raised in him by imagining being at the ocean.

By imagining being at the ocean, and by vividly remembering a time in his life when he felt terrific, Jim reminded his body of what it felt like to feel good. He got both a concrete feeling of what health might include and a tool for pointing himself toward his goal. When he worked with keeping those images in his mind, he shifted the way he felt inside, supporting his physiology into becoming more dynamic. He began to break the pattern of fear that was undermining his health. He took responsibility for having a map of the road to wellness and driving in the direction he wanted to go.

Imagination in Everyday Life

Unconscious negative images can affect any area of our lives. I once worked with a golf player who tended to hook balls to the left when he drove off the tee. He had taken endless lessons to improve his golf swing, but they only helped him marginally. He still had a persistent hook to the left. After putting him into a deep state of relaxation, I guided him through a visualization in which he was to see himself making a clean, straight swing, and observe the ball loop gracefully upwards and out, in a line going directly out from the imaginary tee. He discovered to his surprise that he couldn't do this. His automatic tendency was to see the ball hooking. Since his unconscious program directed the ball to the left, it was no wonder he couldn't hit it straight! He had to work on changing his mental program, and with a little time and patience he was able to do this. Once he could see an image of a golf ball flying straight instead of hooking, his golf performance also improved.

Years ago, I used visualization to deal with an extremely difficult relationship with a tenant of a house I owned in New York City. I had moved out and begun renting the two floors as individual apartments while I put the house on the market. I was new at the rental business, and quite naive. I failed to ask for references from the thirty-five-year-old female pharmacist to whom I rented the top floor of the house. I found out my error soon enough, but not soon enough to avoid financial difficulties and personal turbulence.

This woman, whom I'll call Ava, was a professional rent evader. Over the previous three years she had been evicted from two apartments after long periods of refusing to pay rent. Tenant laws being what they are in New York City, Ava had developed an effective method for lowering her cost of living.

Ava also had severe psychological problems. She was the one who was taking advantage of me, but she genuinely perceived me, along with everyone else in the world, as her tormentor. Substance abuse made her mood swings worse. In addition to refusing to pay rent, she changed the lock on the apartment and wouldn't let me in when I wanted to show the house to prospective buyers. She turned hysterical at the drop of a hat, and telephoned me at all times of the day and night, screaming that I was doing something terrible to her or that the tenants below were torturing her. I was furious at her, and our phone conversations degenerated into mutual shouting matches.

I couldn't handle the financial stress and emotional upheaval. I began to envisage draconian measures. Should I find someone to throw Ava out of the house? That, of course, was illegal. Should I break down the door and put out all her belongings while she was at work? That too might get me in trouble. My fantasies only fed my anxiety and anger. Eventually, I decided to try an alternative tack.

Every afternoon I would sit down in a quiet place by myself, coax myself into a state of relaxation, and visualize Ava. I visualized seeing her heart and addressing her heart to heart. I imagined myself addressing and reaching the solid and good part of Ava, overcoming the fearful side. I visualized myself talking to her, and being warm and open and in my own heart—a state that certainly wasn't my habit when I spoke with her.

Once I had trained myself to visualize my interactions with Ava in this way, the next step was to use my imagination proactively while I was actually dealing with her: when I had to talk to her about the rent (she was by now four months behind), and when she called with a threatening or hysterical message about the downstairs occupants or the next door neighbors. I tried to see her heart center as I talked to her, and to imagine us talking calmly. I reacted less to her provocative behavior. As for her, she had been so used to people treating her with hostility on account of her own paranoid behavior that she was completely taken aback by my increased calmness, my neutrality and what she must have experienced as my kindness. I won her heart.

Something happened deep down inside Ava. She no longer wanted to avoid paying rent, even though from a legal perspective she could certainly do that with impunity for a number of months. As a result, five months after I began visualizing my talks with Ava, she was fully paid up in her rent. She actually came to like me so much that she gave me a birthday present, and despite all our difficulties, I came to like Ava as well. I saw that she was a wounded animal, and that underneath the wounds was a person who really did have a heart.

Ava also allowed me to show her apartment to potential buyers, and eventually I sold the house. Unfortunately, the day after the sale was completed, Ava had a confrontation with her new landlords. She stormed through the house threatening to perform dire acts with a hammer and a large kitchen knife. The police were called, Ava was detained in the local jail, and I lost track of her.

The sad end to Ava's occupancy of what had been my house only highlights the true strength of the power of the imagination. When I held to a story between the two of us that was different from the story of anger and mutual abuse that Ava was used to, she was able to shift into being a new person. She was grateful for being treated as a decent human being, and instead of being manipulative, she did her best to respond in kind. She broke her long-standing pattern of rent abuse and emotional violence. But she wasn't able to trust that she could be decent with everyone and receive kind treatment in return. When we parted ways, she reverted to her self-destructive behavior.

Building Visualization Skills

Visualization enables us to change how we experience ourselves and how we treat the world around us. Since it can generate powerful results, it is unfortunate that few people know how to visualize in more than a rudimentary fashion. Schools don't encourage the use of the inner eye, and by the time most of us are adults, we are so hooked on linear thinking that we can no longer tune in to our imaginations. Like everything else, the imagination suffers from lack of use.

Visualization is not limited to seeing things with the imagination. It is coextensive with the imaginary use of any or all of our sensory modalities: seeing, hearing, feeling, smelling and tasting. Everyone visualizes in a different way. Some people visualize with brilliant detailed images; others may have less vivid images, or have feelings, sensations or sounds associated with visualization. Anyone interested in visualization should start their own visualization training without preconceptions about whether they are good visualizers. We all naturally have vivid imaginations. If we are not in touch with ours, then it just needs to be reawakened. The main guideline in developing visualization skills is to stay away from *thinking about* things in our minds and to stay with *experiencing* them in our imaginations. Visualization is not about analyzing, but about sensing—seeing, feeling, hearing, tasting, smelling, etc.

Books and tapes on visualization are a dime a dozen. Unfortunately, they often lack sufficiently concrete and systematic training tips to enable a person to visualize to maximum advantage. Through my studies, my own experience, and the experiences of hundreds of clients, I have determined that there are four stages in learning to reawaken the imagination and to use visualization effectively. Detailed exercises for these can be found in the Suggestions for Practice at the end of this chapter.

Stage One: Practicing Perceiving

For those of us who have let our imaginations lie dormant for a long time, the first stage in developing visualization skills consists in practicing with what is right around us. When I first noticed that I was constantly thinking and talking to myself, and could rarely see things in my mind's eye, I trained myself to stop thinking and start seeing by closing my eyes and imagining the room around me. I would try to recall the exact shape of the room, the objects it contained, the windows, the colors, etc. Then I would open my eyes and check what I had imagined against the actual room. Initially I was surprised and embarrassed by how much I had missed. I was equally surprised, however, at how quickly my skills developed. And as my inner sight improved, I added other senses. I imagined how the floor would feel under my feet, or what different objects would feel like if I picked them up.

Imagining what is right around us helps us utilize feedback from our eyes, our sense of touch and other senses to improve the accuracy of our internal perception. Then it is only a step from visualizing what is literally in front of our eyes to visualizing what is familiar to us, but not directly in front of us. Sometimes, when I lay in bed at night, I would imagine walking through my entire house, noticing furniture, pictures, curtains, sounds, smells and textures. I also strengthened my inner eye by reviewing in my imagination things that I had done during the day. I would play back to myself my morning run, or a conversation with a friend. I would re-create them in my mind, replaying the sights, sounds, smells and textures of the events.

The first stage of visualization training thus consists in learning to see with our inner eyes the things and events in our immediate surroundings.

Stage Two: Practicing Imagining

The second stage of visualization training consists in creating genuinely imaginary scenes in our mind's eye. Many of us remember the experience, as children, of being transported to another world when our parents read us stories. We not only heard the words of the stories, we saw the events they described. As adults, we may still experience these imaginary worlds when we read gifted authors. We are creating scenes in our mind's eye.

Maximizing our creative abilities depends on using our imaginations constantly in this way. I trained my ability to create imaginary scenes at will by deliberately trying to see, hear and feel scenes and events that I read about. I also would script passages for myself and then project them in my imagination. For example, I would imagine myself walking down a country road in Vermont on a late afternoon, a light breeze fanning my hair and the sun beating on my face. The more detail I could put into my imaginary scenes, the more my focus and visualization abilities improved.

Stage Three: Changing Ourselves through Visualization

Being able to visualize clearly and at will is the key to using our imaginations proactively. Training ourselves in the first two stages of visualization ensures success in the third and most important stage of training. This involves working with our imaginations to create what we want to have in our lives. This has nothing to do with making things happen by wishing them. Visualizing winning the lottery is unlikely to make that happen. Effective visualization is generally not about directly influencing the shape of events around us by imagining them to be as we would like them to be. It is more about influencing the shape of events around us by imagining ourselves the way we would like to be.

Change happens outside us because we transform ourselves inside. We affect events through the impact our own internal changes have on people around us. By becoming different ourselves, we encourage others to respond in kind, and through this indirect impact on others, we influence the events of our lives.

When I visualized a change of relationship with Ava, the woman who had rented my house and who refused to pay her rent, I focused not so much on what I wanted her to be like as on how I wanted myself to be. I tried to change myself by imagining how I could feel in her presence, how I could perceive her, and how I could behave with her. I used visualization to let go of my own negative reactions to her, reactions that only fueled her negativity. This visualization exercise was effective in diffusing a tense situation and establishing communication. But that was not because I imagined Ava reacting differently or because I cast some kind of inner spell. I encouraged Ava to behave differently by behaving differently myself, and I accomplished this by reprogramming myself through visualization. Then, when Ava responded to me by letting go of her paranoia, I no longer had a problem with rent payments. We are always in a feedback loop with other people, influencing them and being influenced by them, and it is by making internal changes in ourselves that we get the world around us to change.

Practicing visualization can reveal a great deal to us about the assumptions we bring to our interactions, and about the way we unconsciously shape events. Let's say we want to use visualization to improve a relationship with someone with whom we are having conflict. The first thing to do is to notice what comes up when we imagine being in the presence of this person. If we feel tense, angry or afraid, then these form our automatic program around that person. They represent the way we feel about this person now and our projection of future interactions.

When we experience tension while thinking about someone, we may be inclined to say that this is because that person is causing us tension. But that isn't accurate. The person we are thinking of isn't anywhere near us, and still we feel tense! It is our associations to the person that are causing us tension. There may be reasons for these associations in our past, but nonetheless our associations are ours alone, and no one else is responsible for them. While we are influenced by our past, how we feel in the present can be independent of the past if we so choose.

In order to become creative, we have to be able to program ourselves to feel the way we want to feel, and not to let our associations with past experiences determine our present and future. After all, if we feel tense merely while thinking about someone, we can be sure that the next time we run into that person we will have a tense interaction. That's what happens to most of us everyday. Then we turn around and say, "He made me so tense!" But that's not it. We make ourselves tense through our own expectations and then find an explanation for that tension in other people and external events. It's simple: anticipating a negative interaction heightens its probability, and anticipating a positive interaction heightens its probability. Once we understand this rule, then we have to learn to use it in a way that is constructive for us. That is what visualization is about: becoming constructive in the way we see ourselves in the future.

If we recognize how we unconsciously bring a negative influence into our interactions with someone by anticipating that we will feel angry, hurt or fearful in that person's presence, we can shift things by focusing on how we want to feel with that person, as opposed to how we have programmed ourselves to feel. Our visceral reactions to other people are strong determinants in our behavior. In reprogramming ourselves, we need to pay special attention to how we want to *feel* in the presence of other people.

If our immediate reaction in thinking of someone with whom we have conflict is to tighten up, we need to practice imagining feeling comfortable while we're in that person's presence. This can be quite a challenge. When I used to work on altering my reaction to someone toward whom I had conflicted or angry feelings, I would start by visualizing myself in a very comfortable or soothing environment. I'd see and feel myself floating in water, or looking at the stars at night, to get in touch with a deep sense of peace. Then I would bring the image of the person whom I associated with conflict into my space of peace. I'd try to feel the peace of nature even while I thought of that person. In this way, I gradually shifted myself out of the feelings of tension that I automatically associated with that person. I learned to connect being peaceful with thinking of that individual. Eventually, visualization changed my behavior with that person and improved our relationship.

Neuro-Linguistic Programming, popularly called NLP, teaches a useful technique for altering our conditioned negative responses to people. The first step is to get yourself into a relaxed frame of mind by meditating, or perhaps imagining yourself in a pleasant and soothing environment. Then let yourself see in your mind's eye a small picture of a person who causes you distress. The picture must be so small, and so far away from you, that it creates no visceral reaction of tension in you. It is just too insignificant. Once you can do this, then begin to make the picture of that person larger and bring it closer to you. Do this at a pace where you can stay comfortable inside. If bringing the picture closer starts to bring up your tension reaction, then back off and move more gradually. Eventually, you will reach the point where you can be totally calm while holding a life-size picture of the person in your mind. When you can do this, you have changed your conditioned response to the person in question. You will feel a lot freer in your dealings with that person.

The stronger our visualizations, the more we can influence our own internal programs and shift ourselves into an empowered state. To make our visualizations powerful, we have to use them frequently. In addition, the more detailed they are, the more effective they are. Can we not only see, but also feel, hear, taste or smell ourselves and the situation we envisage? And are we inside or outside the scene we imagine? When we are outside the scene, it is as though we were watching ourselves in a movie. We are seeing ourselves as we want to be. When we are inside the scene, we are an actor in the movie, feeling how we would like to feel in the situation we envision. In the first case, we are disassociated from what we are imagining. In the second, we are associated.

We should be able to shift back and forth between these two approaches, each of which has its strengths and weaknesses. The strength of watching ourselves from the outside—being disassociated—is that it helps us develop the detachment that's important for emotional self-mastery. It also enhances our ability to see how other people see us. The weakness of the disassociated approach is that it doesn't get us directly in touch with bodily feelings since we are outside our bodies observing ourselves. And it may be a good idea for us to get in touch with those feelings because they can be empowering. It was a good idea for me to get in touch with how I imagined Audrey Hepburn felt inside, because imagining how she felt inside changed the way I felt inside, and reduced my pain. I practiced having an associated image of her. I did not simply see her in my imagination. I pretended I *was* Audrey Hepburn.

The strength of associated images—when we are *in* the movie we are imagining rather than *watching* that movie—is that these images help us get more in touch with the experience of being in the altered state we are seeking. The weakness of associated images is that if we are the type of person who associates all the time, we probably have a tendency to get too identified with our feelings. When we identify with our feelings a lot, it can be hard to free ourselves from the negative ones we want to change, and to move into an altered state identified with more useful feelings.

Learning to disassociate, to see ourselves from the outside, helps us let go of emotions with which we are overly identified. It gives us more flexibility. If we can learn to shift between associated and disassociated imagery, we get the benefits of both. We can use disassociation—see ourselves from the outside—when we need to remove ourselves from strong reactive feelings, and use association—feel how we might want to feel on the inside—to learn more about feelings we want to enhance.

Stage Four: Building Commitment

The fourth stage in building visualization skills involves developing commitment and discipline. Changing our conditioned responses through visualization takes persistent, patient practice. We can't just occasionally visualize how we want to be; we have to do it regularly. Our positive visualizations have to be constant partners in our lives, until they influence us so deeply that we become who we want to be.

Whether we know it or not, we are all constantly visualizing. The brain never stops sending subliminal messages. The question is whether those messages are constructive or not. Our goal in visualization is to use that activity of the brain positively, to access our right-brain creative potential and put it at our service. By making visualization a staple of our lives, we tune in to our underutilized potential. Most creative people use constructive visualization spontaneously and constantly as a matter of habit. It's a good habit to develop.

The Limits of Visualization: Our Bodies

The famous movement educator, Moshe Feldenkrais, developed some exercises for his students that demonstrated the power of visualization. He showed that one can use visualization to obtain all the physical benefits of stretching without actually doing any stretching.

One way Feldenkrais demonstrated this was to have his students lie down and go through a series of gentle stretching movements on the left side of their bodies, getting in touch with how their bodies felt as they did this. He directed students specifically to feel the movements, and then to notice how much their left sides opened up, relaxed, stretched and realigned. Then Feldenkrais would lead his students through exactly the same exercises on the right side of their bodies. This time, however, they performed the exercises *in their imaginations only*.

When they had finished doing the exercises on the right side in their imaginations, the students would notice how the right sides of their bodies felt and moved. Typically, they found that their right sides had benefited at least as much from doing the exercises in their imaginations as their left sides had from actually doing the same exercises. In fact, the right sides often felt significantly better. By imagining the feeling of their muscles going through specific changes, the students changed their physiologies and gave themselves a full workout.

The imagination can work wonders. But it can only work wonders if it has a rich fund of material from which to draw. That's why Moshe Feldenkrais had people stretch the left sides of their bodies before imagining stretching the right side. By the time they started their visualizations, they knew exactly what it felt like to move their bodies in the way they wanted to imagine. The information was stored in their memories from actually stretching their left sides. They then utilized that information to visualize a similar experience on their right sides. If they hadn't had this physiological imprint in their memories, their visualizations would have had less impact because they would have been vague. As an analogy, imagine a thirty-five-year-old couch potato trying to mobilize himself into action by visualizing himself as an energetic dynamo such as tennis star Andre Agassi. If his body is really acclimatized to lethargy, the couch potato's visualization might not get him far. He might not know how to access the feeling of energy, even though he might like to.

It's partly because our powers of visualization are limited by our experience that the person who has been chronically ill from infancy has a harder fight than the person who becomes ill after twenty years of radiant health. A person who has some experience of health to draw on can utilize that experience as a resource, but someone with no experience needs to search more deeply to find healing.

If we are missing experiences that open up higher possibilities for us, that limitation will affect every area of our lives. We may unconsciously short-change ourselves by asking for less than we can actually have. In my work I frequently notice that many people do not dare to envisage radiant health for themselves, in part because they have never experienced it. Their bodies are degraded by emotional suffering compounded by a diet of over-processed foods and chemical additives. They assume that they are as healthy as they can be, or even that they are healthy, when the truth is that they are far from being truly healthy. Low standards of experience lead to low expectations. As a result, people often neither envisage nor strive for the radiant health that is their birthright.

Similar comments can be made about our culture's emotional health. Levels of depression, anger and grief in our society are extraordinarily high. Too many people assume that the way they feel is the norm. They lose sight of alternatives. And since emotions are patterned in the body in the way people hold themselves and move, the body has no memory of better alternatives on which to draw, and no way to change.

Higher forms of intelligence, creativity and expanded states of awareness are, like physical health and emotions, experienced through the body. We can deny ourselves physical health and emotional strength through our failure to experience these as real options. We can also suppress our creativity and higher intelligence if we have not courted the experience of these states. Our mass culture pays virtually no attention to the centuries of tradition—most of it embodied in ancient spiritual texts and practices—that tell us how to develop expanded states of awareness and greater creativity. Yet anyone who persistently pursues the development of higher powers can achieve these. It is absolutely critical for each of us to open the door within ourselves to our higher potential.

We need to look at how we restrict our possibilities because of our own limited experience. We need to explore nutritional alternatives and exercise to see if they can heighten our vitality. We need to explore bodywork to change the way we live and move in our bodies, and to access renewed grace and power. We need to explore expanded states of perception, so as to increase our brain's potential. The more we explore, the more resources we have that can serve as a basis for moving ourselves through visualization into the lives we want. As long as we are curious about the possibilities that experience holds for enriching our lives, then visualization can give us the power to evolve infinitely.

Summary

The brain visualizes constantly, but does it visualize constructively? Do we focus on what we want, or do we focus on what we fear? Creativity involves our ability to visualize ourselves as we want to be, rather than as we fear being.

This chapter has explored four stages in the development of creative visualization skills. The first stage activates the inner eye. In this stage, we train ourselves to see in our imagination places, objects and events familiar to us from everyday life. The second stage builds on the first. In it we develop our ability to imagine not only real scenes from our actual life but also fictional scenes. The third stage applies the strength built through stages one and two to visualizing ourselves as we wish to be. In this stage, we learn to reprogram our automatic reactions to people and situations in ways that are more empowering to us. Through reprogramming our reactions, we also influence events around us. The fourth stage involves the regular, daily practice of visualization. We practice constructive visualization until it has become so much a part of our lives that it is automatic. At this stage we no longer have to think about seeing ourselves and our lives as we wish them to be. Instead, we do that spontaneously. We eliminate negativity and fear from our lives.

Exercises for the four stages of visualization training are outlined in the Suggestions for Practice that follow.

Suggestions for Practice_____

1. Explore Developing Your Mind's Eye. 🖳

Personal creativity depends on the ability to shift perspective. You have to be able to visualize a change in yourself with such intensity that you energize that change into existence, displacing an old habit or perspective. Your ability to change yourself through powerful, creative imagery depends on developing a more basic skill of seeing with your mind's eye. You do this by closing your eyes and inwardly seeing what is right around you. Follow the text below or use the exercise (10 minutes) provided on Cassette 5 of Effortless Practice.

• Practice seeing with your eyes closed.

Sit down in a room at home, and close your eyes. With your eyes closed, see the room around you. Imagine how far away the walls and ceilings are. In your mind's eye, imagine the windows, curtains and doors. See the objects in the room, and their colors. Then open your eyes and check your internal perception against the external reality. Close your eyes and again visualize the room around you, observing whether you can see it more clearly. Give yourself several minutes to complete this exercise.

Repeat the exercise with different rooms in the house until you feel that your ability to see things around you with your eyes closed has improved substantially. Take as many practice sessions as you need to feel that you have improved. Then intensify your visualization workouts by imagining walking through your house, or down the street. Replay events of the day in your imagination. Stretch your ability to see in your mind's eye what you actually see in your daily life.

Notice, when you close your eyes, whether you are thinking about the room around you or seeing it. If you pick up a tendency to think about what is around you rather than actually seeing it, gently refocus your attention on seeing. Because our culture emphasizes control more than creativity, and thinking about things more than imagining them, many of us lose contact with the vivid visual imagination we had as children. You are reawakening that imagination.

Notice, when you open your eyes after inwardly visualizing the room around you, whether there are discrepancies between what you imagined and what is really there. Did you imagine the proportions of the room correctly? Did you miss some of the objects? Was your perception of colors off? Notice how your perception improves with a little practice.

• Include your other senses in your visualizations.

Once you have become familiar with seeing the room around you, and with replaying in your imagination some of the events of the day, expand on your visualization by including senses other than your inner sense of sight. How do you imagine that the floor in the room feels under your feet? What do different objects feel like if you pick them up in your imagination? Check the accuracy of your impressions by walking on the floor and picking up the objects. If you imagine walking down the street, what sounds and smells do you pick up? Do you hear traffic? Do you smell any particular fragrances? Remember a moment earlier in the day when you had a snack. Can you in your imagination recall the taste of what you ate?

Notice that the more senses—sight, hearing, taste, smell, touch—you include in your visualizations, the more vivid your visualizations become, and the more you strengthen your creative ability. Notice that when you practice imagining what is right around you, you use feedback from your eyes, your ears, your sense of taste and smell, and your sense of touch, to improve the accuracy of your internal perception.

2. Practice Developing Your Imagination. 🖭

Once you can see things around you by closing your eyes and re-inventing them in your inner eye, you are ready to strengthen your powers of visualization by creating imaginary scenes. Follow the suggestions below or use the related exercise (15 minutes) on Cassette 5 of Effortless Practice.

• Practice visualizing imaginary scenes.

Have someone read to you, or record and play on tape the following reverie as an exercise in imaginative visualization. When you do this, give yourself enough time between each sentence to fully visualize the content of the sentence.

Begin by finding a quiet place free of distractions. Sit or lie down and place your intention on letting go of your thoughts about the day, and going into your own internal place. Meditate by following your breathing for a minute or two, to calm and center yourself.

Now imagine that you are sitting at a campsite by a clear flowing river. In the distance you can see the mountains with trees growing straight and dark green up to the tree line, and rocky barren areas above. Closer by you see meadows of tall waving grasses and yellow, pink and purple flowers. You can smell the lavender and sage in the air. It is early in the evening of a summer's day, the sun is setting, and the air is getting cool as you warm your hands over an open fire and cook a hearty soup. You dip a spoon into the pot, blow on it to cool the soup, and taste it. It tastes spicy and rich. You look off into the distance and enjoy the purple and orange streaks filling the sky as the sun sets. As you gaze into the distance, you also pick up the sounds of the crackling fire, of crickets and frogs beginning to sing their evening song, of the wind blowing gently through the nearby trees, and of distant traffic. You walk over to the stream, crouch down and rinse your hands, enjoying the cool feel of the mountain water while you gaze down at the smooth, rounded pebbles visible under the rush of the stream. You look up at the first stars as they emerge into view. You sigh softly as you drink in the beautiful evening.

Notice whether your mind wanders during your visualization. Can you keep your attention focused on being fully in the scene that you are imagining? Can you both see, hear, smell, taste and feel different aspects of the scene? Notice how visualization involves all of your senses. Notice that you may be better at imagining with some of your senses than with others. Notice that if you are patient, and simply go back over aspects that you missed of the visualization, it will begin to come into clearer focus. Visualization trains your mind's capacity to focus, and it is this discipline of focus which will enable you to create, through visualization, the life you want.

• Develop your own visualizations.

Once you have practiced visualizing imaginary scenes such as those above, you are ready to develop your own visualizations. Write down a description of an imaginary place, including what it looks like, sounds like, smells, tastes and feels like. Then close your eyes and imagine this place in vivid detail. Make this type of exercise a fun game you can explore in spare moments.

Notice that the more you visualize, the easier it becomes.

3. Practice Imagining How You Want to Be. 🖳

By developing your power of imagination, you develop the ability to use visualization to change your life. You learn to use your imagination to project how you want to feel and behave in various circumstances. *Follow the suggestions below or use the related exercise (10 minutes) on Cassette 5 of* Effortless Practice.

- **Each day, visualize how you want to be during the day.**

Take a few moments in the morning, before you get involved in the rush of the day's activities, and think about what is in store for you during the day. Pick a situation that matters to you, a situation in which you would like to improve upon your habitual responses. Perhaps you would like to be more confident, or more relaxed. Write down how you would like to be, including in detail how you would like to feel and behave. Then close your eyes and in your imagination see yourself feeling and behaving that way. Bring as much detail as possible into your imagination. How will you feel? How will you move? What expression will you have on your face? How will you speak to people, and with what tone of voice? Imagine how you will see people you encounter, and how they will respond to you. See yourself calmly and confidently overcoming obstacles. Commit yourself in your mind to being the type of person you visualize. Then, as you go through the day and face the situations you had visualized, bring your visualization to mind. Allow it to influence the way you feel, look, talk and respond to people.

Notice how your ability to visualize events in your day influences the shape of those events, by affecting the way you deal with them. At the end of the day, notice how much you allowed your visualization to impact the day's events. Did you stay with how you imagined yourself behaving, or did you stray? How can you strengthen your ability to commit to being the kind of person you visualize yourself as being?

4. Develop Discipline in Your Visualizations.

Visualization is only as effective as your commitment to it. The more you use visualization, and take it seriously as a tool to shape your life, the more it serves you.

- **Make visualization a constant practice.**

Keep in mind that you are constantly visualizing, for good or for ill. Train yourself to use visualization to your own benefit. As you get used to visualizing, learn to use it constantly. When you walk into a room, see yourself as you want to be; when you head out the door, see yourself happy and energetic; when you meet friends for a social event, let go of your tension by seeing yourself as radiant and relaxed. Practice directing your attention to being who you want to be.

Notice that the more you use visualization, the more automatic it becomes. You simply train yourself to project yourself with energy, enthusiasm and a positive outlook into every situation in your life.

Suggested Reading

Korra Deaver, *Psychic Power and Soul Consciousness* (Alameda, CA: Hunter House, 1991). Written by a gifted psychic, this book contains superlative tips for visualization training.

Jean Houston, *The Possible Human* (New York: Jeremy Tarcher, 1982). Unquestionably the best book available on multi-sensory visualization and its application to awakening creativity.

chapter 13

The Art of Personal Relationships

Being creative about ourselves leads naturally into being creative in our personal relationships. It's that creativity that makes for improved communication. One of the ways that I help people to become creative in their relationships is by showing them how to tap into their intuition.

During a weekend training program I was offering for people interested in intuition, we were exploring how to become more intuitive about others. I had each person bring to mind the face of someone they knew quite well. Most people chose family members, close friends or sweethearts. Then I asked everyone to close their eyes and imagine that they were that person. If they were thinking of their mother, son or sweetheart, now they became that person in their imagination. They imagined feeling how that person felt from the inside. What kind of emotions was that person feeling? What was it like to be in that person's body? What was it like to talk the way that person talked, and to make the kind of expressions that person made? Each member of the class also walked around the room carrying themselves the way they imagined that person to carry themselves. Then everyone recorded what they had discovered and came back to the group to share their insights.

All the people in the class discovered that they knew things they didn't realize they knew. They tapped into intuitive knowledge that had been unconscious. It had been unconscious because they were not used to making use of their faculties of imaginative identification. When we operate intuitively, we don't think about an object or person in order to know something about it. Instead, we become that object or person in our minds. By identifying with the object of our knowledge we experience it from the inside.

Using the tools of imaginative identification can cause us to rethink how we approach a situation. A young woman in the class had an aunt of whom her family disapproved. They described her as a weirdo. It came as a surprise to this young woman, when she imagined being her aunt, that she felt charismatic, free and exhilarated as if she were floating on air! She discovered that what her family members really disapproved of was her aunt's joie de vivre and freedom from other people's opinions.

Another woman in the class had a tense relationship with her father, whom she viewed as controlling and demanding. She completely changed her perception of him after she imagined being in his body. For the first time, she realized that life on the inside for him was nervous and fearful, and that it was because of these feelings that he behaved in a controlling fashion. She had been taking his behavior toward her too personally, instead of seeing that behavior as an expression of her father's issues. Now she recognized that he wasn't able to do any better. She resolved to work on being less reactive and angry with her father.

Finally, a man in the class imagined occupying the body of his twenty-eight year old son who was having trouble landing a job. He burst into tears when he realized that his son was suffering from deep depression. He had been aware that something was going on but hadn't allowed himself to tune in and appreciate the intensity of his son's experience.

The woman who imagined being her aunt was able to let go of the conventional attitudes of her family and to appreciate her aunt's sense of personal freedom. The woman who imagined being her father changed the way she reacted to him because she no longer saw him from the narrow and exclusive viewpoint of her own needs and desires. The same thing happened with the father who imagined being his son. Intuitive awareness helps us let go of tunnel vision habits of perception that cut us off from people. It heightens our ability to experience other people as they are. It improves our clarity of perception. We enhance our ability to enjoy meaningful relationships.

Intuitive Knowing Through Creative Identification

When we practice intuitive awareness of other people, we use the very same faculty of creative imagination that was discussed in Chapter 12. When I worked on healing my chronic back pain, I identified myself with Audrey Hepburn, imagining being in her body in order to learn how to change the way I lived in mine. When we practice intuitive awareness of another person, we also use our creative imaginations by pretending to occupy that person's body. Our goal, however, is different. Instead of identifying with someone else in order to transform our own subconscious patterns, we identify with someone else in order to understand more deeply how that person experiences life.

The very first time I imagined occupying someone else's body was on a visit to see my brother at the state mental hospital that had been his home for many years. A precocious loner when he was a teenager, my brother had suffered a nervous breakdown during his last year of college, and he never recuperated from that blow. For a while, he managed to function as a computer programmer for several different companies, each time losing his job after fighting with his superiors. Then he drove a taxi for a few years, becoming increasingly obsessive and delusional until finally he was institutionalized. At first, he was sent to the acute wards of various private mental hospitals. Then, as he continued to deteriorate, he was placed for longer periods of time in psychiatric institutions and halfway houses. Finally, after all these interventions failed to help him, he found his way to the chronic ward of the state mental hospital.

My brother lived a caged existence, and unfortunately he did not really want anything better. He was too afraid of the world, and too hallucinatory. His contacts with the outside were limited to the weekly visits by family members. As for me, while I felt that it was my duty to visit him, doing this week after week, month after month and year after year wore on me. Each visit was also difficult because my brother acted unpleasant, demanding and incoherent. He was also dirty, and his end of conversations was limited to asking for food and cigarettes. But after all, he was my brother.

On one particular day, as I was waiting for him to be brought out to the visitors' lounge on his ward, I was feeling irritated at once again having to make this visit. I had a lot of other things on my mind. And then, as I saw his six-foot-two-inch frame lumbering down the long hallway toward me, his belly falling out of pants that were precariously close to falling down, I was suddenly and unexpectedly catapulted inside his body. What I felt gave me pause.

I sensed that an enormous depression and heaviness filled my brother, making it difficult, even close to impossible, to move forward. He was that heavy-laden. I knew that he had in part created this unbearable weight in his own life, and that it was neither possible nor appropriate for me to try to lift it off his shoulders. Nonetheless, the unexpected and instantaneous intuitive knowledge that came when I was my brother for a split second did give me an enhanced appreciation of what it was like to live life through his eyes. And that helped me deal with him more effectively. Our conversation proceeded better than usual. I can't say that this was because I was kinder or softer. The way my insight altered my behavior was subtler than that. I may even have shed some of the caretaking behavior that passed for kindness but that enabled my brother's depression rather than supporting his growth. What I do know is that I felt more connected, and that my brother sensed that. I knew where he was. He knew that I knew it, and that helped him.

My spontaneous experience of empathically identifying with and becoming my brother sowed the seeds of what became a deliberate practice. Both as a healer and in my personal relations, I began regularly imagining being in other people's bodies in order to understand them better and respond appropriately. I also began to teach this practice to clients. They found that identifying imaginatively with others gave them added insight and lessened their ego needs. Then one day I picked up a book that talked about this process of identification. The author was the gifted spiritual teacher, educator and clairvoyant, Rudolf Steiner, and the book

was entitled *Knowledge of the Higher Worlds and Its Attainment.**
The subject of the book is the nature of spiritual growth.
Steiner writes that whoever wants to grow to any spiritual height
must rigorously cultivate within himself a twofold ability. First, he
must learn to evaluate himself, including his own desires, needs,
and behavior patterns, as objectively and dispassionately as if he
were evaluating someone else. He must give himself no special
consideration or leeway just because his feelings and needs are his
and not someone else's. Second, he must learn to quieten himself
inwardly enough to be able to listen to other people with not even
a hint of criticism in his mind, until eventually he can blend completely with another person and become identified with him. In
other words, he must develop deep empathy through intuitive
identification.

The ability to identify empathically with others is not easily
won. It is natural for us to give our own experience priority, and to
see it as more real than the experience of another person. Yet we
can, through practicing seeing through other people's eyes, greatly expand our understanding of them. We can also enlarge our own
perspective in a way that enriches our own lives. By training ourselves in the ability to identify with others, we learn to temper our
own ego needs and develop the art of personal relationships.
Cultivating deep relationships is the highest of arts precisely
because it requires full appreciation of another person's
experience.

Intuitive Knowledge and Personal Growth

Steiner points out that it is impossible to tap into a deeper
empathic understanding of others, let alone into the spiritual perception of our fundamental unity, unless we first develop a love of
tranquility and clarity. We must carry these deep inside ourselves.
That is why the art of healthy relationships is a mature art. It
opens up for us more and more only as a result of undergoing our
own personal healing and finding inner balance.

---

* Rudolf Steiner, *Knowledge of the Higher Worlds and Its Attainment*
(Hudson, NY: Anthroposophic Press, 1947).

When Ellen first came to work with me, she lacked this balance. As a result, she couldn't get along with her family. Her relationship with them was extremely tense. Ellen and her five-year-old son were living with her parents while she went through an acrimonious, long-winded divorce from a man who had managed to keep possession of most of their joint assets. Ellen had returned to school, aiming to obtain a teaching degree while she also worked part-time. Her parents had welcomed her back to live with them, and they assisted in raising her son while she went through the transition to greater financial and professional independence.

Unfortunately, despite her parents' generosity in taking Ellen and their grandchild into their home, Ellen was also the fall guy in the family dynamics. When things went wrong, it was her fault. Her mother, father and sister criticized her for the way she was raising her son, objected to her lifestyle all the way from how she dressed to her religious beliefs and practices, and dragged her to family therapy sessions which focused around why Ellen was making the lives of other family members miserable. Ellen had not yet learned to detach herself from the way her family perceived her, so she inevitably fed their perceptions by being angry, resentful and hurt.

Over the course of a year, Ellen did a lot of work to separate emotionally from her parents and to take responsibility for owning herself. She developed inner equanimity and learned to stop reacting to her family's accusations with hostility and guilt. Instead of focusing angrily on how she was being treated, she started to stand up for herself without reactive rancor. As the months passed she changed from being troubled and uncertain to being a lot more fun loving, open and balanced. She developed more confidence in the way she was raising her son, and this was reflected in his growing maturity. Ellen saw that she was intelligent and self-reliant, that she had good judgment, and that she didn't have to defend herself against her family.

One day toward the end of our work together, Ellen came into my office and described a simple but revealing incident involving her mother. A friend of the family had called to ask her mother to meet her for lunch. Ellen's mother had had plans to take a walk during the lunch hour, but instead of saying this to her friend, she became upset and nervous on the phone, and began hemming and hawing. All of a sudden it was crystal clear to Ellen that her mother, who had been the bane of her existence, had trouble feeling free to do her own thing. She felt constrained by a simple request from a friend. At that moment Ellen realized that her mother's tendency to get angry and to yell at her daughter was connected to the fact that she constantly felt pressured and pushed around by people.

Ellen felt sorry for her mother, and calmly interceded to suggest that she could ask her friend to meet her a little later, for tea instead of lunch. She coached her mother through the conversation, and her mother hung up the phone greatly relieved.

Understanding her mother's insecurity and anxiety in this incident led Ellen to recast how she interpreted her mother's behavior toward herself. She had never before clearly seen the insecurity and pain that generated her mother's hostile behavior. She had always thought that if her mother yelled at her, then either her mother was an ogre or she, Ellen, was doing something wrong. Now those interpretations dissolved in the face of a simple, clear perception of who her mother was.

The anxiety and rage that Ellen had harbored through years of living with her mother had been a reflection of her own inability to see clearly. It's the failure of vision, based in our own inner turmoil, insecurities and needs, that makes for difficult relationships. When Ellen ceased projecting her own needs and fears onto her family, as they had projected their needs and fears onto her, she developed what Buddhists call "direct perception." She could see what was going on for the people around her, and could base her actions on this clear sight. Because she was less focused on her own ego needs, she could also for the first time genuinely help her mother rather than react to her. And this was useful for both of them. Not only did Ellen stop interpreting her mother's behavior as a personal attack, her mother also began to appreciate her more, and therefore to treat her with more respect.

Personal Relationships as Spiritual Teachers

Ellen was able to influence the destructive and co-dependent dynamics within her family because she spent a great deal of time practicing taking responsibility for her own feelings. She did this through working with breathing, meditation, personal exploration of her life history, and visualization. Even while she worked on herself, she continued to live in an angry, accusatory environment. She did not become more balanced because her environment became supportive. She became more balanced in spite of her environment.

Ellen practiced letting go of her resentments and hostilities, not because they weren't in some sense legitimate, but rather because they hurt her more than they hurt anyone else. As long as she stayed reactive, she suffered, eating herself up with rancor. When she decided that she, and she alone, would be responsible for her own moods, she began to be a happier, more balanced person not because others treated her better, but because she decided not to let her moods be dependent on others. This wasn't easy for her. But by accomplishing this, she started breaking the family cycle of resentment.

Like Ellen, all of us experience disappointments in our relationships. People treat us unkindly without due cause, make demands on us that we cannot meet, or fail to meet our own expectations. Like Ellen, most of us also react initially in kind. If others treat us unkindly, it's easy to hold a grudge or to become hostile ourselves. Then we make our own demands, or become ambivalent, or put a hold on understanding the other person until the other person shows that they understand us! Then, of course, the cycle only worsens, because while it may be true that someone else threw the first stone, after a while, who did what first is no longer relevant.

When we experience negative dynamics in our relationships, as Ellen did, we can focus on our sense of bitterness over the disappointments they engender or we can ask ourselves what lesson we can learn from those disappointments. Even the most painful relationships can act as spiritual teachers when we look at what we can learn from them. Usually, this learning has to do with becoming stronger within ourselves, and more personally empowered. Our relationships become spiritual teachers when our dissatisfactions with them motivate us to create for ourselves the peace, strength, and integrity that we mistakenly look for from other people. Once we can create that inner strength in ourselves, then we can enjoy healthy relationships based on mutual empowerment.

Healthy Relationships and Mutual Empowerment

The eminent Buddhist author and teacher Thich Nhat Hanh tells a story about a father and daughter that illustrates how healthy relationships are based on mutual empowerment rather than on mutual need. The father and daughter have a circus act in which the daughter climbs on the father's shoulders to perform acrobatic stunts. One day, the father turns to his daughter and tells her that since their livelihood depends on performing their circus act, they each need the other. Therefore, he says, she must be sure to take care of him, and he will be sure to take care of her. Otherwise, if one of them falls ill or suffers an injury, they will both lose the roof over their heads. The wise daughter, however, replies by chastising her father. No, she tells him, it is neither her function to take care of him nor his to take care of her. Instead, she must take care of herself, so that she remains strong and supple. And he must take care of himself, so that he too remains strong and supple. In this way, they will both guarantee that they can join forces and continue to put on an exciting circus act.

In a growing relationship, each person commits to being one hundred percent responsible for his or her physical, emotional and spiritual well being. That's when the relationship becomes a tool for expressing the creative power and beauty that emerges from joining the forces of its individual members.

How can we evaluate the status of our own relationships? How can we make sure they are spiritually growing, leading us toward greater self-determination, integrity and strength? How can we tell whether our relationships contribute to creating an intimacy that is less tarnished by ego needs and more expressive of love? On a pragmatic level, we can ask ourselves where we use a relationship to protect ourselves from developing an ability that we would need if we were on our own. Where do we ask a relationship to take care of us, instead of requiring that we take care of ourselves? We can ask the same questions about those we love. Where do we protect a spouse, sweetheart, son, daughter or friend from developing capacities and character traits that he or she would need to become independent? Do we keep our loved ones from growing up?

On an emotional level, we can ask ourselves whether we look to our relationships only for comfort and security and not for

growth. Chronic feelings of fear, resentment or anger in relationships are always signs of power struggle and co-dependency. If we
feel them, in some way we are making other people responsible for
our lives. We are rationalizing our own refusal of power by projecting negativity onto others.

Everyone suffers from such feelings to some extent. We must
never judge ourselves harshly when we find negative emotions
within ourselves. But we can be conscious of the importance of letting go of these, rather than finding excuses for holding on to
them. We only stand to gain from learning how to let go of these
feelings, since they can eat up our lives. Negative feelings hurt us
far more than they hurt the people toward whom we feel nega-
tively. We know that we are beginning to approach relationships
in a more enlightened manner when negative feelings no longer
plague us quite as much as they once did.

Spiritual Partnership and Oneness

In the film *Phenomenon*, released in 1996, John Travolta plays
the part of a well-meaning, friendly garage mechanic named
George Malley who lives in a small Western town. George's life is
dramatically and suddenly transformed because of a brain abnor-
mality that causes him to develop special powers of focus and concentration. This easygoing, all American guy starts reading a minimum of four books a night, displays a memory for everything
from foreign languages to the biochemistry of soil nutrients, and
creates inventions, any one of which would take most people at
least a lifetime to conjure up. He also develops extrasensory abilities. He discovers that he can move objects by mere force of will
(telekinesis), and can sense the vibrations preceding earthquakes
long before sophisticated equipment can detect them.

The development of these paranormal abilities both fascinates
and terrifies the community of people amongst whom George
lives, but the deepest insight that he tries to convey goes virtually unnoticed. He recounts this insight through a story about the
largest single organism on the planet: a grove of aspen trees located in one of the forests of the northwest. This grove looks to the
naked eye like an extensive stand of independent trees, but all the
trees are actually shoots of a single giant root. What looks to be
separate is in reality one. Through the image of the aspen grove,

George is drawn to an understanding that life is partnership in a common being. We are all part of one another, just as the aspen trees that seem separate are part of a larger being. Each human being partakes, like a cell in an organism, of the larger organism of humanity. Humanity itself is also part of the larger organism of the planet, including its rocks, plants, animals and atmosphere.

George Malley struggles to convey to people that if we can grasp our oneness with everything on the planet, several major changes will occur. For one, our mental capacities will greatly improve. Malley sees his power of telekinesis—his ability to move things by the power of the mind alone—as the manifestation of a partnership or oneness between himself and the objects he moves. He and the pen are part of the same ultimate stuff of nature. When he tunes in to his oneness with the pen, his mind and the pen cooperate to move the pen in a way that cannot be understood if we believe in separateness, that fundamental illusion of three-dimensional reality.

Even more important than the growth of paranormal abilities are the changes that develop for human beings in their relationships with one another. According to George, when we experience ourselves as parts of a larger whole, then the way we relate to one another changes. Accepting our common partnership, we become more sensitive and tuned in to the evolutionary process in those around us, support each other more, eagerly share what we know, and willingly take the opportunity to learn from others. We manifest a deeper form of love, and treat each other as natural extensions of ourselves.

Unfortunately, while George is trying to share his increasing goodness of spirit, his power is scaring everyone senseless. The FBI investigates him and puts him in isolation. They are afraid he will use his extraordinary intelligence against the national interest. His neighbors think that an alien force possesses him. He is both too weird and too good to be true. Things take a turn for the worse in another way as well. It turns out that George's exceptional abilities are the result of a tumor that magnifies his brain's functioning as long as he is alive, but that is rapidly bringing his life to a close. George dies surrounded by a few very close friends, and only once he is gone does the community he lived in absorb some of his message and celebrate the gifted and loving man he was.

George's message that we are all one is an age-old spiritual truth. As with most spiritual truths, the reality of our oneness is easy to intone but hard to experience. Spiritual partnership is built not on a conceptual understanding but on an experiential revelation of oneness. We are the other person. The other person is us. If we are the other person and the other person is us, then of course we will want to see that person grow, not because of some direct benefit we'll get back (affection, security, money) but because we experience ourselves as being parts of a larger being whose nature is to evolve. If we are the other person and the other person is us, we will also act on the assumption that the other person wants us to grow, not in order to do something for us or to get something from us, but just because the two of us together form part of something larger.

In his own mid-Western American way, George Malley asked people to think about healing their divisions and becoming one with one another. If we evaluated our lives by reference to how much we were able to do this, we would probably end up being sorely uncomfortable with ourselves. Yet the principle of our ultimate oneness can provide us with some healthy guidelines for thinking about our experience. After all, Malley himself became a profoundly happy person when he grasped the truth of oneness. He was happy despite being persecuted by a community who viewed him as dangerously weird, and he was happy despite knowing he was going to die. Could it be that seeing ourselves as one with others could make us more happy?

George Malley spent the last months of his life giving to others without thought of reward. He gave up the desire for payback. He apparently felt so identified with everyone and everything around him that by giving to others he was giving to himself. Although this seems paradoxical, we can see from Ellen's experience why it might actually be true that the more we identify with others, the happier we can be. When Ellen was involved in her own pain, she was unkind to her parents and unaware of their pain. When she stopped being involved in her pain, and took responsibility for releasing it, she was both happier inside herself and kinder to her parents. It was easy for her to be kind because she didn't need anything from them anymore, and at the same time she could see their pain. She was more generous because she had fewer needs. She could also afford to be more generous because, having fewer needs, she could appreciate the fears that kept her parents in pain. She had nothing to lose and everything to gain from giving.

The more empowered we are within ourselves, the more readily we can give up the need for payback from other people. The more we give up the need for payback, the more able we are to support them in a productive manner, even when they cannot give back to us.

Practicing Oneness

Imagine that you have a close friend who goes through some personal experiences that are painful and unsettling for her. Despite your friendship, she withdraws into her own world. You try to communicate with her and show her your support, but she fails to respond. Even worse, she takes your attempts to support her and show your care as irritating. She snaps at you on the phone, or hangs up.

Your friend is so involved in her own issues that she cannot see that you care, let alone be considerate toward you. At a certain point, it's only natural for you to say, "Okay, have it your way." You might want to walk away from the friendship at this point. Or you might feel resentful and angry. These are normal reactions. And it may be the healthy response for you to let go of supporting someone who fails to reciprocate. But sometimes you may find within yourself the strength for a different response.

Maybe that old friend needs your support precisely because she is too tied up in her self-destructive anguish. Maybe she is foolishly snapping at everyone who loves her. You may not want to throw pearls in her direction right now. But maybe if you maintain an open door even when you have been slighted one too many times, this could help her a great deal without costing you too much. Maybe when she comes around, she will remember with gratitude how you were there for her when she wasn't there for you. Maybe that will open her heart, and change her on a deep level. In those times when someone treats you poorly but you still want to love them because you know that that's what they need in order to grow, you are practicing spiritual partnership. You affirm your oneness with someone else.

A good friend of mine once told me the story of her friendship with a man who had years before caused her great disappointment. That disappointment sowed the seeds for her learning to experience and practice oneness. For a while, she had been deeply hurt, and that forced her to look at herself. She saw that she had three choices. She could try to make this man do what she wanted him to do. That choice already wasn't working. She could let go of him, while nursing pain and resentment. That was a choice she had made before, and she didn't want to travel down that road again. It ate up too much of her life and was definitely unsatisfying. But there was only one last alternative. She could let go of this man and continue to cherish him with love. That was a difficult choice to make because it required her to be selfless! It required her to give without any expectation of return.

As she considered this option in her heart, it became clear to the woman that she loved this man for more than what he gave or didn't give her. She loved him for who he was. She decided to work on letting go of him with love. That meant loving him whether or not she ever saw him again. It meant not holding on. It also meant avoiding using letting go as an excuse for feeling wounded. She had to let go *and* feel love.

Through some hard work, my friend got to the place where she could do this. If she never saw her friend again, that was fine with her. And if she saw him, that was great too. She stopped being invested in how he behaved toward her. She stopped having expectations and stopped needing a payback. And when she let go completely, something interesting happened: her friend felt that she was not making demands on him, and he began to love her for that, to want her in his life. He recognized in her a beautiful woman who loved him freely. That was something that he had never before experienced. Their relationship was reborn on a new level, and today, just as she loves him for who he is, he too loves her for who she is.

Giving without the need for a payback from someone else has nothing to do with being a martyr. It is not about sacrificing ourselves or about doing everything for someone else and getting nothing back. Giving up expectations is really about committing ourselves to a more joyful existence. In its own way, it's even hedonistic! Ellen wasn't a stoic when she decided to be happy even if her parents attacked her, or to be supportive to them even if they didn't support her. She was practical and realistic. She realized that she would be happier that way. She realized that by focusing on making each interaction more constructive, she was only helping herself. And she was also helping those around her. Practicing oneness may seem idealistic. But it is also extremely realistic and practical.

When we consciously work on supporting another person's growth, we focus not on that person's weaknesses but on their inner core. In the moments where we can do this, we are able to put aside that person's personality which may, like our personality, be flawed and to focus instead on their soul. We focus our attention on what that person can become, on their potential for growth, and try to do what we can to support that growth.

Helping someone else to grow can require us to let go of our own egos for a time, to let go of our demands to be special, different, apart and preferred. This is extremely difficult. All our lives we struggle to get other people to satisfy our ego needs. All our lives we fail. When we ask someone else to treat us as special—instead of doing the work of becoming special inside whether or not anyone notices—we can't win. It's a zero sum game. It takes us so long to recognize that we find personal fulfillment and love not in getting our ego needs met but in going through the many struggles that teach us to temper our ego needs, and to help others do the same, even when that seems to work at our own expense.

George Malley thought that, like the aspen trees with a common root system, we were all one. The Indian spiritual teacher Vivekenanda put the same thought in other words when he said, "Why should we do good to the world? Apparently to help the world, but really to help ourselves." We have arrived at spiritual partnership when we become strong enough within ourselves to know in our hearts that there is no difference between ourselves and others. When we reach that point, we have also fostered in ourselves a deep longing to grow what is pure and holy in our own hearts. And when we are strong enough to embrace our own purity, our hearts' growing abundance teaches us also to embrace and serve what is pure and holy in those who cross our path.

Summary

Healthy relationships come into our lives as a natural result of our own struggle to become personally healthy and self-empowering. When we stop allowing our fears to control us and focus instead on developing inner balance and vision, then we become capable of deeper partnership.

Developing personal relationships depends, first of all, on learning how to identify with the people around us by imaginatively stepping into their skins. This is the practice of direct perception, which allows us to view life from perspectives other than our own. Second, healthy relationships depend on understanding that relationships are not in our lives to support our needs or foster our dependency. Instead, relationships teach us, often through difficulties, how to transcend our own limitations and to share with others from a place of mutual empowerment. Third, the more empowered we become within ourselves, the more able we are to share in spiritual partnership with people around us by identifying with and supporting them in their own growth.

The Suggestions for Practice below offer several tools for developing healthy relationships.

*Suggestions for Practice*_____

1. Practice Direct Perception.

Direct perception is the art of intuitively knowing someone or something outside ourselves by experiencing that person or thing from the inside.

- **Explore direct perception by imaginatively identifying with others.**

Pick someone you know, and imagine that you are that person. Imagine that you feel, gesture and move the way that person feels, gestures and moves. Imagine that you see things the way that person does. Occupy that person's body. Let yourself be interested in what it is like to be that person.

Notice how, by imagining being someone else, you pick up things about that person that you didn't know before, or that you didn't know as clearly as you do now. How does your deepened insight into the person change the way you think about that person, or how you might act? Notice also that to be accurate in your perceptions, you have to give up being invested in your own views. You have to be interested in just letting the other person in.

2. Recognize that Relationships Act as Spiritual Teachers.

Relationships are meant to teach us how to become personally more empowered and self-reliant, because it is only through personal empowerment that we can learn to love.

• Examine your personal relationships.

When you experience anger, pain or disappointment in a relationship, ask yourself whether you have been using that relationship to avoid taking responsibility for your own inner balance. How do you make someone else responsible for your happiness? What do you need to do, inwardly or outwardly, to break the addiction to others? Ask yourself where the blessing is in the pain you may experience. Does it challenge you to develop a quality that you are lacking? Finally, ask yourself if you protect your loved ones from their own responsibility to grow into self-determining individuals.

Notice that while you may need to rid yourself of some dependencies and needs in your relationships, this is true of everyone else as well. The willingness to explore your imperfections is not a sign of your deficiency but of personal maturity.

3. Consider How You Can Empower Others.

• Practice oneness with others.

Develop your capacity for spiritual partnership by observing where you have expectations in your relationships, and where you look for a payback. Ask yourself if you can sometimes let go of your need for payback.

Notice that when you commit yourself to giving without expectation, you can free yourself up to be happier and more at peace. You're not waiting for someone else to give you what you want. Notice also how people respond to your giving more freely. Are they more receptive? Do they also give more freely in return?

Suggested Reading

Caroline Myss, *Anatomy of the Spirit* (New York: Harmony, 1996). A brilliant study of the challenges to spiritual growth created by our attitudes toward relationships, and of the damaging emotional and physical consequences that result from seeing relationships as a struggle for power.

chapter 14

Becoming Ourselves

Our world is in the throes of both inner and outer transformation. Many of the triggers behind the changes we are experiencing are extremely uncomfortable. We change only when we need to, and it is pain that tells us we need to change. The fear that has guided our lives, and the all too superficial focus on material pursuits and individual satisfaction, have created devastation everywhere. Our external life, obsessed with competition, consumption, waste, and an appalling irreverence for the planetary forces that sustain us, faithfully reflects back to us the consequences of our relationship to ourselves. That relationship to ourselves, built up through generations of materialism and of the promises that have made that philosophy appealing, is a relationship of neglect. For all our culture's so-called individualism, most people have very little true sense of themselves, or of a purpose to their lives that they can eagerly espouse. It is no wonder that, if we focus on externals and find our validation primarily in what we do and in what we get for what we do, we will never find ourselves.

This book presents one way to journey into ourselves. The art of effortless living, presented as an antidote to the effortful lifestyle of doing and performing, is a pathway of being. It's a practice for becoming ourselves. It includes creating our own sources of well being and learning how to give richly to the world around us.

I have presented the art of effortless living as a way to begin creating solutions to the sufferings of life that every single one of us encounters. I have also presented it in an attempt to encourage our culture to raise its sights from its present barbaric focus to a higher vision for humanity. While raising our sights takes more discipline than staying down in the mud, the rewards are far greater.

Every day I work with people who are in pain. All of them are in some degree of psychic pain and many of them suffer physical pain as well. This suffering, which was personally familiar to me for many years, reflects the heritage of a society that gives no importance to inner development. Some time in their adult lives, most people who want something real from their lives break down. The breakdown is sometimes physical, sometimes emotional or spiritual, and sometimes all three. It acts as a symptom, and is a way of crying out for experiences that will make life more substantial. It's an expression also of the inner longing to create that something more or bust.

There may be other cultures which have vied with our own for the prize for superficiality. But ours must surely be one of the front runners. We can't go on this way, many of us know it, and we're looking for a way out of the impasse. That way out has to be a way in. Whatever the other challenges are that we face for the twenty-first century, there is no question that inner development forms a huge piece of the answer to our personal, cultural and global crises.

Inner growth is a slow and incremental process that accomplishes extraordinary results through what often look like minute daily changes. Look back over the suggestions in this book, and you will see that most of them involve making small but definite shifts in your life. Sooner or later those small changes transform not only who you are but also what and whom you draw into your world. Living the philosophy of being, just like living the philosophy of doing outlined earlier in this book, expresses itself in a holographic pattern that spreads through all of our lives. We alter our relationship to our bodies, our emotions, our spiritual life, our creativity, and our relationships. Seemingly insignificant shifts in each of these areas support shifts everywhere else, until there comes a time when our entire lives take on a new aura and we have become new and different people.

Some of the changes I have suggested involve altering the way you breathe or move. Some of them involve learning to feel more deeply and to release emotions fully. Some of them involve valuing solitude, cultivating your dream life, and developing a sense of inner guidance. Some involve investing in the life of the imagination. Many of them involve embracing techniques that lead you to perceive your relationships with other people along novel dimensions. All of them are about enhancing self-awareness.

Self-awareness is key, and it grows quietly and without fanfare. It is a powerful force that moves mountains through its subtlety. One of my clients, a highly successful entrepreneur who has been coming to see me for a number of years, said to me recently, "I look back at my life, and I cannot believe how much my world has changed since I began doing this work. There were times that it seemed so subtle that I couldn't believe it would make a change. But now I understand that things change far more deeply when the change is subtle, because it's a real change in myself."

Cherish this truth: It is through regular practice of timeworn, simple techniques such as those I rediscovered and present in this book that your inner power grows. And it is through the growth of that inner power that you begin to see that you have been holding back on all the gifts you are meant to give to life. You are not meant to wait for someone else to tell you that you are okay. You are meant to teach yourself how to feel okay inside and then cultivate your inner fire. You are not meant to ask someone else to give you what you need. That is so much less rewarding than discovering that you can give yourself what you need. You are not meant to accept the low standards that rule our world. You have the capacity to transform those standards and to inspire others to follow in your footsteps. And you are not meant to hold back your love for others. Rather, the more you can bring yourself to others, the more you nurture the foundation of your own life and the lives of those who follow you. Take courage, and give others courage through your example. May your earnest heart and honest mind shine through all your endeavors.

Effortless Practice Audio Program
Order Form

Effortless Practice, the audiocassette program designed to accompany *The Art of Effortless Living,* will assist you in fully integrating the principles of effortless living into your life. The audio program, conveniently packaged in a binder, consists of six cassettes, each approximately 45 minutes long. An introductory cassette provides an overview, and the remaining five cassettes offer guided exercises based on the suggestions for practice included in the book.

To order *Effortless Practice,* fill out and mail the form below (or send a separate sheet with the information requested).

Name: _____

Address: _____

Telephone: _____ E-mail: _____

Effortless Practice Audio Program (Quantity) _____ @$45.95 $ _____

Shipping and Handling

	QUANTITY		
	1	2-5	
Priority mail	$5.25	$8.00	
OR			
Express Mail	$18.00	$25.00	

Subtotal (*Effortless Practice* + shipping and handling)   **SUBTOTAL** _____

Tax (For delivery to New York State only, please add 6.75% to price.) _____

TOTAL _____

Send check or money order (credit card orders not accepted) payable to:

Vision Works
PO Box 147
Croton-on-Hudson, NY 10520-0147

For inquiries, contact Vision Works at 1-888-450-1241 or visionworks@ingridbacci.com

About the Author

Ingrid Bacci, Ph.D., is a health care practitioner and motivational consultant to corporations, educational institutions, hospitals and churches. A licensed teacher of the Alexander Technique and a Craniosacral Therapist, Dr. Bacci has published articles in scientific, management and spiritual journals, has produced television shows on mind-body training, and has demonstrated the techniques of effortless living on major networks.

The author's training and expertise in mind-body healing grew out of her own experience with a serious medical condition. Twenty years ago, she was a young philosophy professor on the academic fast track, with degrees from Harvard and Columbia Universities, and a fellowship to Cambridge University. At thirty-one years of age, her career was abruptly shattered by a mysterious and crippling collagen disease that defied cure by highly respected traditional medical doctors.

For three years Bacci was a bedridden invalid in constant pain. During this time she turned her own mind and body into a laboratory for self-study. She explored and subsequently trained in alternative therapies based on the mind-body connection, and studied spiritual traditions that focus on accessing the higher powers of the mind.

Ten years later all signs of illness were gone, and Dr. Bacci had transformed herself from a cripple to a triathlete. In addition, she had committed herself to a lifelong professional goal of assisting others in achieving optimum health and creativity.

To receive current information about workshops and seminars offered by Dr. Bacci, or to inquire about private sessions, contact www.ingridbacci.com, send e-mail to visionworks@ingridbacci.com or write to Ingrid Bacci, P.O. Box 147, Croton-on-Hudson, NY 10520-0147.